VARIANT VERSIONS
OF TARGUMIC TRADITIONS
WITHIN CODEX NEOFITI 1

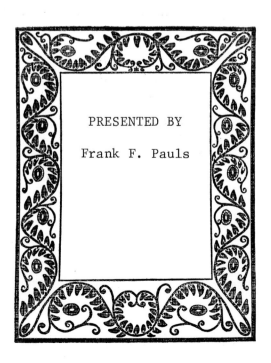

PRESENTED BY

Frank F. Pauls

SOCIETY OF BIBLICAL LITERATURE
ARAMAIC STUDIES

Number 2

VARIANT VERSIONS
OF TARGUMIC TRADITIONS
WITHIN CODEX NEOFITI 1

by
Shirley Lund and Julia A. Foster

SCHOLARS PRESS
Missoula, Montana

VARIANT VERSIONS
OF TARGUMIC TRADITIONS
WITHIN CODEX NEOFITI 1

by

Shirley Lund and Julia A. Foster

Published by
SCHOLARS PRESS
for
The Society of Biblical Literature

Distributed by

SCHOLARS PRESS
University of Montana
Missoula, Montana 59812

VARIANT VERSIONS
OF TARGUMIC TRADITIONS
WITHIN CODEX NEOFITI 1

by

Shirley Lund and Julia A. Foster

Library of Congress Cataloging in Publication Data
Lund, Shirley
Bible. O. T. Pentateuch. Aramaic. Targum Yerushalmi.
Selections. 1977.
    Variant versions of Targumic traditions within Codex
Neofiti 1.

    (Aramaic studies ; 2)
    English or Aramaic.
    Includes bibliographical references and index.
    I. Bible. O.T. Pentateuch. Aramaic. Targum
Yerushalmi. I. Lund, Shirley. II. Foster, Julia A.
III. Bible. O. T. Pentateuch. English. Lund.
Selections. 1977. IV. Codex Neofiti 1. V. Title.
VI. Series: Aramaic studies series ; 2.
BS1224.A76 1977   222'.1'046   77-5389
ISBN 0-89130-137-2

Printed in the United States of America

1   2   3   4   5

Bitterroot Litho
Missoula, Montana

ACKNOWLEDGMENTS

Some of the research underlying this study was done originally by Julia Foster for a doctoral dissertation, completed in 1969, at Boston University under Professor H. Neil Richardson, whose encouragement and direction is deeply appreciated. Further work has been supported by a Piedmont University Center research grant, sponsored jointly by the Piedmont University Center and Pfeiffer College, Misenheimer, North Carolina.

The research by Shirley Lund is based upon research originally done for a doctoral thesis, completed in 1967, at the University of St. Andrews under Reverend Professor Matthew Black, whose support and guidance then and continuously is gratefully acknowledged. Recent research has been supported in part by a grant from the Boston University Graduate School.

We wish to express our profound gratitude to Reverend Professor Black for his interest, invaluable assistance, and encouragement as we undertook the writing of the monograph.

We wish also to express our appreciation to Professor Leander E. Keck of Atlanta, Georgia, and Professor Emeritus William F. Stinespring of Durham, North Carolina, for guiding the manuscript through its first stage; to Professor Richardson for continual encouragement and helpful suggestions as the work progressed; to Professors Geoffrey J. Cowling, of Sidney, Australia, and Gerard J. Kuiper, of Atlanta, Georgia, to whom we are indebted for assistance in many ways, not least of which their critical comments on the original draft.

We have acknowledged individually elsewhere those who provided microfilms and/or photocopies of manuscripts, but we wish to express here our sincere thanks for the use of these materials.

We want to thank also Ruth Kopelman and Rebecca Low, of Boston University, who so patiently and so carefully typed their way through rough drafts to final copies; Iris Tobin of Brandeis University and Judith Furness of Boston University, who submitted to the boredom of proofreading Aramaic texts letter by letter; and Jonathan Miller of Boston University, who not only proofread, but also rendered valuable assistance in the translating of the Aramaic texts.

v

TABLE OF CONTENTS

TABLE OF CONTENTS (Cont.)

SOURCES OF TARGUMIC TEXTS:
MANUSCRIPTS AND EDITIONS

Ms. Codex Neofiti 1 of the Vatican Library:	Microfilm, courtesy of the Vatican Library, Rome; photocopies of microfilm, courtesy of Reverend Professor Matthew Black, St. Andrews, Scotland.
Ms. Vaticanus Ebr. 440 of the Vatican Library:	Folios 198-227 of Codex Antiquus, microfilm of original supplied by the Vatican Library to Andover-Harvard Library, Harvard Divinity School, Cambridge, Massachusetts; photocopy, courtesy of Professor Malcolm C. Doubles, Laurinburg, North Carolina.
Bomberg fragments:	Published in Biblia Hebraica Rabbinica, Basle, 1618-19, of Andover-Harvard Library, Harvard Divinity School, Cambridge, Massachusetts.
Ms. Hebr. 110 of the National Library of Paris:	Photocopy, courtesy of Professor Gerard J. Kuiper, Atlanta, Georgia.
Pseudo-Jonathan:	Microfilm of British Museum Ms. Targum Yerushalmi 'Al Hat-Torah, Add. 27,031, courtesy of Professor Joseph A. Fitzmyer, Cambridge, Massachusetts; photocopy, courtesy of Professor Gerard J. Kuiper, Atlanta, Georgia.
Cairo Genizah fragments:	Paul Kahle, Masoreten des Westens, II. Stuttgart: W. Kohlhammer Verlag, 1930, 1-62.
Vatican 440 group:	Malcolm C. Doubles, "The Fragment Targum: A Critical Re-examination of the Editio Princeps, Das Fragmententhargum by Moses Ginsburger, in the Light of Recent Discoveries," Ph.D. thesis, University of St. Andrews, 1962, pp. 81*-102*, 1-122.
Targum Onkelos:	Alexander Sperber, ed., The Bible in Aramaic, I. Leiden: Brill, 1959, 1-353.

ABBREVIATIONS AND SYMBOLS

B	Bomberg fragments; printed edition of the Fragment Targum.
BM	In the margin at the bottom of the page.
CG	Cairo Genizah manuscripts designated A through F in P. Kahle, Masoreten des Westens, II.
CG A	Cairo Genizah Manuscript A.
CG B	Cairo Genizah Manuscript B.
CG C	Cairo Genizah Manuscript C.
CG D	Cairo Genizah Manuscript D.
CG E	Cairo Genizah Manuscript E.
CG F	Cairo Genizah Manuscript F.
F	Cairo Genizah Manuscript F.
FT	Group of Fragment Targum manuscripts and printed edition: Ms. Vaticanus Ebr. 440; Bomberg fragments; Ms. Codex 1 of Nuremberg; Ms. Codex 1 of Leipzig; Ms. Hebr. 110 of the National Library of Paris (VBNLP).
L	Fragment Targum Manuscript Codex 1 of Leipzig.
LM	In the left margin of the page.
M	Variant reading in the margin of a manuscript.
Mgg	Variant readings in the margin(s) of a manuscript.
Ms;Mss	Manuscript; Manuscripts.
MT	Masoretic Text.
N	Fragment Targum Manuscript Codex 1 of Nuremberg.
Ni 1	Manuscript Codex Neofiti 1 of the Vatican Library.
Ni M	Variant reading in the margin of Codex Neofiti 1.
Ni Mgg	Variant readings in the margin(s) of Codex Neofiti 1
O	Targum Onkelos.
P	Fragment Targum Manuscript Hebr. 110 of the National Library of Paris.
PJ	Targum Pseudo-Jonathan.
PT	Palestinian Targums.
RM	In the right margin of the page.

ABBREVIATIONS AND SYMBOLS (Cont.)

TJ   Targum Jerushalmi.

TJ I   Targum Jerushalmi I (Targum Pseudo-Jonathan).

TJ II   Group including Cairo Genizah Manuscripts A
            through F, Ms Vaticanus Ebr. 440, Bomberg frag-
            ments, Codex 1 of Nuremberg, Codex 1 of Leipzig
            and Ms Paris 110.

V   Fragment Targum Manuscript Vaticanus Ebr. 440.

V 440   Group including Ms Vaticanus Ebr. 440, Bomberg
group   fragments, Codex 1 of Nuremberg, Codex 1 of
            Leipzig (VBNL).

I   Type I marginal variant.

II   Type II marginal variant.

*   Refers reader to a note at the bottom of the page.

.   Sign for a variant reading employed in Codex
            Neofiti 1.

[ ]   Used in the transcriptions of texts for clarifica-
            tions of the text; do not function to enclose ac-
            tual textual readings found in Codex Neofiti 1.

            Used in the translations of transcribed texts to
            enclose the translation of the text which is not
            included in the marginal variant in Aramaic.

]   Used in the transcription and translations of texts
            to mark end of textual reading and beginning of
            marginal variant.

( )   Used to enclose explanatory material.

- -   Used in the transcription of texts to show the re-
            lationship of a marginal variant to the Neofiti 1
            text or to the Pseudo-Jonathan text.   Between
            words in a marginal variant, indicate words before
            and after belong to the one variant.   Used before
            or after a marginal variant, indicate that the
            corresponding word, or words, in the Neofiti 1
            text, or the Pseudo-Jonathan text, is (are) can-
            celled out by the variant reading.

| Used in the transcription of texts to separate
            marginal variants.

            Lacuna of one word or less.

            Lacuna extending beyond one word. Nothing is to be
            inferred as to the size of the lacuna.

The numeration system we have used is that of the
Masoretic Text with that of English translations
where different given in parentheses.   The exception is Deut. 5:29(26) where the numeral in parentheses is the number of the verse in some Targums,
including Codex Neofiti 1.

CHAPTER I

INTRODUCTION

A. Targum Jerushalmi

A "Targum," from the Aramaic word understood to mean
"translation," is a rendition of the sacred Hebrew text into
Aramaic, the language which came into common use after the Babylonian Exile. There are extant Targums to the Pentateuch, the
Prophets and the Hagiographa.[1] This monograph, however, is
limited to a study of certain Jewish Targums to the Pentateuch,
the Targum Jerushalmi (TJ), also known as the Palestinian Targum
(PT), and Targum Onkelos (O).[2] Its focus is on the TJ.

Because of the ambiguity of the term "TJ," it seems wise to
include a few explanatory words. In the first place, "Targum"
has been used in the literature to refer, not only to one Targum, but to a number of Targums. Secondly, the term TJ is not
used consistently, so that it is often difficult to be sure to
what Targums reference is being made when the term is used. The
Targums designated by the term differ depending both on who is
using the term and at what time in the history of Targumic research it is being used. Also, as research goes on it is be-
coming increasingly more apparent that the use of "Palestinian"
and "Jerusalem" synonymously increases problems of identification.

The earliest explicit reference to the PT (תרגום ארץ
ישראל) is found in the Responsa of R. Hai Gaon (c. 1038). According to this Responsa, there was a tradition that the PT was
recited (in Africa? in Palestine?) as early as the 4th century
A.D. From this reference, however, we learn nothing as to what
the PT actually was.[3] Inasmuch as some Targumists hold that
all the Targums are to be connected with Palestine, to these
Targumists all Targums are Palestinian. However, O, in its
extant texts, at least, is a distinctly different version from
the other extant Targums called "Palestinian." The date given
by Jewish tradition for the original composition of O is A.D.
140.[4] By the time of the composition of the Babylonian Talmud
(c. A.D. 500), O had become a carefully standardized "official"
Targum with, usually, a literal translation of the Hebrew and

1

in close agreement with the interpretations of the Mishnah.
It was quoted as "our Targum" in the Babylonian Talmud (Kidd.
49a). The language, however, was quite different from the
Babylonian Aramaic of the Talmud. If O is included under the
rubric "PT," the term becomes meaningless for extant Targums
whose relationship to one another and to Palestine can be demonstrated to be closer than is their relationship to O or is the
relationship of O to Palestine. It seems reasonable to exclude
O from the group of Targums referred to as PT.

G. Dalman designated all Pentateuchal Targums then known
other than O as "Jeruschalmi" Targums.[5] Dalman, then, included
in the PT as "Targum Jeruschalmi I" a complete Targum to the
Pentateuch attributed to Jonathan ben Uzziel, but commonly referred to as Pseudo-Jonathan (PJ).[6] Medieval authors, who knew
both PJ and a number of texts in fragmentary form (see below),
referred to all as TJ and considered them variant versions of the
same tradition. Dalman agreed with this view. Since Dalman,
however, there have been many studies of PJ. These studies have
made clear how difficult it is to determine the relationship of
this Targum to O, on the one hand, and to the fragmentary Targums, on the other. The basic problem is whether PJ is delib-
erately a composite work in which O and the PT tradition have
been combined, or whether it is an authentic form of the PT tradition and, as such, a branch of the TJ. Thus, over a period
of time, for some Targumists TJ came to designate a limited
group of Targums (in fragmentary form), exclusive of O and PJ.
For others TJ included PJ as the bearer of an authentic PT tradition (TJ I) and the fragmentary Targums as the best witnesses to TJ (TJ II).

The term "Fragment Targum" (FT) for these texts of a fragmentary nature is used both as an individual and as a collec-
tive appellation, not for fragments of incomplete and/or damaged
texts, but for texts which contain a collection of selected
readings. The collections differ to a greater or lesser degree
among the texts. A reading may be as brief as one word (e.g.,
Ex. 36:3), frequently includes a complete verse with expansion
(e.g., Gen. 15:1), rarely renders an extended passage (e.g., Deut. 32-34).

Historically, the FT have consisted of an editio princeps,
four manuscripts, and citations. The editio princeps was published in the Bomberg edition of the Rabbinic Bible in Venice,
1517-1518.[7] This text is known as "B" and has been published
in the subsequent editions of the Rabbinic Bible and in Poly-

glots.   The four manuscripts, which date from the twelfth to
the sixteenth centuries, are the Ms. Vat. Ebr. 440 (V), Rome;
the Ms. Codex 1 of Nuremberg (N); the Ms. Codex 1 of Leipzig
(L); and the Ms. Hebr. 110 of the National Library of Paris
(P).[8]   M. C. Doubles has re-emphasized that of these five texts
those of VBNL (V 440 group) are closely related to one another
and may be considered "a family," while the text of P is distinct from them.[9]   Citations of the PT are found in Sepher he
Arûk, a lexicon compiled by R. Nathan ben Jehiel (c. 1100), and
in various Jewish literature (e.g., in Midrashim of Palestinian
rabbis and in the writings of D. Kimhi, Elias Levita).   PT
readings are also found in the Tosefta to Onkelos, but these are
written in the Aramaic of Targum Onkelos.

   Before 1930 TJ II was known only in the FT.   In 1930 Paul
Kahle published fragments of Mss of the PT from the Cairo Genizah (CG) and designated them as Mss A through F.[10]   He dated
these Mss from the seventh to the tenth or eleventh centuries.
The CG fragments, therefore, are the earliest witnesses extant
to the PT.[11]   In text and language these Mss most closely re-
semble the FT, but they contain, not individual verses or portions of verses, but a complete verse by verse rendering of portions of the Pentateuch.[12]   The impression gained from these
fragments is that the texts preserved were once parts of complete Targums.   Also, unlike VBNL, which represent a single
version of the PT, the CG fragments represent several versions.
Inasmuch as Mss E and D overlap at three places, these two
texts can be studied comparatively at these points.   Such study
reveals that they differ from each other much more than any text
of VBNL differs from any other.

   Additional Mss belonging to each group have come to light
in recent years.[13]   Yet every text of the FT and CG is a fragmentary one.   So it was with great delight that Targumists, and
others, received the announcement in 1956 of the discovery of a
complete TJ to the Pentateuch.   This copy of TJ is a sixteenth
century Ms, the Codex Neofiti 1 (Ni 1), discovered by A. Díez
Macho.[14]   Not only is the text a virtually complete copy of the
Pentateuch, but the Ms is replete with marginal (Ni M) and interlinear (Ni I) glosses.[15]   As might be expected, the Codex
has been and is the subject of much research.   The first discovery, of course, was that the text belonged with TJ represented
by the texts of the FT and CG (TJ II) rather than with that of
PJ (TJ I).   The Ni 1 text shows no striking affinity for any

4

other extant witness within the TJ II group. S. Speier, in a
series of articles, has called attention to the relation of a
large number of citations in the <u>Sefer</u> <u>he</u> <u>Arûk</u> to readings doc-
umented only in Ni 1.[16] This same observation has been made
independently by G. Cowling.[17] We thus have evidence for the
existence of the Ni 1 text type as early as 1100. With the
discovery of Codex Ni 1 there are now extant three complete
texts of the Targum to the Pentateuch: Onkelos (Babylonian),
Pseudo-Jonathan (TJ I), and Codex Neofiti 1 (TJ II). There
are also a large number of fragments: FT, CG, Ni Mgg, Ni I.
In Chapter II of the monograph we adduce evidence which we hope
will help to clarify the relationship of these various TJ II
texts.

B.   <u>History</u> <u>of</u> <u>Targumic</u> <u>Research</u> <u>in</u> <u>Palestinian</u> <u>Aramaic</u>
     The great flowering of Biblical scholarship in the 19th
century produced a renewed interest in all kinds of evidence
which might help the scholar to get behind the facade of tra-
ditional interpretation. Specific attention was focused on
the Targums and their language because of the possibility of
gaining insight into the life and language of pre-Talmudic Juda-
ism, or -- from a Christian viewpoint -- into the life and language of the time when Jesus lived. In the 20th century, several new discoveries have added to our store of material for the
study of Palestinian Aramaic. These are the CG material, the
Dead Sea Mss, and, most recently, Codex Ni 1. Each of these
has produced new studies. The following discussion can be con-
veniently divided into periods following each discovery.
     1. <u>Nineteenth</u> <u>and</u> <u>Early</u> <u>Twentieth</u> <u>Century</u>. The Aramaic
texts of O, PJ, and the FT had all been published by the end of
the sixteenth century and reissued thereafter in various Rabbinic
Bibles and Polyglots. One result of the renewed interest in Targumic materials was an effort to make these texts, as well as
heretofore unpublished manuscript materials, more readily acces-
sible.
     In 1862 an English translation of O, PJ, and FT B by J. W.
Etheridge was published.[18] This translation was specifically
intended to be an aid in working with the Targums in the original
Aramaic and was therefore rendered in an extremely literal, word-
for-word style. A. Berliner's new edition of O appeared in
1884.[19] In 1899 Moses Ginsburger published P in its entirety,
together with an apparatus of variant readings in VNL collated

against B (which was not reproduced).[20]   He also included a
list of citations from the PT found in various Jewish works.   A
few years later, Ginsburger published an edition of PJ based on
the only extant Ms.[21]

During this period considerable attention was given to the
Aramaic of the various Pentateuchal Targums, and efforts were
made through textual and linguistic studies to understand the
history of these works and the traditions underlying them.
Some of the chief questions raised were:

Was there one PT from which all later ones developed, or
a variety of traditions which were collated and edited into the
final official version?

Were the earliest traditions transmitted orally, in writing,
or in both forms?

Did the developing tradition move from literal rendition to
embellishment and paraphrase, or from free and expanded versions
to a more disciplined form?

Which type of language should be regarded as literary, which
as a closer reflection of the everyday spoken language?

How were the various Pentateuchal Targums related to one
another, to the Masoretic Text (MT), to the Mishnah, Talmud, and
(particularly) to the Midrashim?

Was the FT simply a set of glosses, or was it the remains
of a complete text?

An early treatment of these questions was given by Leopold
Zunz in 1832.[22] He maintained that there must have been written
Aramaic translations in the time of the Hasmonaeans and dated O
to the time of Philo. He considered Targum Jonathan to the
Prophets somewhat different in dialect from O and subsequent to
it; both, however, were prior to passages in Talmud and Midrashim, which were dependent upon the Targums. He regarded PJ and
the FT as different recensions of the same work, and described
their language as a Palestinian dialect with a mixture of Hebrew,
similar to the Jerusalem Talmud, the Midrashim, and the Targums
to the Writings. Although he believed that free or expanded
translation was the older usage, on the basis of a number of late
readings he dated the PT, which contained free or expanded translations, to the second half of the seventh century A.D.

Frankel, Geiger, and Nöldeke placed more value than had Zunz
on the extant PT as sources for the oldest traditions.[23] Hermann
Seligsohn, on the other hand, believed that O was the earliest
Targum; that the FT had never existed in a full recension but had

been composed as a series of glosses to O; and that the still
later PJ had completed the work, creating a new Targum, but one
dependent on and later than O.[24]   W. Bacher believed that O,
the FT, and PJ had a common origin in an older PT; his views on
the nature and dating of FT and PJ were similar to those of
Seligsohn.[25]

An early work dealing more specifically with linguistic
problems was that of S. D. Luzzato.[26]   He distinguished four
dialects in addition to Biblical Aramaic and the language of the
Babylonian Talmud: O and Jonathan to the Prophets, which represented a literary dialect in use in Babylon, whereas the Babylonian Talmud was written in the common language of the Babylonian
Jews; PJ, the literary language of Palestine; the Palestinian
Talmud and Midrashim, the common dialect of the Jews of Palestine; and the Targums to the Writings.

Gustaf Dalman's Grammatik des Jüdisch-Palästinischen
Aramäisch gave the first systematic grammatical treatment of
all dialects which could be regarded as Palestinian.[27]   In the
second edition of his Grammatik he described O and Jonathan to
the Prophets as the best witnesses for an early Judean dialect
in spite of their "literary" character. He took the Aramaic
portions of the Palestinian Talmud and Midrashim as examples of
Galilean Aramaic of a somewhat later period. He described the
language of the PT as "mixed" and not earlier than the fifth
century A.D. because of the presence of Babylonian Aramaic words
and signs of dependence upon O. Dalman evidently saw no reason
to attempt to distinguish between the languages of Targums
"Jeruschalmi I" (PJ), "Jeruschalmi II" (FT), and "Jeruschalmi
III" (Tosefta to Onkelos). He was heavily influenced by the
language of PJ, which was by far his most extensive source, in
his judgment that the PT was a source of "mixed" language.

Dalman's view of the PT as late and "mixed" was also that
of Jacob Bassfreund, who followed Zunz in most other respects.[28]
He found this Targum to be dependent on the Talmud and the youn-
ger Midrashim and dated it in its basic form to the second half
of the seventh century A.D. Both the FT and PJ were described
as later versions of the one original PT. Since time had to be
allowed for the development of divergent recensions, these recensions could be dated at the earliest from the eighth century A.D.

Dalman's grammar took into account all Targumic Aramaic
sources then known. Similarly, Jastrow's Dictionary,[29] which
appeared in 1903, was complete for all Targums then available.

Scholars of that era must have felt a certain sense of completion. Dalman's grammatical system was widely accepted and remained the dominant one for several decades. After 1930, however, a quite different view, identified with the name of Paul Kahle, gained ascendancy.

2. <u>1930</u>: <u>The Cairo Genizah Fragments</u>. In 1930 Kahle published the CG Mss.[30] The earliest of the Mss was dated by him to the seventh century A.D., or, at the latest, the beginning of the eighth. A theory such as that of Bassfreund that the PT first came into existence in the seventh century thus became untenable, since time had to be allowed for the dissemination of the Targum from Palestine to Egypt. The presence of multiple recensions of the Targum, moreover, suggested that it was held in high esteem and was in regular use in the West long after Targum O had become established in the East.

The language of the CG Mss, furthermore, did not show the relationship to the language of O found in PJ, but resembled more closely the dialects of the Palestinian Talmud, Christian Palestinian Aramaic, and Samaritan Aramaic. Thus there was no barrier to dating this Targum to a period contemporary with, or earlier than, the Palestinian Talmud. Kahle took this language relationship as a sign that the PT had been the original Targum of Palestine, written, like the Palestinian Talmud, in the language of the people. He described the language of Targum O as an artificial, literary one, and pointed out that Dalman had also regarded it as literary. PJ was seen as a combination of O and the older PT.[31]

In 1941, Kahle gave the Schweich Lectures on the CG materials.[32] He emphasized further the Babylonian provenance of Targum O and the artificial nature of its language. He maintained, in addition, that the text (and language) of the PT could be dated, not merely to a period contemporary with the Palestinian Talmud, but to pre-Christian times. This conclusion was based on a passage from PJ (Deut. 33:11), which is understood by many to refer to John Hyrcanus in a manner not possible after his reign (135-105 B.C.), and upon the non-Mishnaic interpretation of Ex. 22:4,5 in CG Ms A.[33] On the basis of these two passages, the generally popular, Midrashic character of the translation, and its lack of a fixed text, Kahle concluded that "in the Palestinian Targum of the Pentateuch we have in the main material coming from pre-Christian times....And we possess this material in a language of which we can say that it is very similar to that spoken by the earliest Christians."[34]

Kahle's view was very widely accepted by his own students and others, and his position concerning the antiquity of the language of the CG Targums was taken as proved.   Unfortunately, little was accomplished until very recently toward the completion of thorough, systematic studies of these texts and their language.   A proposed grammar based upon the CG fragments, to be published by Kahle and William B. Stevenson,[35] was never completed.   In the years following the publication of the fragments, Prof. A. J. Wensinck of Leiden made a study of the language of the PT and of the closely related Aramaic of the Palestinian Talmud.   His intent was to produce a lexicon and grammar which, unlike Dalman's, would be based entirely upon Palestinian material.   His source for this material was to be "the language spoken in Palestine at the time of the beginning of Christianity there."[36]   This project was still incomplete at Wensinck's death in 1939.   By 1956, when Codex Ni 1 was discovered, it had still not been completed.   Since that time, the focus of attention has been upon the production of a grammar of Palestinian Aramaic by utilizing Codex Ni 1.   Such a work is planned by students of Díez Macho.[37]

In the meantime, a completely new body of Aramaic material became available when the Dead Sea Scrolls came to light, and a new approach was made to the whole question of Palestinian Aramaic.

3.   1947: The Dead Sea Scrolls.   Since 1947, a considerable number of Aramaic documents from Qumrân, Murabba'at, and other locations in the area east and southeast of Bethlehem have been published with accompanying linguistic apparatus such as concordances and descriptive grammars.   These MSS can be dated, on external and internal grounds, between the second century B.C. and the first part of the second century A.D.   The impact of these discoveries on Targumic studies is twofold.

First, the Job and Leviticus fragments demonstrate the existence of written Targums at an early date.[38]   Secondly, all the Aramaic material discovered provides a new datable corpus for comparison with previously known Aramaic materials, including the Targums.   The implications with regard to the language of O are particularly important.

Linguistically, the Dead Sea materials show varying degrees of development from Imperial Aramaic, with which they show strong affinities.   Kahle had classed Biblical Aramaic and the Aramaic

of O together as "the same literary language," which is essen-
tially undatable.[39]   A quite different view has been developed
by E. Y. Kutscher.   He sees the period between the composition
of the book of Daniel and the appearance of the Talmudic dialects as a time of linguistic transition when Imperial Aramaic
gradually broke down into separate dialects.   During the earlier stages of this development, Eastern and Western dialects
were not yet clearly distinguished.   Nabatean and Palmyrene
inscriptions, dated from the first century B.C. through the
third century A.D., are not in Syriac but in a language closer
to Imperial Aramaic -- and to the Aramaic of the Dead Sea documents.   On the basis of a detailed study of the language of the
Genesis Apocryphon in comparison with such dated materials,
Kutscher dates the language of this particular document to the
latter part of the first century B.C.[40]   He also finds a re-
semblance between this dialect and that of O and, accordingly,
maintains a Palestinian, probably Judean, origin for O.

> The T.O. represented, like our scroll, R.
> [Reichsaramäisch] coloured by Western Aramaic.
> After the destruction of the Temple and the crush-
> ing of the Bar-Kochba revolt, which destroyed the
> cultural centres of Judaea, this literary style,
> a cross between R. and the Western Aramaic, died
> out, and instead the local spoken Western Aramaic
> dialects started to be used as means of literary
> expression and the Palestinian Targum came into
> being.   But in Babylonia the language of the T.O.
> had always been a stranger, because of the western
> colour.   Therefore the events in the west did not
> affect its position.[41]

It is to be noted that Kutscher, like Kahle, connected the
PT with the local spoken dialect.   However, Kutscher did not
believe the Western dialects existed unchanged from the Christian
era to the period for which they are attested; that is, beginning with the fourth or, at the earliest, the third century A.D.
He distinguished three dialects of Western Aramaic -- Galilean
Aramaic (Palestinian Talmud, Midrashim, Targums), Samaritan
Aramaic, and Christian Palestinian Aramaic -- and stated that
"all of these reflect the linguistic situation of about the
middle of the first millennium C.E."[42]

Joseph Fitzmyer accepts Kutscher's evaluation of the
Aramaic of the Genesis Apocryphon as "a transitional type between the Biblical Aramaic of Daniel and that of the Palestinian Targums or Christian Palestinian Aramaic."[43]   His
classification of Aramaic dialects is in essential agreement
with that of Kutscher although their terminologies are not
identical.

Study of the language of the various Dead Sea materials
and publication of the texts was in progress when the discovery
of Codex Ni 1 produced publications which, following Kahle's
view, hailed the newly discovered Targum as a rich source for
the language of Jesus' day.[44]   The opposing viewpoints are well
exemplified in an exchange of views between Kahle and Kutscher.

4. Codex Ni 1 and the Kahle-Kutscher Controversy.   In
1958 Kahle wrote an article in which he restated his view concerning the antiquity and linguistic value of the PT.   Referring to the newly discovered Codex Ni 1, he said, "Das Palästinische Pentateuchtargum wird sprachlich und sachlich von
grösster Bedeutung sein, nun da wir es vollständig in Händen
haben."[45]   He criticized Kutscher for referring to the language
of the Palestinian Talmud, Midrashim, and the PT as "Galilean
Aramaic," since, in Kahle's view, this was the spoken language
of all the people of Palestine.   He also criticized Kutscher
for neglecting to use this language as a criterion for the dating of the Genesis Apocryphon, emphasizing, however, that a full
evaluation could not be made until new editions and critical
works had appeared for the Aramaic texts involved.

Kutscher's indignant reply to Kahle's criticism appeared
two years later.[46]   Kutscher insisted that, in dating a language, one must work from materials having an established date.
Thus, his emphasis had been on inscriptions and other materials
whose date and place of origin were certain.   He questioned the
validity of employing the language of the Palestinian Talmud
(third-fifth centuries A.D.) for the dating of a text, necessarily on purely external grounds, no later than the first century
A.D.   The same argument would apply a fortiori to the CG Targums
(not to mention Ni 1, a sixteenth century manuscript!).

Wir wären Prof. Kahle zu grossen Dank
verpflichtet wenn er uns zeigen könnte, wie man
mit Hilfe dieser Texte, aus dem 7.-9. Jh., unsern
Text ins 1 (!) Jh. datieren kann.[47]

Kutscher concluded that Kahle had no evidence for assuming the language of Palestine had not altered during a period of 500-700 years, even if there were evidence for the antiquity of the ideas found in the Targum. "Was Kahle...bezüglich des Inhalts behauptet, ist für die Sprache dieses Targum demnach vollkommen belanglos."[48]

In the same issue a brief reply from Kahle appeared, in which he stressed that new publications and language studies were being made by his students and the students of his students. He expressed the hope that with this additional study the issue would be clarified.[49] This controversy made the scholarly world more aware that the status of the Aramaic dialects found in the various Targums was far from settled. The work accomplished in the years since has made for much more effective communication among proponents of differing views, if not yet for consensus.

It is beyond the scope of this monograph to review all the recent work on the Pentateuch Targums. A survey of work in the field to date has appeared in the introduction to each volume of Díez Macho's editio princeps of Codex Ni 1, and a number of other useful summaries and bibliographies are available.[50] We have attempted here to give only enough background to make clear the rationale for the present work. Since the time of Dalman we have moved from a situation in which all Targumic materials known were available in published form, and data from them incorporated in a dictionary and a grammar, to the current position; namely, the possession of vastly expanded resources which are being actively utilized by scholars, even though the resources have not yet been completely published or analyzed. It is obvious that no full re-evaluation of the Targums can be made without the full publication of new texts, without new editions of previously published texts which take into account new evidence, and without the processing of all linguistic data in these texts, as a first step toward the updating of Aramaic lexicons and grammars.

The present work is offered as a contribution to the first effort. At this writing, the publication of the editio princeps of Codex Ni 1 is near completion. It may well be asked why we have chosen in this monograph to publish and translate portions of Ni 1 already included in the editio princeps. Our reason is related to the complexity of the Ni 1 Ms, which contains, in addition to a continuous text of the Pentateuch, a large number of interlinear and marginal notations constituting a textual apparatus to variant Targumic versions.[51] Prof.

Pérez Castro has pointed out that in Ni 1 the world has gained
not one but three new Targumic texts, "ya que en los márgenes
del Neofiti aparecen constantemente variantes de otros dos
manuscritos."[52]   In addition, there is evidence that the beginning (Gen. 1:1-3:4) and end (Deut. 29:17(18)-34:12) of the
main text of the Ni 1 Ms have been copied from a number of
Targum versions distinct from that of the central portion of
the text.[53]   In order for an accurate evaluation to be made
of the historical relationships of the texts, language patterns,
and traditions of the Targums, it is very important that separate
texts not be confused.   The chief purpose of this work is to
draw attention to the multiplicity of texts within Ni 1.

Because the variant texts of Gen. 1:1-3:4 and Deut. 29:
17(18) ff can be examined easily in the editio princeps, they
have not been reproduced here.   The continuity of one set of
Mgg has been recognized by us and others, and we reproduce individual and extended passages to demonstrate this continuity
to those unfamiliar with the Ms.[54]   The chief problem of identification centers around those verses in Ni 1 provided with
two or three sets of Mgg.   Since these are not so easily located
and studied from the editio princeps, we have attempted to reproduce in full the texts and Mgg for all verses with undoubted
multiple marginal variants.[55]

When these verses had been assembled, certain further decisions had to be made.   Where other texts, such as CG or FT,
were present, one marginal text regularly corresponded with
these.   The second marginal text conformed closely to no known
text, and often included unusual word forms and distinctive
traditions.   Furthermore, it showed affinities (but not a close
identity) with PJ and raised hopes that it might provide an important link in the puzzle of PJ's relation to the other Targums.
We have, therefore, pursued this second marginal text some dis-
tance into the realm of hypothesis, using linguistic data from
firmly identified texts to reach decisions about more problem-
atical ones.

Much of what is presented here is necessarily tentative.
The classification of texts which exist only as marginal notes
to another text presents many problems.   Nevertheless, we believe the present situation can be clarified considerably beyond
the point now reached.   Further, we consider the best possible
identification and classification of the abundant new material
of Codex Ni 1 invaluable for the advancement of understanding

of the textual history of the Targums and of Palestinian Aramaic.

We hope that the transcriptions and translations which make up the major portion of this work will serve both as useful working papers for further detailed study by specialists, and as an illustrative sampling of diverse Targumic versions for those with a more general interest in the traditions represented by these texts.

CHAPTER II

VARIANT VERSIONS IN Ni 1 MGG

A.   Type I Mgg

That there is a close relationship between Ni 1 Mgg and
certain TJ II texts has been rather widely observed.[1] However,
the fragmentary nature of the FT and CG texts makes it difficult to appreciate the nature of this relationship.   Much of
the material of Ni 1, both text and Mgg, is paralleled by no
other member of the TJ II group.   Even where other members
are extant not all members are extant for the same passage.
Thus, one is limited to certain sections or certain verses of
Ni 1 for comparison with other texts.   By using examples taken
from many passages of the Ms, whether or not paralleled by
TJ II texts, but accompanied by TJ II text(s) if and where
extant, we present the evidence for the conclusion that Ni Mgg
and FT-CG are closely allied.   The examples also illustrate
the homogeneity and continuity of these Mgg.   This continuity
has been noted by others, but to our knowledge it has not been
demonstrated.[2]

In Appendix I to this chapter (pp. 20-31) we set forth a
selection of verses with Mgg from Ni 1.[3]   For the verses in
the first group, "A," there are extant complete, or nearly
complete, TJ II texts, so that comparison of Ni Mgg with at
least one TJ II text is possible.   One may note, for example,
that the Ni Mgg to Gen. 7:14 and 9:9 are in exact agreement,
and those to Gen. 29:13 nearly so, with the text of CG E.   In
fact, if the Mgg are substituted for the Ni 1 text at the ap-
propriate places, texts (almost) identical to those of CG E
are produced.   This is also true of the Ni Mgg at Lev. 23:2
and Nu. 28:23, except that the text is that of CG F instead
of E.   At Deut. 15:11 the Ni Mgg correspond to the text of
VB.   At Ex. 20:1, where the M can be compared with three texts,
the M agrees with V and CG F, but not with P; while at Nu.
4:20 and 34:6 the Mgg agree with both VB and P.   At Ex. 13:20
the Ni M agrees with the extant portion of V, but not with P.
On the other hand, the Ni Mgg to Ex. 9:29 are not in agreement with CG D; rather there are differences in both vocabulary and grammar; CG D agrees with Ni 1 text against Ni Mgg.

From the comparison of texts in group A, Ni Mgg can be
seen to be identical, or nearly identical to various   TJ II

14

texts.   The text may be V, VB, VBP, or CG E or F.   Where P
differs from VB, the Mgg are closer to VB.   A correspondence
does not exist with the one illustration using CG D.

The next group of verses, "B," illustrates the possibility
of comparison where only a portion of a verse is paralleled by
another TJ II text.   One may note, for example, that the Ni Mgg
at Ex. 36:3, Lev. 3:9 and 27:14, and Nu. 30:17(16) are identical,
or nearly so, to the portion of V text extant.   At Lev. 3:9 a
good deal of the V text parallels the Ni Mgg.   At Ex. 36:3 a
one-word fragment parallels the longer Ni Mgg.   At Lev. 27:14
the Ni Mgg are a series of one-word Mgg, two of which parallel
the V text, but at the third M the V text is not extant.   At
Gen. 34:12 the FT text is not extant parallel to the Ni Mgg.
Where it is extant, it is in close agreement with Ni 1 text.
CG C, for which the entire verse is extant, agrees with Ni 1
text as closely here as does the FT.   CG C continues in close
agreement to the end of the verse.   The two Mgg disagree with
CG C.   At Deut. 5:29(26) the portion of the V text extant parallels one of the Ni Mgg and agrees with it.   The verse is
wholly extant in CG D.   Where CG D parallels the V text and Ni
Mgg, however, CG D is closer to the Ni 1 text than to that of
Ni Mgg and V.   This agreement with the Ni 1 text against Ni Mgg
is evident also for the remainder of the verse.   As at Ex 9:29
(Group A), the Ni Mgg do not correspond to CG D.   Besides the
M which corresponds to the V text, a part of one M, ‏ולזרעיית[ו]‎
‏בניה/]‎, parallels the CG E text at Gen. 9:9 (Group A).

For the third group, "C" there are no parallel passages
extant in TJ II.   Yet the underlined variants which could be
compared with a TJ II text in group A, and are found with variants which can be compared with a TJ II text in group B, appear
again, singly or in context, in the Mgg in group C.

One may also note that these underlined words or phrases
are found not only in all three groups, but also in various
combinations with one another.   While ‏הנון‎ is the only member
of this group of words or phrases at Gen. 7:14, it is found with ‏דאית‎
at Nu. 34:6, with ‏דאית‎ and ‏כן‎ [‏בגין]‎ at Deut. 15:11, with ‏כן‎ at Nu.
21:14.   While ‏זרו‎ is found alone (of this group) at Ex. 34:8,
it is found with ‏עוד‎ at Gen. 24:20.   While ‏דאית‎ is found alone
at Lev. 19:9 and Ex. 13:20, it is found, besides with ‏הנון‎ at
Nu. 34:6 and with ‏הנון‎ and ‏כן‎ at Deut. 15:11, with ‏מימריה דיי/‎
and ‏מן בגין כן‎ at Ex. 20:11.   While [‏ה]אליין‎ is found alone
at both Gen. 29:13 and Nu. 28:23,   it is found with ‏הנון‎ at

16

Lev. 23:2.   While ליורא׳ (illustrative of gentilic ending
"א״י") is found alone at Nu. 4:20, "א״י-" is found with כן at Gen.
10:18.   All of these combinations, and others, are found in the
texts in group A.   In group B עוד and הנון are found in the M
at Ex. 36:3.   The Mgg at Nu. 30:17(16)   include מימריה די׳/ and
אל׳ין.   In group C זרז occurs with מן בגין כן at Gen. 19:22 (In
A it was found with עוד.);   הנון is found with מצראי at Ex. 8:22(26)
and with אל׳ין at Nu. 13:28.   לליורא׳is found with הנון and
דאית at Nu. 1:50 and with מימריה די׳/ and כן at Nu. 8:20.
מימריה די׳/ is found with עוד at Deut. 3:26.   Other combinations, also, exist in group C.

    We recapitulate below the occurrences of the underlined
words in the various groups.

[ה]אל׳ין]	Group A: Gen. 29:13; Lev. 23:2;
	Nu. 28:23.
	Group B: Nu. 30:17(16).
	Group C: Gen. 26:3; Nu. 13:28;
	Deut. 15:5.
דאית	Group A: Ex. 13:20; 20:11; Lev.
	19:9; Nu. 34:6; Deut. 15:11.
	Group B: Lev. 3:9.
	Group C: Gen. 19:22; Nu. 1:50;
	Deut. 12:12.
ה]י[נון	Group A: Gen. 7:14; Lev. 23:2;
	Nu. 21:14; 34:6; Deut. 15:11.
	Group B: Ex. 36:3.
	Group C: Ex. 8:22(26); Nu. 1:50;
	Nu. 13:28; Deut. 20:15.
זרז	Group A: Gen: 24:20; Ex. 34:8.
	Group B: None.
	Group C: Gen. 19:22.
זרעיית בני/	Group A: Gen. 9:9.
	Group B: Deut. 5:29(26).
	Group C: Gen. 26:3.
טליתה	Group A: Deut. 22:20, 21.
	Group B: Gen. 34:12.
	Group C: Ex. 2:5.
[מן] בגין כן or כן	Group A: Gen. 10:18; Lev. 24:20;
	Nu. 13:23; Nu. 21:14;
	Deut. 15:11.

‏[מן] בגין כן‎ or ‏כן‎	Group B: Lev. 27:14. Group C: Gen. 19:22; Nu. 8:20; Deut. 20:15.
‏מימריה דיי/‎	Group A: Ex. 20:1,11; Nu. 21:14; Deut. 28:68. Group B: Nu. 30:17(16). Group C: Nu. 8:20; Deut. 3:26.
‏עוד‎	Group A: Gen. 24:20; Ex. 9:29; Nu. 32:14; Deut. 28:68. Group B: Gen. 8:10; Ex. 36:3. Group C: Deut. 3:26.
Gentilics in ‏אי‎	Group A: Gen. 10:18; Nu. 4:20. Group B: Nu. 35:2,4. Group C: Ex. 8:22(26); Nu. 1:50; Nu. 8:20; Deut. 12:12.

Many of the Mgg in Ni 1, including those previously discussed, are one-word citations which alter vocabulary or morphology, frequently without effect on the meaning of the text (e.g., ‏הנון‎ for ‏אינון‎, ‏עוד‎ for ‏חוב‎, ‏דאית‎ for ‏די‎ or ‏ד‎). The three extended passages reproduced in Appendix II (pp. 32-43), two with comparative material from TJ II (Gen. 6:18-7:15; Gen. 9:5-23) and one without (Nu. 18:21-32), illustrate this use of one-word variants in the margins of Ni 1. It can be seen from these passages that variants under discussion are also found in TJ I (e.g., ‏ה[י]נון‎ at Gen. 7:14; Nu. 18:21; ‏עוד‎ at Gen. 9:11 (twice); ‏בגין כן‎ at Nu. 18:24). However, a collation of TJ II and/or TJ I texts against the Ni 1 text and margin shows that, while the words are related linguistically to TJ I, as marginal variants in Ni 1 they do not correlate as well textually with TJ I as with CG E and/or FT. On the contrary, a study of the extended passages makes clear that these short variants, together with the other variants, are to be understood as evidence for one variant text. The transcriptions with comparative texts from TJ II in Appendices I and II also illustrate the affinity of this text to those of the FT-CG E and F, on the one hand, and its independence of them, on the other. The Mgg of this text we designate, "Type I Mgg."

B. Multiple Mgg

The majority of verses in Codex Ni 1 have but one variant reading to any one portion of the verse, and the evidence is

rather impressive that these variant readings stem from a
common textual tradition.   There are verses, however, for
which there are two (rarely three) variant readings to the
same portion of the verse.   In order truly to illustrate the
relationship of these sets of multiple variants in respect to
occurrence, we would need to transcribe a tremendously long
passage.   One set occurs infrequently.   As can be seen from
the extended passage transcribed in Appendix IIIA (pp. 44-55),
the other set is continuous with verses before and after those
verses at which the multiple variants occur (Ex. 19:3,18). The
continuous set of Mgg is now familiar as Type I Mgg.   The
other set, as can be seen from a comparison of texts, approx-
imates the text of TJ I, although the correlation is by no
means as close as is that of Type I Mgg and TJ II texts.
This approximation of one set of Mgg to TJ I can be seen also
in the individual verses with multiple Mgg transcribed in Appendix IIIB (pp. 55-59).

In order to facilitate further study of the passages with
multiple variants, we have transcribed the verses with undoubted multiple marginal readings (pp. 83-117).[4]   The approximation of one set of Mgg to TJ I was not always as clear as in
the above examples.   Therefore, for purposes of study, those
Mgg which showed a distinct relationship to TJ I were classed
together as "Type II Mgg."   These Type II Mgg were most easily identified where Type I witnesses (CG, FT) were extant and
could be correlated with Type I Mgg.   As the study proceeded,
some other Mgg were added to the group on the basis of their
use of language elements unknown or extremely infrequent in
TJ II witnesses, but typical of TJ I and/or O (see pp. 66,67).

The remaining Mgg were further subdivided.   Mgg marked
with ס"א were grouped together, since the special mark suggested they were distinct in origin from those surrounding
them.   Passages with three sets of Mgg were also grouped. The
remaining passages with two sets of Mgg were divided into
"Similar" and "Unclassified" groups.

By the method of comparison of texts, then, we found one
set of variants which appear to be homogeneous and continuous
and to be collations from a TJ II text heretofore unknown, similar to FT-CG E and F, and recoverable to a significant degree
by substitution of these Mgg for a Ni 1 text.   We found, in-
termittently appearing, second and third sets of variants, and

we isolated a subgroup within these both as significantly
"different" from TJ II witnesses and as bearing a relationship
to the TJ I text type.   In Chapter III, we turn to a consideration of the linguistic character of "Type I" and "Type II"
Mgg.

APPENDIX I*

A. Ni 1 Texts and Mgg with Complete, or Nearly Complete,
    TJ II Texts

Gen. 7:14

	Gen. 7:14
Ni 1	אינון וכל חיתה למינה וכל בעירה למינה וכל רחשא דרחש על
Ni M	רמסא דרמס <u>הנון</u>
CG E	הנון וכל חיתה למינה וכל בעירה למינה וכל רמסה דרמס על

Ni 1	ארעא למינהו וכל עופה למינה וכל דפרח וכל דטייס:
Ni M	צפר - - דטייס למינהון
CG E	ארעה למינהון וכל עופה למינה וכל צפר דטאייס:

Gen. 9:9

	Gen. 9:9
Ni 1	ואנ/ הא אנה מקיים ית קיימי עמכון ועם בניכון
Ni M	רית <u>זרעיית בניכון</u>
CG E	ואנה הא אנה מקיים ית קיימי עמכון רית זרעיית בניכון

Ni 1	בתריכון:
Ni M	מן בת/
CG E	מן בתרכון:

Gen. 10:18

	Gen. 10:18
Ni 1	רית ארוודייא רית זימרייא רית אנטוכיא ומן בתר כדין
Ni M	לוטסאי חמצאי רית <u>אנטירבאי</u> <u>כן</u>
V	רית אנטרדיאי רית חמצאי רית אנטוכייא מן בתר כן

Ni 1	אתפרשו זרעיהון דכנעניא:
Ni M	זרערותהון דכנענאי
V	איתפרשו ניסי אומייא:

Gen. 24:20

	Gen. 24:20
Ni 1	ואוחיית ופנית קולתה לגו מורכיון ורהטת חוב
Ni M	<u>וזרזת</u> ואוחיit קו/ <u>עוד</u>
V	וזרזת ואחתת מורכייה לגו שיקיא ורהטת עוד

Ni 1	לבאירה למימלי ומלת לכל גמלוי:
Ni M	ואשקיית
V	לבירא למימלי ומלת ואשקיאת לכל גמלוהי:

*In the Appendices to Ch. II obvious and insignificant scrib-
al errors in Ni 1 text and Mgg have been corrected.

20

Gen. 29:13   Gen. 29:13

והוי כדי   שמע לבן ית שמעה דיעקב בר אחתה ורהט   Ni 1
כיון דשמע   Ni M
והווה כדי   שמע לבן ית שמעיה דיעקב בר אחתה ור▨▨   CG E

לקדמותיה וגפף יתה ונשק יתה ואעיל יתה לגו   בייתיה ותני   Ni 1
ועל   - - - - לבייתיה   Ni M
וחבק
לקדמותה ו▨▨ק יתה ונשק יתה ואעל יתה   לבייתה ות▨   CG E

ללבן ית כל פתגמא ׃ האילין׃   Ni 1
האליין   Ni M
▨יה האליין׃   CG E

Ex. 9:29   Ex. 9:29

ואמר ליה משה   במפקי ית קרתא אפרש ית כפי ידי קדם יי/   Ni 1
כד נפוק מן   כף   Ni M
ואמר ליה משה   במפקי ית קרתא אפרוס   כפי ידיי קדם יי/   CG D

קלייא יתמנעון וברדא לא יהוי תוב מן בגלל דתדע ארום דיי/   Ni 1
יפסקון   עוד   Ni M
קלייא יתמנעון וברדא לא יהוי תוב מן בגלל דתדע ארום דיי/   CG D

היא   ארעא׃   Ni 1
היא כל ארע/   Ni M
היא כל ארעא׃   CG D

Ex. 13:20   Ex. 13:20

ונטלו מסכות ושרון באיתם   בסיפה מדברה׃   Ni 1
ראית בסייפי   Ni M
ראית בסייפי מדברה׃   V
ונטלו מסכות ושרו   באיתם   דבסיפוי דמדברא׃   P

Ex 20:1   Ex. 20:1

יי/ ית כל שבח דיבדרייא האליין למימר׃   Ni 1
מימרי/ דיי/   Ni M
ומלל מימרא דיי/ ית כל שבח דבירייא האילין למימר׃   V
ומלל מימריה דיי/ ית כל שבח דביריה האליין למימר׃   CG F
ומליל דיבדריה דיי/ ית כל שבח דבריא   האילין למימר׃   P

Ex. 20:11   Ex. 20:11

שמיא	ארום לשתא יומין ברא יי/	Ni 1
ושכלל מימרי/ דיי/	_אשתה_	Ni M
ית שמייה	ארום אישתה יומין ברא יי/ ושכלל	CG F
ית שמיא	ארום שיתא יומין עבד יי/	P

דכהון והוה _שבא_	וית ארעא ית ימיה וית כל מה	Ni 1
דאי/ בהו – – – –		Ni M
וית ארעא וית ימייה וית כל מה דאית בהון		CG F
דכהון	וית ארעא וית ימיא וית כל	P

בגין כדין ברך	ונייח קדמוי ביומא שביעיא	Ni 1
מן בגין כן ברך מימרי/	ואתניח – – – ביום/	Ni M
מן בגין כדן בריך ממ/	ביומה שביעייה:	CG F
על כן ברך	ביומא שביעאה	P

יי/ ית יומא דשבתא וקדש יתיה:		Ni 1
דיי/		Ni M
דיי/ ית יומה דשובתה וקדש יתיה:		CG F
יי/ ית יומא דשבתא וקדיש יתיה [text continues]		P

Ex. 34:8   Ex. 34:8

משה ועקד לארעא ואודי ושבח:	ואוחי	Ni 1
על/ א	_וזריז_	Ni M
וזריז [read, וזריז] משה ועקד על ארעא ואודי ושבח:		V

Lev. 19:9   Lev. 19:9

ובחצדכון ית חצדא דארעכון לא תשיצון אומנה אחריה		Ni 1
חצד אר/		Ni M
ובחצדכון ית חצד ארעכון לא תשיצון אומן אוחריא		V
לא תשיצון אומנא מחדיא		P

דחקלכון למחצד ולקטה דחצדיכון		Ni 1
דאית בחקליכון למחצד ולקט חצדכון		Ni M
דאית בחקלכון למחצוד ולקט חצדכון		V
[read, אחריא] דאית בה בחקליכון למחצד:		P

לא תלקטון:	Ni 1
לא תלקטון:	V

Lev. 23:2   Lev. 23:2

Ni 1	מלל עם בני ישראל ותימר להון מועדוי דיי/ די
Ni M	סדר
CG F	מלל עם בני יש/ ותימר להון סדרי מועדיי דיי/ די

Ni 1	תאריעון יתהון יומין טבין ואירעון קדישין אלין אינון
Ni M	וארועין קדישין אליין הנון
CG F	תאריעון יומין טבין ואירועין קדישין אליין אינון

Ni 1	זמן סדרי מועדוי׃
Ni M	סד/
CG F	זמן סדרי מועדיי׃

Lev. 24:20   Lev. 24:20

Ni 1	תבר תשלומי דתבר עין תשלומי עין שן תשלומי שן היך מה
V	תבר תשלומי תבר עין תשלומי עין ושן תשלומי שן היך

Ni 1	דיתיהב מום כבר נשא כדן יתייהב ביה׃
Ni M	בחבריה כן
V	דיהב מום כבר נשא כין יתיהב ביה׃

Nu. 4:20 [*]   Nu. 4:20

Ni 1	ולא ייעלון למיחמי כד משקע כהנה
Ni M	ליראי יהוון כהנייא משקעין - -
V	ולא ייעלון ליוואי למיחמי כד יהויין כהנייא משקעין
P	ולא יעלון ליואי למיחמי כד יהוון כהניא משקעין

Ni 1	רבה ית כל מני בית קודשה דלא ימותון׃
Ni M	- - - - - מאני בית קודשא דלא ימו/
V	מני בית קודשא דלא ימותון׃
P	מאני בית קודשא ולא ימותון׃

Nu. 13:23   Nu. 13:23

Ni 1	ומטון עד נחל סגולה ולקטו מן תמן עוברה וסגולה
Ni M	ואתון וקטעו וביה סגול
V	ואתו עד נחל סגולה וקטעו מתמן עוברא וביה סגול

Ni 1	דעניבין חד וטענו יתיה בקופה בתרין וכן מן
Ni M	דענ/ וסובלוהי באסלה\ביני תרין גוברין וכן
V	דעינבין חד וטענו יתיה בקופה ביני תרין גוברין וכן מן

Ni 1	רמונייה וכן מן תאינייה׃
Ni M	ומן - -
V	רימוניא ומן תינייא׃

[*]See also, p. 94, for multiple Mgg.

Ni 1	כתיב ומפרש בספר אורייתה דיי/	בגין כדן
V	בספר אוריתא דיי/	בגין כדין יתאמר
P	יתאמר כתיב ומפרש בספר אוריתא	מן בגין כן

Ni 1	דמתילה בספר קרבייה נסייה	דעבד	יי/
Ni M	<u>מימריה דיי/</u>		
V	דמתיל בספר קרבי/ ניסיא וגבורתא דעבד	יי/	
P	דמתילא בספר קרביא נסיא וגבורתא דעבד מימרא דיי/		

Ni 1	ישראל כד הוון קיימין על ימא דסוף וגבורתה עם
V	לעמיה בני ישר/ כד הוו קיימין על ימא דסוף
P	עם בני ישראל כד הוון קיימין על ימא דסוף

Ni 1	דעבד עמהון	כד הוון עברין	בנחלי
Ni M	<u>כן</u> יעבד להון (<u>מימריה</u>) <u>דיי/</u> כד <u>הנון</u> עבר/		בנחלי
V	כן עבד עמהון	כד הוו עברין ית	נחלי
P	כן יעבד להון	כד אינון עברין ית	נחלי

Ni 1	ארנונה:
V	ארנונא:
P	ארנון:

Ni 1	בר מן עלתה דצפרה די לעלתה דתמידה תקרבון ית
Ni M	דסמיך לעלתה תמידה
CG F	בר מן עלתה דצפרה דסמיך לעלת תמידה תקרבון ית

Ni 1	אילין:
Ni M	<u>אליין:</u>
CG F	אליין:

Ni 1	והא קמתון חלף אבהתכון תרבו דגברין חייבין למוספה
Ni M	חולף ותסגון גובר/
VB	תסגון* גוברין חייבין למוספא
P	תסקון גוברין חייבין:

Ni 1	תוב על תקוף רוגזה דיי/ על ישראל:
Ni M	<u>עוד</u>
VB	עוד על תקוף רוגזא:

*
Reading of B.

Nu. 34:6   Nu. 34:6

Ni 1	ותחום ימה רבה אוקיינוס אינון מי בראשית ניסוי
Ni M	הוא אוקייאנוס – – – – – – – ניסוי
VB	ותחום ימא* רבא*הוא אוקינוס ניסוי
P	ותחום ימא רבא הוא אוקיאנוס ניסוי

Ni 1	מעוזוי וספינתה עם מיא קדמייה די בגווה
Ni M	ומחוזוי וספינתה קדמייה ראית בגווה הנון מיה
VB	ומחוזוי וספינתא עם מיא קדמיא* ראית בגווה הינון מי
P	ומחוזוי וספינתא עד ימא קמאה ראית בגויה הינון מי

Ni 1	דין יהווי לכון תחום ימא:
Ni M	בראשית די/ תחומה מערבייה
VB	בראשית דין יהוי לכון תחומא מערבי:/
P	בראשית דין יהוי לכון תחומא מערבאה:

Deut. 15:11   Deut. 15:11

Ni 1	ארום אין נטרין בני ישראל אולפן אורייתה ועבדין
Ni M	אין – – – בני\ישראל מצוותה דאורייתה – – –
VB	אין נטרין הינון ישראל מצוותא דאורייתא

Ni 1	פיקודיה לא הוי ביניהון מסכינייה
Ni M	– – – – לא הווי בהון מסכינין ברם אין שבקין הנון
VB	לא הווי* בהון מסכנין* ברם אין שבקין הינון

Ni 1	בגו ארעא
Ni M	מצוותה דאורייתא ארום לא פסקין מסכינייה בגו ארעא
VB	מיצוותא דאורייתא ארום* לא פסקין מיסכיניא בגו* ארעא

Ni 1	בגין כדין אנה מפקד יתכון יומא הדין למימר מפתח
Ni M	כן למימר מיפתוח
VB	בגין כן אנא מפקד יתכון למימר מיפתוח

Ni 1	תפתחון ית ידיכון לאחיכון למסכינייה ולצריכיכון
Ni M	ולצריכייה ראית
VB	תיפתחון ית ידיכון לאחיכון מיסכיניא ולצריכיא ראית

Ni 1	בארעכון:
Ni M	בא/
VB	בארעכון:

*Reading of B.

Deut. 22:20   Deut. 22:20

Ni 1   ואין קשוט הוה פתגמא הדין לא אשתכחו סהדוון לרביתה:

Ni M   קושטה   אשכחון   <u>לטליתה</u>

VB   ואין* קושטא הוה פיתגמ/ הדין לא אשכחו* סהדוון לטליתא*:

P   לא אשכחו סהדין לטליתא:

Deut. 22:21   Deut. 22:21

Ni 1   ויפקון ית רביתה   לתרע בייתה דאבוה וירגמון יתה עמא

Ni M   ויפקון ית <u>טליתה</u> מן תרע בית

VB   ויפקון ית טליתא מן* תרע ביתה דאבוהא וירגמון יתה עמה:

Ni 1   דקרתה באבנייה ויקטלון יתה ארום עבדת מרחקתה הדה בישראל

Ni M   ביש/

Ni 1   למזנייה בייתיה דאבוה ותבעדרון עבדי בישתה מן ביניכון:

Ni M   תה   ותישיצון

Deut. 28:68   Deut. 28:68

Ni 1   ויחזר   יי/ יתכון למצרים בלברנייה

Ni M   ויחזור יתכון <u>מימריה דיי</u>/ - - -

V   ויחזר יתכון מימריה דיי/   למצרים בלברנייא

Ni 1   ובאלפייה באורחה די אמרת לכון לא תוספון תוב למחמי

Ni M   <u>עוד</u>

V   באורחא די אמרית לכון לא תוספון עוד למיחמי

Ni 1   יתה   ותזדבנון תמן לבעלי דבביכון לעבדין ולאמהן ולית

V   יתה:

Ni 1   דזבין יתכון:

B.   <u>Ni 1</u> Texts <u>and</u> Mgg <u>with</u> Incomplete TJ II Texts

Gen. 8:10   Gen. 8:10

Ni 1   ושרי תוב לממני   שבעה יומין אחרינין ואוסף למשלחה

Ni M   - - לוחוי <u>עוד</u> *זר*/

V   ושרי   למימני

Ni 1   ית יוונה מן תיתבותא:

*Reading of B.

Gen. 34:12   Gen. 34:12

Ni 1   אסגון עלי לחדא פרן וכתובה ואתן היך מה די תאמרון לי כל
Ni M
V   אסגין עלי   פורן וכתוב:/
CG C   אסגון עלי לחדא פרין וקדשין ואתן היך מה די תימרון לי נדן וכתובה
P

Ni 1   ואסכו לי ית רביתה לאתה:
Ni M   __טליתא__
CG C   והיבו לי ית רביתא לאנתא:

Ex. 36:3   Ex. 36:3

Ni 1   ונסכו מן קדם משה ית כל אפרשותה די אפרשו בני ישראל אייתון
Ni M

Ni 1   לעבידת פלחן בית קודשא למעבד יתה ואנון אייתון לוותה
Ni M   __והנון__ אייתון יתה

Ni 1   חוב נדבה בכל צפר וצפר:
Ni M   __עוד__ נסיבה בכל
V   נסיבה

Lev. 3:9   Lev. 3:9

Ni 1   ויקרב מנכסת קדשיה קרבן קדם יי/ תרבחה
Ni M   מן נכסת מתקבל לשמה דיי/ תרבה
V   תרבא

Ni 1   אליתה שלמתה לקבל שזרתה ועבר יתה ית תרבה דחפי ית
Ni M   ורניעה שלמה לוקבל עצייה ועבר ית/ על
V   ורנעא שלימא לקביל עיציא יעבר יתה רית תרב דחפי על

Ni 1   כרסה רית כל תרבה די על בני גווה:
Ni M   __דאית__
V   כריסה:

Lev. 27:14   Lev. 27:14

Ni 1   וגבר ארום יקדש ית ביתה קדש לשמה דיי/ ויעלי יתה ויסדר
Ni M
V   קודש/ לשמא דיי/ ויסדר

Ni 1   כהנה בין טב ובין ביש היך מה די יעלי יתיה כהנה כדן
Ni M   סדר __כן__
V   כהנא היך מה די סדר יתיה:

Ni 1   יקום:

28

Nu. 30:17(16)   Nu. 30:17(16)

יי/ ית משה בין גבר לאתתיה   אלין קיימיה די פקד   Ni 1
ית /מימריה דיי   אליין   Ni M

דאבוה: ברביותה בביתה   בין אב לברתה   Ni 1
ביומי טליותה   Ni M
דאבואה:/   ביומי טליותה בבית   V

Nu. 35:2   Nu. 35:2

פקד ית בני ישראל ויתנון לליוויי מן ירתות אחסנתהון
אחסנות/   ללוראי

קורייין למישרי ופרוירין לקרוין   די   חזור חזור יתהון   Ni 1
להון   דח/   ופרוילי לקורייתה   Ni M
ופרוולי לקוריתא   חזור חזור להון   V

תתנון לליוויי: Ni 1
תתנון ללואי: V

Nu. 35:4   Nu. 35:4

מכותלה דקרתה   ופרוירי קרייתה די תתנון לליוויי   Ni 1
דק/   שורה   ללוראי מן   ופרוילי   Ni M
ופרוולי   V

לברה אלף אמין מן חזור חזור: Ni 1
דאומין   Ni M

Deut. 5:29 *   Deut. 5:29*

להון למדחול מן   לוי מן יתן ויהוי לבה שלמה   Ni 1
אלורי מי יתין יהווי לבה טבה הדין להון   Ni M
אלורי מי יתן יהווי לבא טבא הדין להון: V
למדחול מן   לוי מן יתן דיהוי ליבה שלמה הדין   CG D

קדמי ולמטור ית כל מצוותה דאורייתי כל יומיה מן בגלל   Ni 1
ית כל פיקודי/   - - -   כל יומיא   Ni M
כל יומיה מן בגלל   קדמי ולמטור ית כל מצותי   CG D

לעלם׃   דייטיב להון וליבניהון   Ni 1
למייטבה להון ולזרעעית בניה/   Ni M
לעלם: למייטבה להון ולבניהון   CG D

*Verse 26 in Ni 1 and other Targums.

C. <u>Ni</u> <u>1</u> <u>Texts</u> <u>and</u> <u>Mgg</u>

Gen. 19:22   Gen. 19:22

Ni 1   אוחי אשתיזב לתמן ארום לא • אוכל למעבד פתגם עד זמן

Ni M   <u>זריז</u>   לית אנא יכיל למ/

Ni 1   דתיעול לתמן   בגין כדין קרא <u>שמה</u> דקרתא זער:

Ni M   תמן <u>מן</u> <u>בגין</u> <u>כן</u>

Gen. 26:3   Gen. 26:3

Ni 1   אתותב בארעא הדא ואהווה במימרה עמך ואברך יתך ארום לך

Ni 1   ולבנך   אתן ית כל ארעתא האלין   ואקים ית <u>שבועתה</u>

Ni M   ול<u>זרעיית</u> <u>בניך</u>   <u>האליין</u>

Ni 1   די קיימית לאברהם אבוך:

Ex. 2:5   Ex. 2:5

Ni 1   ונחתת ברתה דפרעה למתקררא על   נהרא ורבייתה מהלכיין על

Ni M   על גב נהרא ו<u>טלייתא</u>

Ni 1   גוף נהרא וחמא ית תיבתה בגו אפרה   ושלחת ית אמהתה

Ni M   גומיא

Ni 1   ונסבת יתה:

Ex. 8:22 (26)   Ex. 8:22 (26)

Ni 1   ואמר משה לא תקן כדן ארום   מרחקא אינון

Ni M   אמרייה – – -· <u>הינון</u>

Ni 1   טעוותיהן דמצריי מנהון נסב למקרבא קדם יי/ אלהן הא אין

Ni M   מרחקתהון ד<u>מצראי</u> מנהון נסב ונקרבה קדם

Ni 1   מקרבן אנן ית טעוותהון דמצריי קדמיהון לית אפשר דלא

Ni M   מרחקתהון ד<u>מצראי</u>

Ni 1   ירגמון יתן:

Nu. 1:50 '   Nu. 1:50

Ni 1   ואת מני   ית לוויי על משכנה דסהדותה ועל כל מנוי   ועל

Ni M   מאני ית <u>לוואי</u>   מאנוי

Ni 1   כל מה   דליה אינון יטענון ית משכנה וית כל מנוי

Ni M   מה <u>דאית</u> ליה <u>הנון</u> יסבלון   מאנוי

Nu. 1:50 (cont.)　　　　　　　　　　　　　Nu. 1:50 (cont.)

Ni 1　ואינון ישמשון יתיה וחזור חזור למשכנה ישרון:

Ni M　והנון　　　　　　　חזור

Nu. 8:20　　　　　　　　　　　　　　　　　Nu. 8:20

Ni 1　ועבד משה ואהרן וכל　כנשתה דבני ישראל ללווי　כל מה

Ni M　　　　　　　　　　עם　　　　　　　לליוואי|בכל

Ni 1　די פקד　　דיי/ ית משה על ליווי　כדן עבדו להון בני

Ni M　מימריה דיי/　　　ליוואי כן　ע/

Ni 1　ישראל:

Nu. 13:28　　　　　　　　　　　　　　　　Nu. 13:28

Ni 1　להוד ארום חציפין אינון עמה　די　שריין בארעא

Ni M　תקיפין הנון　עמא אליין　דש/

Ni 1　וקרווה　תקיפן רברבן לחדה ואוף בנוי דענק　גיברה

Ni M　וקורייתה　תלילן רבר/　עפרון גברה

Ni 1　חמינן תמן:

Deut. 3:26　　　　　　　　　　　　　　　　Deut. 3:26

Ni 1　ותקף רוגזיה דיי/ בי מן בגללכון ולא שמע בקל צלותי ואמר

Ni M　קבל מני - - ואמר

Ni 1　יי/ לי אמר משה סגין לך לא תוסף למללה קדמי תוב

Ni M　מימריה דיי/ לי אמר משה סגי　לך לא תוסף למללה עמי עוד

Ni 1　בפתגמא הדין:

Ni M　בפ/

Deut. 12:12　　　　　　　　　　　　　　　Deut. 12:12

Ni 1　ותחדון קדם יי/ אלהכון אתון ובניכון ובנתכון ועבדיכון

Ni 1　ואמהתכון וליוויי די　בקורייכון ארום לית להון חלק

Ni M　וליוואי דאית בק/　חולק

Ni 1　ואחסנה עמכון בפלוג ארעא:

Ni M　עמכון*

*Version being rendered ended with this word.

Deut. 15:5   Deut. 15:5

Ni 1   לחוד אין משמע תשמעון בקל ממרה דיי/ אלהכון למטור

Ni M   משמוע

Ni 1   למעבד ית כל מצוותה הדה   די אנה מפקד יתכון יומא

Ni M   ולמעבד ית כל פיקודייה האליין די אנה

Ni 1   הדין:

Deut. 20:15

Ni 1   כדן תעבד   לכל קרייתה דרחיקן מנכון לחדה די לא מן

Ni M   כן   תעבדון לכל קורייתה

Ni 1   קרי   אומייה האליין אנון:

Ni M   קורייה   הנון:

A.   Extended Passages of Ni 1 with Mgg and Texts of TJ II and
     TJ I

Gen. 6:18-7:15   Gen. 6:18-7:15

Ni 1   (6:18) ואקיים ית קיימי עמך ותיעול לתיבותה את ובניך
CG E   ואקיים ית קיימי עמך ותיעול לתיבותה את ובניך
TJ I   ואקים ית קימי עמך ותיעול לתיבותא אנת ובנך

Ni 1   ואתתך ונשי בניך עמ/: (19) מן כל חייא מן כל
CG E   ואתתך ונשי בניך עמך: ומכל חיתה מן כל
TJ I   ואינתתך ונשי בנך עמך: ומן כל דחי מכל

Ni 1   בשרא תרין מן כולא תעיל לתיבותה למקיימה עמך דכר
Ni M   תריין   תיעול
CG E   ביסרה תריין מן כולה תעל לתיבותה למקיימה עמך דכר
TJ I   בישרא תרין מכולא תעיל לתיבותא לקיימא עימך דכר

Ni 1   ונקבה יהוון: (20) מן עופא למינה ומן בעירא
Ni M   וזוגה
CG E   וזוגה יהוון: מן עופה למינה ומן בעירה
TJ I   ונוקבא יהון: מעופא ליזניה ומבעירא

Ni 1   למינה ומן כל רחשא דארעא למינה תרין מן כול
Ni M   רמסה דארעא למינהון תריין
CG E   למינה מן כל רמסה דארעה למיניהון תריין מן כולה
TJ I   ליזניה ומכל ריחשא דארעא ליזניה תרין מכולא

Ni 1   יעלון לוותך
Ni M   יעלו עמך
CG E   יעלון לתיבותיה
TJ I   ייעלון לוותך על יד מלאכא כאחד ומעל יתהון לך

Ni 1   למקיימה: (21) ואת סב לך מן כל מיכל די יתאכל
CG E   למחקיימה: ואת סב לך מן כל מזון די יתאכל
TJ I   לקיימא: ואנת סב לך מכל מיכל דמיתאכול

Ni 1   ותכנש לוותך ויהוי לך ולהון למיכל: (22) ועבד נח כל
Ni M   למזון
CG E   ותכנש לוותך ויהווי לך ולהון למזון: ועבד נח ככל
TJ I   ויהי לך ולכון למיכל: ועבד נח ככל

32

Gen. 6:18-7:15 (cont.)

Ni 1 מה דפקי/ יתיה יי/ כדין עבד: (7:1) ואמר
Ni M ממריה דיי/ כן עבד
CG E מה די פקד ממ דיי/ כן עבד: ואמר
TJ I דפקדיה ה:/ ואמר

Ni 1 יי/ לנח עול את וכל אנשי ביתך לתיבותא ארום יתך
Ni M ממריה דיי/
CG E ממ דיי/ לנח עול את וכל אנשי ביתך לתיבותה ארום יתך
TJ I ה:/ לנח עול אנת וכל אינש ביתך לתיבותא ארום יתך

Ni 1 חמי/ צדיק קדמי בדרה הדין: (2) מן כל בעירא דכיא
CG E חמית צדיק קודמיי בדרה הדין: מן כל בעירה דכייה
TJ I חמית זכאיי קדמי בדרא הדין: מכל בעירא דכיא

Ni 1 תסב לך שבעה שבעה דכר ונקב/ ומן בעירא די לא דכיא
Ni M וזוגה
CG E תסב לך שבעה שבעה דכר וזוגה ומן בעירה די לא דכי
TJ I תיסב לך שובעא שובעא דכר ונוקבא ומן בעירא דליתא דכייא

Ni 1 הוא תרין דכר ונקבה: (3) אף מן עוף שמיא
Ni M תריין דכר וזוגה לחוד עופא די שמ/
CG E הוא תריין דכר וזוגה להוד מן עופה דשמייה
TJ I תרין דכר ונוקבא: ברם מן צפרי שמיא

Ni 1 שבעא שבעה דכר ונקבה למקיימא בנין על אפי
CG E שבעה שבעה דכר וזוגה למקיימה זרע על אפי
TJ I שובעא שובעא דכר ונוקבא לקיימא מנהון זרעא על

Ni 1 ארעא: (4) ארום בתר שבעה יומין הא
Ni M כל - - - - - ליומין קליילין שבעה -
CG E כל ארעה: ארום ליומין קליילין שבעה
TJ I ארעא: ארום הא

TJ I אנא יהיב להון ארבא שובעא יומין אין יתובון ישתביק להון

Ni 1 אנה מחת מטר על
Ni M אנה מחת מטרא על
CG E אנה מחית מיטרה על
TJ I ואין לא יתובון לזמן יומין תוב שיבעא אנא מחית מיטרא על

Gen. 6:18-7:15 (cont.)

ארעא ארבעין יממין וארבעין לילון   ואישצי ית כל ברייתיה   Ni 1
יומין וארבעין לייין   Ni M
ארעה ארבעין יומין וארבעין לילוון   ואישצי ית כל בירייתה   CG E
ארעא ארבעין יממין וארבעין ליליון ואישצי ית כל גוויית   TJ I

די ברריית   מעלווי אפי ארעא: (5)   ועבד נח   Ni 1
די ברית מן עלווי אפי ארעה: ועבד נח   CG E
אינש ובעיר   ארעא: ועבד נח   TJ I

כל מן די פקד   יתיה   יי:/   (6)   ונח בר שית   Ni 1
בכל   ממריה דיי/   Ni M
ככל מה די פקד   יתה ממ   דיי/   ונח בר שת   CG E
ככל   דפקדיה   ה:/   ונח בר שית   TJ I

מאה   שניין הווה ומבולא הוה מיא   על ארעא: (7)   ועל   Ni 1
מים   Ni M
מאורן שניין   ומבולה הווה מיין על ארעה: ועל   CG E
מאה   שניין   וטובענא הוה מיא   על ארעא: ועל   TJ I

נח ובנווהי ואתתיה   ונשי בנוהי עמה: לתיבותא מן קדם   Ni 1
בנוי   Ni M
נח ובנוי ונשוי   ונשי בנויי עמיה לתיבותה מן קודם   CG E
נח ובנווהי ואינתתיה ונשי בנוי   עימי לתיבותא מן קדם   TJ I

מוי דמבולא: (8)   מן בעירא דדכיה ומן בעירה   דלית   Ni 1
מוי דמבולה: מן בעירא דכייה ומן בעירה די לית   CG E
מוי דטובענא: מן בעירא דכייא ומן בעירא   דליתא   TJ I

היא דכיה ומן עופא וכל   דרחיש על ארעא: (9)   תרין   Ni 1
די   תרמס   תריין   Ni M
הוא דכי   ומן עופה וכל די   תרמוס על ארעה: תריין   CG E
דכייא ומן עופא וכל   דרחיש על ארעא: תרין   TJ I

תרין   עלו עם   נח לתיבותא דכר וזוגה היך מה די   פקד   Ni 1
תריין   לוות   Ni M
תריין עלו לוות נח לתיבותיה דכר וזוגה היך מה די   פקד   CG E
תרין עלו   לנח לתיבותא דכר ונוקבא היכמא   דפקיד   TJ I

יי/ ית נח: (10)   והוה לסוף שבעת יומי   Ni 1
ממריה דיי/   שבעתי יומיא   Ni M
ממ   דיי/ ית נח: והווה לסוף   יומין קלילין   CG E
והוה לסוף שובעת ימי   P
ה/ ית נח: והוה לזמן שובעא יומין   TJ I

אבלא דמתושלח   Ni 1
אבליה דמתושלח   P
מן בתר דשלים איבליה דמתושלח חמא ה/ והא לא תהו בני נשא   TJ I

Gen. 6:18-7:15 (cont.)

Ni 1	ורמי דמבולא הוון על ארעא:
Ni M	ורמי
CG E	רמי מבולה הוון על ארעה:
P	רמי דמבולא הורין על ארעא:
TJ I	ורמי דטובענא הוו נחתין רתיחין מן שמיא עילוי ארעא:

Ni 1	(11) בסוף שית מאה שנין לחיוהי דנח בירחה תניינא
Ni M	לסוף שת מאוון דשנין לחוי
CG E	בשנת שת מאה שנין לחיי דנח בירחה תנינה
TJ I	בשנת שית מאה שנין לחיי דנח בירחא תניינא

TJ I	הוא ירח מרחשין דעד כדין לא הוו מתמנן ירחייא אלהן

Ni 1	בשבעה עשר יומין לירחא
CG E	בשבעת עשר יומין לירחה
TJ I	מתחשרי דהוא ריש שתא לשכלול עלמא בשבסרי יומין לירחא

Ni 1	היך זמן יומא הדין אתבזעו כל מבועי תהומא
Ni M	עיינות תהום
CG E	ומן יומה הדין אתבזעו כל עיינות תהום הדין
TJ I	ביומא הדין איתבזעו כל מבועי תהומא

Ni 1	רבה
CG E	רבה
TJ I	רבא והוון בני גיברייא משוויין תמן בניהון וסתמין יתהון

Ni 1	וכווי שמיא אתפתחו: (12) והוה מטרא
Ni M	וחרכי
CG E	וחרכי שמיה אתפתחו: והווה מיטרה
V	וחרכי דשמי/ איתפתחו:
TJ I	ובתר הכי חרכי שמיא איתפתחו: והוה מיטרא נחית

Ni 1	על ארעא ארבעין יומין וארבעין לילוון: (13) בזמן
Ni M	היך זמן
CG E	על ארעה ארבעין יומין וארבעין לילוון: היך זמן
TJ I	על ארעא ארבעין יממין וארבעין לילוון: בכרן

Ni 1	יומא הדין על נח ושם וח/ ויפת בנוי דנח ואנתתיה דנח
CG E	יומה הדן על נח ושם וחם ויפת בנוי דנח ואנתתיה דנח
TJ I	יומא הדין על נח ושם וחם ויפת בני נח ואיתת נח

Ni 1	ותלתי נשי בנוהי עמהו/ לתיבותה: (14) אינון וכל
Ni M	עמה הנון
CG E	ותלתי נשי בנוי עמהון לתיבותה: הנון וכל
TJ I	ותלת נשי בנוהי עימיה לתיבותא: הינון וכל

Gen. 6:18-7:15 (cont.)

חיתה למינה וכל בעירה למינה וכל רחשא דרחש על ארעא — Ni 1

רמסא דרמס — Ni M

חיתה למינה וכל בעירה למינה וכל רמסה דרמס על ארעה — CG E

חיתא ליזנהא וכל בעירא ליזנהא וכל ריחשא דרחיש על ארעא — TJ I

למינוֹהו* וכל עופה למינה וכל דפרח וכל דטייס: — Ni 1

למינהון צפר - - - - דטייס — Ni M

למינהון וכל עופה למינה וכל צפר דטאייס: — CG E

ליזניה כל עופא ליזניה כל ציפר כל דפרח: — TJ I

(15) ועלו עם נח לתיבותא תרין תרין מן כל בשרא — Ni 1

תריין תריין — Ni M

ועלו לוות נח לתיבותיה תריין תריין מן כל ביסרה — CG E

ועלו לות נח לתיבותא תרין תרין מכל בישרא — TJ I

דאית בה נשמה דחיין: — Ni 1

נפש — Ni M

דאית ביה רוח דחיין: — CG E

דביה רוחא דחיי: — TJ I

Gen. 9:5-23

ולחוד ית אדם נפשתכון אתבע מלות כל חיא — Ni 1

אדמכון לנפ/ | אתבוע מן לוות חייתא — Ni M

אדמכון לנפשתכון אתבוע מן יד כל חייתה — CG E

וברם ית דימכון לנפשתיכון אתבוע מן ידא דכל חיתא — TJ I

אתבע יתיה ומלות — Ni 1

אתביע יתיה מן לוות — Ni M

אתבוע יתיה מן יד — CG E

דקטלא לבר נשא איתבועיניה לאית קטלא עליה ומידא — TJ I

בר נשא ומלוות אחוי דבר נשא — Ni 1

בני אנשא מן לוות גבר ואחוי - - - - — Ni M

ברנשה ומן יד גבר ואחוי — CG E

דאינשא מיד גבר דישוד ית דמא דאחוי — TJ I

אתבע ית נפשה דבר נשה: (6) מן דשפך אדמיה דבר נש — Ni 1

אתבע יתיה — Ni M

אתבוע ית נפשיה דברנשה: דשפך אדמיה דברנש — CG E

אתבוע ית נפשא דאינשא: דישוד דמא דאינשא — TJ I

*sic

Gen. 9:5-23 (cont.)

Ni 1   על ידי בר נש   ישתפך אדמיה

Ni M   אדמיה משתפך - - -

CG E   על ידי ברנש אדמיה משתפך

TJ I   בסהדין דייניא מחייבין

TJ I   ליה קטול ודישוד בלא סהדין מרי עלמא עתיד לאיתפרע/

Ni 1   ארום בדמו   מן קדם יי /   ברא

Ni M   אר/

CG E   ארום בדמו   מן קודם יי /   ברא

TJ I   מיניה ליום דינא רבא ארום בדיוקנא   אלקים עבד

Ni 1   ית אדם: (7)   ואתון תקופו וסגון ואתילדון בארעא

Ni M   בר נשא   שרוצו

CG E   ית ברנשה: ואתון תקופו וסגון שרוצו בארעה

TJ I   ית אינשא: ואתון פושר וסגו אתילדו בארעא

Ni 1   וסגון בגווה: (8)   ואמ/   יי /   לנח ולבנוהי עמה

Ni M   ביה   ממריה דיי/

CG E   וסגון בה: ואמר ממ   דיי /   לנח ולבנוי עמיה

TJ I   וסגו בה: ואמר   אלקים לנח ולבנוי עימיה

Ni 1   למימר: (9)   ואנ/ הא אנה מקיים ית קיימי עמכון ועם ורית

Ni M

CG E   למימר: ואנה הא אנה מקיים ית קיימי עמכון וית

TJ I   למימר: אנא הא אנא מקיים   קיימי עמכון ועם

Ni 1   בניכון בתריכון: (10)   וית כל נפש חייתא

Ni M   זרעיית בניכון מן בת/   דחייתא |

CG E   זרעיית בניכון מן בתרכון: וית כל נפש דחייה

TJ I   בניכון בתריכון: ועם כל נפשת חייתא

Ni 1   די   עמכון בעופא ובבעירא ובכל חיתא דארעא   עמכון

Ni M   דאית עמכון בעופה   דאית עמכון

CG E   דאית עמכון בעופה ובבעירה ובכל חייתה דארעה   עמכון

TJ I   דעימכון בעופא ובבעירא ובכל חית ארעא   דעימכון

Ni 1   מכל נפקי תבותא לכל חיתא דארעא: (11)   ואקים ית

Ni M   מן כל

CG E   מכל נפקי תבותה לכל חייתה דארעה: ואקיים ית

TJ I   מכל נפקי תיבותא לכל חית   ארעא: ואקיים ית

Gen. 9:5-23 (cont.)

Ni 1	קיימי עמכון ולא ישתצי כל בשרא תוב מן מוי דמבולא
Ni M	עוד
CG E	קיימי עמכון ולא ישתצי כל ביסרה עוד מן מוי דמבולה
TJ I	קימי עימכון ולא ישתיצי כל ביסרא עוד ממוי דטובעא

Ni 1	ולא יהווי תוב מבול למחבלא ארעא: (12) ואמר
Ni M	ממריה עוד
CG E	ולא יהוי עוד מבול למחבלה ארעה: ואמר ממ
TJ I	ולא יהי עוד טובענא לחבלא ארעא: ואמ/

Ni 1	יי/ דין סימן קיים/ די אנה משוי בין ממרי
Ni M	דיי/ דאנה יהיב בין בממרי
CG E	דיי/ דין סימן קיימה די אנה יהב בין מימרי
TJ I	אלקים דא את קימא דאנא מקיים בין מימרי

Ni 1	וביניכון ובין כל נפש חיתא די עמכון לדרי ארעא:
Ni M	דחיא דאית עמכון לדורת עולם
CG E	וביניכון ובין כל נפש דחייה דאית עמכון לקיים עלם:
TJ I	וביניכון ובין כל נפשת חיתא דעימכון לדרי עלמא:

Ni 1	(13) ית קשתי אשוי בעננא ותהי לסימן קים בין
Ni M	שורית
CG E	ית הזוון קשתי יהבית בעננה ותהוי לסימן קיים בין
TJ I	ית קשתי יהבית בעננא ותהי לסימן קיים בין

Ni 1	ממרי ובין ארעא: (14) ויהי כד יהוון עננא פרסין
Ni M	יפרוס עני - - -
CG E	מימרי ובין ארעה: ויהוי כד אפרוס עני
TJ I	מימרי וביני ארעא: ויהי כד אפרוס עני יקרא

Ni 1	על ארעא ותחחמי קשתא בעננא:
Ni M	על
CG E	על ארעה ותחחמי קשתה בעננה:
TJ I	עילוי ארעא ותתחמי קשתא ביממא עד לא יטמע שימשא בעננא:

Ni 1	(15) ואדכר ית קיימי בין ממרי וביניכון ובין
Ni M	דאית
CG E	ואדכר ית קיימי דאית בין מימרי וביניכון ובין
TJ I	ודכירנא ית קיימי דבין מימרי וביניכון ובין

Ni 1	כל נפש חיה בכל בשרא ולא יהוי מיא למבולא
Ni M	דחיה לכל עוד מים למבול
CG E	כל נפש דחייה בכל ביסרה ולא יהוי עוד מייה למבול
TJ I	כל נפשת חיתא בכל ביסרא ולא יהי תוב מיא לטובענא

Gen. 9:5-23 (cont.)

Ni 1	לחבלא כל בשרא: (16) ותהוי קשתא בעננא ואחמי יתה
Ni M	למחבלה ארעא
CG E	למחבלה כל ביסרה: ותהוי קשתה בעננה ואחמי יתה
TJ I	לחבלא כל ביסרא: ותהי קשתא בעננא ואחמינה

Ni 1	למדכרה קיים עלם בין מימרא דיי/ ובין כל נפש חיתה
Ni M	ואדכר קיים דחיה
CG E	ואדכר קיים עלם בין מימר דיי/ ובין כל נפש דחייה
TJ I	למידכר קים עלם בין מימרא דאלקים ובין כל נפשת חיתא

Ni 1	בכל בשרא די על ארעא: (17) ואמר יי/
Ni M	דאית ממריה דייי/
CG E	בכל ביסרה דאית על ארעה: ואמר ממ דיי/
TJ I	בכל ביסרא דעל ארעא: ואמר אלקים

Ni 1	לנח דן סימן קימא די קיימית בין ממרי ובין כל
CG E	לנח דין סימן קיימה די קיימית בין ממרי ובין כל
TJ I	לנח דא את קים דקיימית בין מימרי ובין מימר כל

Ni 1	בשרא די על ארעא: (18) והוון בני נח די
Ni M	דאית בנוי דנח -
CG E	ביסרה דאית על ארעה: והוון בנוי דנח אלין
TJ I	ביסרא דעל ארעא: והוו בני נח

Ni 1	נפקו מן תיבותא שם וחם ויפת וחם הוא אבוהון דכנענאי:
Ni M	דנפקו
CG E	דנפקו מן תיבותה שם וחם ויפת וחם הוא אבהדן דכנענאי:
TJ I	דנפקו מן תיבותא שם וחם ויפת וחם הוא אבוי דכנען:

Ni 1	(19) תלתא אינון אלין בנוי דנח ומאלין איתמלית
Ni M	ומן אלין
CG E	תלתה אלין בנוי דנח ומן אלין אתמלית
TJ I	תלתא איליין בנוי דנח ומאילן איתבדרו

Ni 1	כל ארעא: (20) ושרי נח גבר צדיקא
Ni M	גברא למהוי כל ארעה:
CG E	ושרי נח גברה צדיקה למהוי כל ארעה:
V	ושרי נח גברא צדיקא למיהוי
P	ושרי נח גבר צדיקא למהוי:
TJ I	ושרי נח למיתב בכל ארעא: למיהוי גבר

40

Gen. 9:5-23 (cont.)

Ni 1 למפלח בארעא:
Ni M פלח
CG E פלח בארעה
TJ I פלח בארעא ואשכח גופנא דמושכיה נהרא מן גינוניתא דעדן

Ni 1 ונצב כרם:
Ni M לה
CG E ונצב לה כרם:
V ונצב כרמא:
TJ I ונצביה לכרמא וביה ביומא אנייצת ובשילת עינבין ועצריניין:

Ni 1 (21) ושתה מן חמרא ורווה ואתגלי בגו משכנה:
Ni M יינא|ורבה | ואתרשל
CG E ושתה מן חמרה ורבה ואתערטל בגו משכניה:
TJ I ושתי מן חמרא ורבי ואיתערטל בגו משכניה:
Ni M ירוש/ ואתפרסם במצע משכניה

Ni 1 (22) וחמא חם אבוהו/ דכנענאי
CG E וחמה חם אבוהון דכנענאי
TJ I וחמא חם אבוי דכנען
Ni M דסוראי ואתבזי במ/ מש/

Ni 1 ית עריתה דאבוי ותני לתרין אחוי בשוק/: (23) ונסב שם
CG E ית עריתה דאבוי ותני לתרין אחוי בשוקה: ונסב שם
TJ I ית עריתא דאבוי ותני לתרין אחוי בשוקא: ונסב שם

Ni 1 ויפת ית אסטליתה ושרון על כתף תריהון והוון
Ni M יתה
CG E ויפת ית אסטליתה ושרון יתה על כתפתהון
TJ I ויפת ית אסכטלא ושריו על כתף תרויהון ואזלו

Ni 1 מהלכין לבתרהון וכסון ית עריתה דאבוהון ואפיהון
Ni M מן בתר
TJ I מאחזריין וכסיו ית עריתא דאבוהון ואפיהום

Ni 1 הפיכו לבתרהון ועריתה דאבוהון לא חמון:
Ni M הפיכן מן בתר
TJ I מאחזריין ועריתא דאבוהון לא חמון:

B.　Extended Passage of Ni 1 with Mgg and Text of TJ I

Nu. 18:21-32　　　　　　　　　　　　　　　　　　Nu. 18:21-32

(21) ולבנוי דלוי הא יהבית　　כל מעשר　דישראל לאחסנה	Ni 1
מעשרה	Ni M
ולבנוי דלוי הא יהבית ית כל מעשרא　בישראל באחסנ/	TJ I

חלף פלחנהון די אנון פלחין ית פלחן משכן זימנה:	Ni 1
חולף　　　　הנון פל	Ni M
חולף פולחנהון　　　דהינון פלחין ית פולחן משכן זימנא:	TJ I

(22) ולא יקרבון תוב בני ישראל למשכן זימנה למקרבה	Ni 1
עוד	Ni M
ולא יקרבון תוב בני ישראל למשכן זימנא לקבלא	TJ I

למסבול חוכין דלא ימותון: (23)　ויפלחון לוויי אנון ית	Ni 1
הנון	Ni M
חובא　ליממת:　ויפלחון ליואי הינון ית	TJ I

פלחן משכן זימנה ואינון יקבלון ית חוביהון	Ni 1
יסבלון　חובה	Ni M
פולחן משכן זימנא והינון יקבלון ית חוביהון אין לא	TJ I

קיים עלם לדריהון ובגו בני ישראל	Ni 1
דעל/　　וביני - - יש/	Ni M
מזדהריו בפולחנהון קיים עלם לדריכון ובגו בני ישראל	TJ I

לא יחסנון אחסנה: (24) ארום ית מעשרין דבני ישראל	Ni 1
יתאחסנון　　　מעשרהון	Ni M
לא יחסנון אחסנא:　ארום ית מעשרא דבני ישראל	TJ I

די יפרשון לשמה דיי/ אפרשו יהבית ללוויי אחסנה בגין	Ni 1
ללוואי לאח/	Ni M
דיפרשון קדם יי/ אפרשותא יהבית ליואי לאחסנא בגין	TJ I

(25) כדן אמרית להון בגו בני ישראל לא יחסנון אחסנה:	Ni 1
כן	Ni M
כן אמרית להון דבגו בני ישראל לא יחסנון אחסנא:	TJ I

ומליל יי/ עם משה למימר: (26) ועם ליוויי	Ni 1
מימריה דיי/　　וללואי	Ni M
ומליל יי/ עם משה למימר: ולליואי	TJ I

תמלל ותימר להון ארום תקבלון מן לוות בני ישראל ית	Ni 1
תקבלון [תסבלון probably read,	Ni M
תמליל ותימר להון ארום תיסבון מן　　בני ישראל ית	TJ I

Nu. 18:21-32 (cont.)

Ni 1   מעשרה די יהבית לכון מן לוותהון באחסנותכון ותפרשון

TJ I   מעשרא דיהבית להון באחסנתהון ותפרשון

Ni 1   מיניה אפרשותה דיי/ חד מן עשרה ממעשרה: (27)

TJ I   מיניה אפרשותא קדם יי/ מעשרא מיגו מעשרא:

Ni 1   ותתחשב לכון אפרשותכון כאפרשות עיבורא מן אדרה

Ni M   רית/

TJ I   ואתחשב לכון אפרשותכון הי כעיבורא מן אידרא

Ni 1   וחמרה מן מעצרתה: (28) כדן תפרשון אוף

Ni M   כן

TJ I   והי כחמרא דמליתא מן מעצרתא: הכדין תפרשון לחוד

Ni 1   אתון אפרשותה דיי/ מכל מעשריכון די תקבלון מן

Ni M   מן כל

TJ I   אתון אפרשותא קדם יי/ מכל מעשריכון דתיסבון מן

Ni 1   לוות בני ישראל ותתנון מניה ית אפרשותה דיי/ לאהרן

TJ I   בני ישראל ותיתנון מיניה אפרשותא קדם יי/ לאהרן

Ni 1   כהנה: (29) מן כל מתנתכון תפרשון ית כל אפרשותה

Ni M   רבה מתנוותכון

TJ I   כהנא: מכל מתנתיכון תפרשון אפרשותא

Ni 1   דיי/ מן כל תרבה ית טובה מנה:

Ni M   טוביה ית קודשה מנה

TJ I   קדם יי/ מן כל שפר טוביה ובי.ה:

Ni 1   ותימר להון באפרשותכון ית טובה מניה (30)

TJ I   ותימר להון לכהניא באפרשותכון ית שפר טוביה מיניה

Ni 1   ויתחשב ללוויי כאפרשות עיבורא מן אדרה

Ni M   עב/

TJ I   ובי.ה ויתחשב לליואי הי כאפרשות עיבורא מן גוא אידרא והי

Ni 1   וחמרה מן מעצרתה: (31) ותיכלון יתיה

TJ I   כאפרשות חמרא מיגו מעצרתא: ותיכלון יתיה אתון

Ni 1   בכל אתר אתון ואינשי בתיכון ארום אגר הוא לכון

TJ I   כהניא בכל אתר אתון ואינש בתיכון ארום אגרא הוא לכון

Ni 1   חלף פולחנכון במשכן זימנה: (32) ולא תקבלון עלוי

Ni M   חולף תסבלון

TJ I   חלופי פולחנכון במשכן זימנא: ולא תקבלון עלוי

Nu. 18:21-32 (cont.)

Ni 1	חוביך באפרשותכון ית טובה מניה
Ni M	חובה
TJ I	חובא בזמן אפרשותכון ית שפר טוביה מיניה וביה לאוכלי
Ni 1	וית קדשיהון בני ישראל לא תפסון ולא
Ni M	תספון
TJ I	מיניה לדסאיב וית קודשיא דבני ישראל לא יתפסון דלא
Ni 1	תמותון:
TJ I	תמותון:

A. Extended Passage of Ni 1 with Multiple Mgg and Texts of
    TJ II and TJ I

Ex. 19:1-25   Ex. 19:1-25

ישראל דבני אפיקתהון   בזמן תליתיא בירחא (1)   Ni 1
           במפקותהון   - -   Ni M
/יש דבני   במפקותהון   תליתייה בירחא   V
/יש דבני   ון   ת בירחה   CG F
ישראל דבני אפקותהון   לזמן תליתאה בירחא   P
ישראל בני   לאפקוח   תליתאה בירחא   TJ I

הדין יומא   זמן היך דמצרים ארעא מן פריקין   Ni 1
הדין יומא   זמן היך מצרים   V
            זמן היך דמצרים ארעה מן פריקין   CG F
דין יומא   זמן היך דמצרים ארעא מן פריקין   P
הדין ביומא   /דמ מארעא   TJ I

מן ונטלו (2)   : דסיני למדברא עלו   Ni 1
               : דסיני למדברא עלו   V
מן ונטלו   : דסיני למדברא עלו   CG F
ונטלו   : דסיני למדברא עלו   P
ונטלו   : דסיני למדברא אתו לירחא בחד   TJ I

וכוונו במדברא ושרון דסיני למדברא ואתון רפידים   Ni 1
ושרון   Ni M
ושרון במדברא דסיני ושרון למדברה ואתו רפידים   CG F
וכוינן במדברא ושרון דסיני למדברא ואתו מרפידים   P
ושרא במדברא דסיני ו ושר למדברא ואתו מרפידים   TJ I

טורא: קבל כל   ישראל   תמן   Ni 1
כלוקבל   Ni M
טורא: וקבל   V
טורא: לקבל כליה   יש   תמן   CG F
טורא: קבל כל   ישראל בני   תמן   P
טורא: קבל כל מייחד בלב ישראל   תמן   TJ I

44

Ex. 19:1-25 (cont.)

Ni 1	ומשה סלק (3)	למתבע אולפן
Ni M		למתבוע
VB	ומשה סליק	למתבוע אולפן
CG F	ומשה סליק	למתבוע אולפן
P	ומשה סליק	למיתבע אולפן
TJ I	ומשה סליק ביומא תניינא לריש טורא	

Ni 1	מן קדם יי / וקרא ליה דבירה דיי / מן טורא למימר כדין
VB	מן*קודם יי / וקרא ליה דבירה יי / מן טורא למימר כדין
CG F	מן קודם יי / וקרא ליה דברי דיי / מן טורה למימר כדן
P	מן קדם יי / וקרא ליה דבריה דיי / מן טורא למימר כדין
TJ I	וקרא ליה יי / מן טורא למימר כדנא

Ni 1	תימר לדבית יעקב ותתני לשבטא	דבני
Ni M	לאנשי ביתיה דיעקב	
VB	תימר לאנשי ביתיה דיעקב ותתני אולפן לכנישתהון	דבני
CG F	תימר לאנשי ביתיה דיעקב ותתני אולפן לכנישתהון	דבני
P	תימר לאינשי ביתיה דיעקב ותתני לשבטיא	דבני
TJ I	תימר לנשייא דבית יעקב ותתני	לבית
Ni M	לנשיא דבית יעקב ותתני לגברי	דבית

Ni 1	ישראל: (4) אתון חמיתון ית קלא	דעבדית
Ni M	- די אתפרעת מן
VB	יש./: אתון חמיתון יתד*מה די איתפרעית מן
CG F	יש: אתון חמיתון ית מה די אתפרעת מן
P	ישראל: אתון חמיתון ית מא די דאתפרעית מן
TJ I	ישראל: אתון חמיתון מה די עבדית
Ni M	ישראל

Ni 1	למצריי וטענית יתכון בעננין	איקר שכינתי
Ni M	מצראי וסבלית יתכון על עננין קלילין - - - - - -	היך
VB	מצראי וסבלית יתכון על עננין קלילין	היך
CG F	מצראי וסבלת יתכון על עננין קלילין	היך
P	מצראי וטענית יתכון על ענני	יקר שכינתי היך
TJ I	למצראי וטענית יתכון על ענניו	הי

Ni 1	על כנפי נשירין קלילין
Ni M	על כנפי נשרין
VB	על כנפי נישרין
CG F	על כנפי נשרין
P	על גדפי נשרין קלילין
TJ I	כעל גדפי נשרין מן פילוסין ואובילית יתכון לאתר

* Reading of B.

Ex. 19:1-25 (cont.)

בית מוקדשא למעבד תמן פיסחא ובההוא ליליא אתיבית יתכון   TJ I

(5)   וקרבית יתכון לאולפן אוריתי: Ni l
וקריבית יתכון לאולפן אוריתי*:   VB
וקרבית יתכון לאולפן אוריתי: CG F
וקריבית יתכון לאולפן אוריתי: P
לפילוסין ומתמן קריבית יתכון לאולפן אוריתי: TJ I

וכדון אם אין משמע תשמעון בקל ממרי ותטרון ית   Ni l
וכדון - אין משמע   Ni M
וכדו* אין משמוע תשמעון בקול מימרי* ותטרון ית   VB
וכדון אם משמוע תשמעון בקל מימרי ותטרון ית   CG F
וכדון אי משמע תשמעון נקל מימרי ותטרון ית   P
וכדון אין קבלא תקבלון למימרי ותינטרון ית   TJ I

קיימי ותהוון לשמי לעם חביבין היך סגלה מן כל   Ni l
אחרן   Ni M
קימי ותיהוון לשמי לעם אחרן וחביבין היך סגולא מן כל   VB
קיימי ותהוון לשמי לעם חביבין היך סגולה מכל   CG F
קיימי ותהוון לשמי עם חביבין והיך סגלה מכל   P
קימי ותהון קדמיי חביבין מכל   TJ I

אמיה ארום דידי היא כל ארעא: (6) ואתון   Ni l
לשמה דיי/ היא כל   Ni M
אומיא ארום לשמא* דיי/ היא* כל ארעא: ואתון   VB
אומייא ארום לשמיה ▨ כל ארעה: ואתון   CG F
אומיא ארום דיי/ היא כל ארעא: ואתון   P
עממייא דעל אפי ארעא: ואתון   TJ I

תהוון לשמי מלכין וכהנין ואמה קדישא   Ni l
קדישא   Ni M
תהוון לשמי מלכין וכהנין ואומא קדישא   V
תהוון לשמי מלכין וכהנין ואומה קדישה   CG F
תהוון קדמי מלכין וכהנין ואומא קדישא   P
תהון קדמי מלכין קטרי כלילא וכהנין משמשין ועם קדיש   TJ I

*Reading of B.

Ex. 19:1-25 (cont.)

Ni 1	פתגמיא די תמלל עם בני ישראל:(7)ואתא		
Ni M	אליין - - דבידריא די		
V	אילין די דבידריא די תמלל עם בני ישראל: ואתא		
CG F	אליין דבירייא די תמלל משה עם בני יש: ואתא		
P	איליין שבח דיבריא דתמלל עם בני ישראל: ואתא		
TJ I	איליין פיתגמיא דתמליל עם בני ישראל: ואתא		

Ni 1	משה וקרא לחכימי עמא וסדר קדמיהון ית כל
Ni M	לחכיניי דיש/
V	משה וקרא לחכימיא דישד/ וסדר קודמיהון ית כל
CG F	משה וקרא לחכימי עמא
P	משה וקרא לחכימי עמא וסדר קומיהון ית כל
TJ I	משה ביומא ההוא וקרא לסבי עמא וסדר קדמיהון ית כל

Ni 1	פתגמיא האיליין די פקד יתיה יי: (8)
Ni M	דברii/
V	דבידריא האילן די פקיד יתיה מימריה דיי/:
CG F	האליין די פקד יתיה מימ/ דיי/:
P	שבח דיבריא האילין דפקיד יתיה מימרא דיי/:
TJ I	פיתגמיא האילין דפקריה יי

Ni 1	וענון כל עמא כחדא בלבא שלמא ואמרי/ כל מה דמלל
V	וענון כל עמא כחדא בלבא שלימה ואמרין כל מה די מליל
CG F	בלבה שלמא ואמרין כל מה די מליל
P	ועניין כל עמא כחדא ואמרו כל דמליל
TJ I	ואתיבו כל עמא כחדא ואמרו כל דמליל

Ni 1	יי/ נעבד וחזר משה ית מליהון דעמא בצלו קדם
Ni M	מימרי/ דיי/ פתגמ/ עמ/
V	מימרא דיי/ נעביד וחזר משה ית פיתגמי עמא בצלו קודם
CG F	ממרה דיי/ נעב פתגמי עמא בצלו קודם
P	מימרא דיי/ נעביד וחזר משה ית מליהון דעמא בצלו קדם
TJ I	יי/ נעביד ואתיב משה ית פיתגמי עמא קדם

Ni 1	יי: (9) ואמר יי/ למש/ הא
Ni M	מימרי/ דיי/
VB	יי: ואמר מימרי/ דיי/ למשה הא
CG F	יי: ואמר ממרה דיי/ למשה הא
P	יי: ואמר מימרא דיי/ למשה האי
TJ I	יי: ואמר יי/ למשה ביומא תליתאה הא

Ex. 19:1-25 (cont.)

מן	דעננא	ממרי מתגלי עלך בתקפא	Ni 1
מן	דעננא	מימרי מתגלי עלך בעביא*	VB
מן	דעננא	מימרי מתגלי עליך בעביה [**also,בתוקפה]	CG F
מן	דעננא	מימרי מיתגלי לך בתוקפיה	P
דענן יקרא מן		אנא מתגלי עלך בעיבא	TJ I

בנבואתך משה	בגלל דישמעון עמא במללותי עמך ואף	Ni 1
נבואתך משה	בגלל ישמעון עמא במללותי עימך ולחוד*מלי	VB
בנבואתך משה	בגלל ישמעון עמה במללו⸱⸱⸱ עמך ולחות	CG F
בנבואתך משה	בגלל דישמעון עמא במללותי עמך ולחוד	P
בך	בגלל דישמעון עמא במללותי עימך ואוף	TJ I

קדם	עבדי יהמנון לעלם ותני משה ית מליהון דעמא	Ni 1
עמא בצלו קודם	עבדי יהימנון* לעלם ותני*משה ית פיתגמי	VB
עמא בצלו קדם	עבדי יהמנון לעלם ותני משה ית פתגמי	CG F
יהמנון לעלם ותני משה ית מליהון דעמא בצלו קדם		P
קדם	יהימנון לעלם ותני משה ית פיתגמי עמא	TJ I

איזל	יי :/ (10) ואמר יי/ למשה	Ni 1
	מימרי/ דיי/	Ni M
איזל	יי :/ ואמר מימרי/ דיי/ למשה	V
אזל	יי / ואמר יי/ למ/	CG F
איזל	יי :/ ואמר מימרא דיי/ למשה	P
איזל	יי :/ ואמר יי/ למשה ביומא רביעאה	TJ I

יתהון יומא הדין ולמחר ויחוורון	לות עמא ותקדש	Ni 1
יתהון יומא הדין ולימחר ויחוורון	לות עמא ותקדיש	V
יתהון יומא הדין ולמחר ויחוורון	לות עמא ותקדש	CG F
יתהון יומא הדין ולמחר ויחוורון	לות עמא ותקוייש	P
יומא דין ויומחרא ויחוורון	לות עמא ותזמינינון	TJ I

ויהוון מזומנים ליומא תליתייא	(11) לבושיהון:	Ni 1
ויהוון מזמנין ליומא תלתייה	לבושיהון:	V
ויהוון מזמנין לתלתה יומין	לבושיהון:	CG F
ויהויין מזומנין ליומא תליתאה	לבושיהון:	P
ויהון זמינין לימא תליתאה	לבושיהון:	TJ I

*
Reading of B.
**
Textual revision.

Ex. 19:1-25 (cont.)

Ni 1	ארום ביומא תליתייא תתגלי איקר שכינתא דיי/ לעיני
Ni M	אתגלי מימרי/ דיי/ חמיין
V	ארום ביומא תלתייה יתגלי מימרא דיי/ חמיין
CG F	ארום ביומא תליתייא יתגלי מימ/ דיי/ לקבל
P	ארום ביומא תליתאה יתגלי מימרא דיי/ לקבל
TJ I	ארום ביומא תליתאה יתגלי יי/ לעיני

Ni 1	כל עמא על טורא דסיני: (12) ותתחם ית עמא
Ni M	כל
V	כל עמא על טורא דסיני: ותתחם ית עמא
CG F	כל עמא על טורא דסיני: ותתחם ית עמא
P	כל עמא על טוורא דסיני: ותתחם ית עמא
TJ I	כל עמא על טורא דסיני: ותתחים ית עמא ויקומון

Ni 1	חזור חזור למימר אזדהרו לכון דלא למיסק
V	חיזור חיזור למימר איזדהרו לכון דלא למיסוק
CG F	חזור חזור למימר אזדהרו לכון דלא למסוק
P	חזור חזור למימר איזדהרו לכון דלא למסוק
TJ I	חזור חזור לטורא למימר הוו זהירין מלמיסק

Ni 1	לטורא ודלא למקרב בשפולוי כל דיקרב לטורא
Ni M	בטורא ולא ׀ למקרב בסייפי/ דיקרב בטורא
V	בטורא ולא למיקרב בסייפוי כל די קריב בטורא
CG F	לטורא ולא למקרוב בסייפוי בשפולוי כל די יקרוב בטורא
P	בטורא ודלא למקרב בשיפולוי כל דיקרב לטורא
TJ I	בהר ולמיקרב בסייפיה כל דיקרב בטוורא

Ni 1	יתקטל יתקטיל: (13) לא תקרב ביה ידא דאנש ארום
Ni M	מתקטל
VB	מתקטל יתקטיל: לא תקרוב ביה יד דאנש ארום
CG F	מתקטלא יתקטל: לא תקרוב בה יד ברנש ארום
P	יתקטלא יתקטיל: לא תיקרב ביה ידא דקטלא ארום
TJ I	איתקטלא איתקטל: לא תיקרב ביה ידא ארום

Ni 1	מתרגמא יתרגם או גירין דאשא יזדרקון
Ni M	יתקשטין
VB	מתרגמא יתרגבים או גירין דאשא יתקשטון
CG F	מתרגמה יתרגם או גירין דאשא יזדרקן
P	איתרגמא איתרגם או גומרין דאישא יזדרקון
TJ I	יתרגמא יתרגם באבנא ברדא או גירין דאישא ודריקון

Ex. 19:1-25 (cont.)

Ni 1	ביה אן בעיר אין גבר לא יחי במתקע
Ni M	ביה במתקעה
VB	ביה אין בעיר אין גבר* לא יחי* במתקעה
CG F	ויתקשטן בה אן בעירא אן ברנש לא ייחי במתקעה
P	ביה אין בעיר אין בר נש לא יחי במתקע
TJ I	ביה אין בעירא אין אינשא לא יתקיים ברם במיגד

Ni 1	שופרא משה ואהרן אינון יהוון רשיין
Ni M	דשיפורא - - - - - הנון - - - - -
VB	דשיפורא הינון
CG F	דשיפורא אינון ומשה ואהרן יהוון רשיין
P	שיפורא משה ואהרן אינון יהוד רשאין
TJ I	קל שופרא הינון מרשן

Ni 1	למיסק לטורא: (14) ונחת משה מן טורא
Ni M	יסקון לטורא
V	יסקון לטורא: ונחת משה מן טורא
CG F	למסוק בטורא: ונחת משה מן טורא
P	למסוק בטורא: ונחת משה מן טורא
TJ I	למיסק בטורא: ונחת משה ביומא ההוא

Ni 1	לוות עמא וקדש ית עמא וחוורו לבושיהון: (15) ואמר
VB	לות עמא וקרי/ ית עמא וחוורו לבושיהון: ואמר
CG F	לות עמא וקדיש ית עמא וחוורו לבושיהון: ואמר
P	לות עמא וקדיש ית עמא וחוורו לבושיהון: ואמר
TJ I	לות עמא וזמין ית עמא וחוורן לבושיהון: ואמר

Ni 1	לעמ/ הוון מזמנין לתלתא יומין לא יקרב מנכון גבר
Ni M	תקרבון
VB	לעמא הוון מזמנין לתלתה יומין לא תקרבון
CG F	לעמא הוון זמנין לתלתה יומין לא תקרבון
P	לעמא הוו זמנין לתלתא יומין לא יקרב גבר
TJ I	לעמא הוו זמנין לתלתי יומין לא תקרבון

Ni 1	לתשמיש דערס: (16) והוה ביומא תליתיא
VB	לתשמי/ דערסא*: והוה ביומא תליתייה
CG F	לתשמיש דערס: והווה ביומה תליתייה
P	מנכון לתשמיש דערס: והוה ביומא תליתאה
TJ I	לתשמיש דעריס: והוה ביומא תליתאה

*
Reading of B.

Ex. 19:1-25 (cont.)

Ni 1   לעדוני צפרא והווה קלין   וברקן
Ni M   בער/
V   בעידוני צפרא והוה קלין   וברקין
CG F   בעידוני צפרה והווה קלין   וברקין
P   בעידוני צפרא והוון קלן   וברקין
TJ I   בשיתא בירחא בעידוני צפרא והוה קלין דרעיב וברקין

Ni 1   וענן תקיף   על טורא   ושופרא   ותקף
Ni M   תק/
V   וענן תקיף   על טורא וקליה דשיפורא   תקיף
CG F   וענן תקיף   על טורא וקליה דשיפורה   תקיף
P   וענן תקיף   על טורא וקליה דשיפורא אזיל ותקיף
TJ I   ועננא תקיף קטיר על טורא וקל   שופרא   תקיף

Ni 1   ולחדא ואזדעזעו כל עמא די   במשריתא: (17)   ואפיק משה
V   ולחד וזעו כל עמא דאית במשריתא: ואפיק משה
CG F   ולחדא וזע כל עמא דאית במשריתיה: ואפיק משה
P   ולחדא ואזדעזעו כל עמא די   במשריתא: ואפיק משה
TJ I   ולחדא וזע כל עמא די   במשריתא: ואנפיק משה

Ni 1   ית עמא לקדמות איקר שכינתא דיי/ מן משריתא
V   ית עמא לקדמות יקר שכינת/ דיי/
CG F   ית עמא לקדמותיה דשכינתיה דיי/ מן משריתא
P   ית עמא לקדמותיה דמימרא דיי/ מן משריתא
TJ I   ית עמא לקדמות שכינתא דיי/ מן משריתא ומן יד

TJ I   תלש מדי עלמא ית טורא וזקפיה באוירא והוה זייג הי

Ni 1   ואתעתדו בשפלוי דטורא: (18)   וטורא
V   ואיתעתדו בשיפולוי דטורא: וטורא
CG F   ואיתעתדו בשיפולוי דטורה: וטורה
P   ואיתעתדו בשיפולי טורא: וטורא
TJ I   כאספקלריא ואתעתדו תחותי טורא: וטורא

Ni 1   דסיני הוה תנן   כוליה מן בגלל
V   דסיני   עטר כוליה מן קודם
CG F   דסיני הוה תנן ועטה כוליה מן קודם
P   דסיני הוה תנן   כוליה מן קדם
TJ I   דסיני   תנין   כוליה מן בגלל דארכין ליה יי/ *שמיא*
Ni M   אתרגביף

– – – – – – – – – – – – – – – – – – –

Ex. 19:1-25 (cont.)

דאתגליית עלוי איקר שכינת/ דיי/ באשתא	Ni 1
בשלהובא דאשא	Ni M
די איתגלית עלוי יקר שכינתא דיי/ בשלהבא דאישא	V
די אתגליית עלוי יקר שכינתיה דיי/ בשלהבית דאשה	CG F
דאיתגלי עלוי יקר שכינתיה דיי/ בשלהוכית דאישא	P
ואיתגלי עלוי באישא	TJ I
ואתמלי מזיו יקר שכינתיה דיי/ - - -	Ni M

וסלקת תננא כתננא דאתונא ואזדעזע כל	Ni 1
וסלק תננא כקטור תנן אתונה וזעו כל	Ni M
וסליק תניניה כתנן אתונא וזעו כל	V
וסלק תנניה כקיטור תנן אתונא ואזדעזע כל	CG F
וסליק תנניה כקיטור תננא דאתונא ואזדעזע כל	P
מצלהבא וסליק קוטריה הי כקוטרא דאתונא וזע כל	TJ I
- - - וסלק קוטרי/היך קוטרא דאתונ/	Ni M

טורא לחדא: (19) והוה קלא דשיפורא	Ni 1
- - - - עמא דאית במשרית/	Ni M
עמא דאית במשריתא: והוה קליה דשיפורא	V
טורה לחדא: והווה קליה דשיפורה	CG F
טורא לחדא: והוה קליה דשיפורא	P
טוורא לחדא: והוה קל שיפרא	TJ I

אזל ותקף לחדא משה הוה ממלל בקול נעים ומן קדם יי/	Ni 1
אזיל ותקיף לחדא משה הוה ממלל ומן קודם יי/	V
אזיל ותקיף לחדא משה הווה ממלל ומן קודם יי/	CG F
אזיל ותקיף לחדא משה הוה ממליל ומן קדם יי/	P
אזיל ותקיף לחדא משה הוה ממליל ומן קדם יי/	TJ I

הוה מתענה ליה בקל:	Ni 1
הוה מתעני ליה בקל נעים:	V
הווה מתעני בקל בסם ונעים:	CG F
מתעני ליה בקל בסים ובנעימה קלא:	P
הוה מתעני בקל נעים ומשבח ונעימתא	TJ I

Ex. 19:1-25 (cont.)

Ni 1	ואתגליית איקר שכינתא דיי/ על טורא (20)	
Ni M	ואתגלית ממרי/ - - - דיי/	
V	ואיתגלי מימרא דיי/ על טורא	
CG F	ואתגליית יקר שכינתיה דיי/ על טורה	
P	ואיתגלי מימרא דיי/ על טוורא	
TJ I	חלייא: ואיתגלי יי/ על טוורא	

Ni 1	דסיני על ריש טורא וקרא מימריה דיי/ למשה מן
V	דסיני בריש טורא וקרא דבירה דיי/ מן ריש
CG F	דסיני על ראש טורה וקרא מימריה דיי/ למשה על ראש
P	דסיני לריש טורא וקרא ליה דברא דיי/ למשה מן ריש
TJ I	דסיני על ריש טוורא וקרא יי/ למשה לריש

Ni 1	טורא וסלק משה: (21) ואמר יי/ למשה חות
Ni M	מימרי/ דיי/
V	טורא וסליק מש/: ואמר מימרי/ דיי/ למשה חות
CG F	טורה וסלק משה: ואמר מימריה דיי/ למשה חות
P	טורא וסליק משה: ואמר מימרא דיי/ למשה חות
TJ I	טוורא וסליק משה: ואמר יי/ למשה חות

Ni 1	אסהיד בעמא דלא ידחקון קדם יי/ למיחמיה ויפל
V	אסהיד בעמא דלא ידחקון קודם יי/ למיחמי ויפל
CG F	אשהד בעמה דלא ידחפון קודם יי/ למחמי ויפול
P	אסהיד בעמא דלא ידחקון קדם יי/ למחמי דלא יפיל
TJ I	אסהיד בעמא דילמא יכוונון קדם יי/ לאיסתכלא ויפיל

Ni 1	מנהון אוכלסין סגין: (22) ולחוד כהניא
V	מנהון אוכלסין סגיין: ולחוד כהניא
CG F	מנהו]ן אוכלסין סגין: ולחוד כהניה
P	מנהון אוכלוסין סגיעין: ולחוד כהניא
TJ I	מנהון רב דכהון: ואוף כהניא

Ni 1	דקיימין ומשמשין קדם יי/ יתקדשון דלא יהוי בהון
Ni M	דקרבין יתקוף בהן
V	דקיימין ומשמשין קודם יי/ יתקדשון דלא יתקוף בהון
CG F	דקיימין ומשמשין קודם יי/ יתקדשון דלא יתקוף בהון
P	דקיימין ומשמשין קדם יי/ יתקדשון דילמא יתקוף בהון רב
TJ I	דקריבין לשמשא יי/ יתקדשון דילמא יקטול בהון

Ex. 19:1-25 (cont.)

לא ייכלין   (23)   :/יי קדם מן רגוז   Ni 1
                                        רגוז   Ni M
ואמר משה קודם יי/ לא יכלין   :/יי קודם מן רגוז   V
ואמר משה קודם יי/ לא יכלין   :/יי קודם מן רגיז   CG F
ואמר משה קדם יי/ לא יכלין   :/יי קדם אמר רגוז   P
ואמר משה קדם יי/ לא יכלין   :/יי   TJ I

למימר בן אסהדת את ארום דסיני לטורא   למיסק עמא   Ni 1
                                         למסוק   Ni M
למימר בן אסידת את ארום דטיני לטורא   למיסוק עמא   V
למימר בן אסהידת את ארום דסיני לטורה   למסוק עמא   CG F
למימר בן אסהידת את ארום דסיני טוורא על   למסוק עמא   P
למימר בנא אסהידת אנת ארום דסיני לטוורא   למיסק עמא   TJ I

ואמר ליה   (24)   :יתיה וקדש טורא ית תחם   Ni 1
ואמר ליה מימריה   :יתיה וקדש טורא ית אתחיים   V
ואמר ליה מימריה   :יתה ותקדש טורה ית תחם   CG F
ואמר ליה מימרא   :יתהון וקדש טורא ית תחם   P
ואמר ליה   :וקדשהי טוורא ית תחום   TJ I

עמך וכהניא   ואהרן את ותיסק חות איזל/ יי   Ni 1
עימך וכהנייא   ואהרן את ותיסוק חות איזל/דיי   V
וכהנייה עמך אחוך ואהרן את ותסוק חות אזיל/דיי   CG F
עמך וכהניא   ואהרן את ותיסוק חות איזול/דיי   P
עימך וכהנייא   ואהרן אנת ותיסק חות איזל/ יי   TJ I

יהוי דלא/ יי קדם   למיסק ידחקון לא ועמא   Ni 1
                                     יתקוף   Ni M
יתקוף דלא/ יי קודם   למסוק ידחקון לא ועמא   V
יתקוף דלא/ יי קודם   למסוק ידחפון לא ועמא   CG F
יתקוף דלמא/ יי קדם   למסוק ידחקון לא ועמא   P
יקטול דילמא/ יי קדם למסתכלא למיסוק יכורונון לא ועמא   TJ I

טורא מן משה ונחת   (25)   :רגוז   בהון   Ni 1
טורא מין משה ונחת   :רגוז   בהון   V
טורא מן משה ונחת   :רגוז   בהון   CG F
טורא מן משה ונחת   :רגוז רב בהון   P
טוורא מן משה ונחת   :בהון   TJ I

Ex. 19:1-25 (cont.)

Ni 1	לורות עמא ואמר להון קרובו קבילו עשירתא
V	לות עמא ואמר להון קרובו קבילו עסרתי
CG F	לורות עמא ואמר להון קריבו קבילו עשרתי
P	לעמא ואמר להון קריבו וקבילו ית עשרא
TJ I	לות עמא ואמר להון קריבו קבילו אורייתא עם עשרתי ית עשרא

Ni 1	דבירייא:
V	דבירייה:
CG F	דבירייה:
P	דבריא:
TJ I	דבירייא:

B.   Ni 1 Texts with Multiple Mgg and Texts of TJ I and, Where Extant, TJ II

Gen. 14:14   Gen. 14:14

Ni 1	ושמע אברם ארום אשתבי לוט בר אחוי וזאין ית עלמוי
Ni M	עולמוי
TJ I	וכד שמע אברם ארום אשתבי אחוי וזיין ית עולמוי

Ni 1	תורכוות ביתיה
Ni M	מרכיוני ביותה
V	מרכיצי ביתיה
TJ I	דחניך לקרבא מרכייני ביתיה ולא צבו למהלכא עמיה
Ni M	מרכייניי ביתיה ולא צבו למהלכה עימיה

TJ I	ובחר מינהון ית אליעזר בר נמרוד דהוה
Ni M	ואיתבחר מניהון - אליעזר - - - - דהוות שקיל קבל

Ni 1	תלת מאה עשר ורדף
Ni M	מאוות ותמנת
V	תלת מאה ותמנת עשר ורדף מן
TJ I	מתיל בגבורת/ בכולהון תלת מאה ותמניסר ורדף
Ni M	- - - - - - - - - - - מאה: ותמנת עשר מן

Ni 1	בתריהון עד קיסריון:
V	בתריהון עד דן דקיסריון:
TJ I	עד דן:
Ni M	דן דקי/*

---

*Note Type II M before colon; Type I M after colon.   See
p.   for transcription of text and Mgg.

Gen. 28:11   Gen. 28:11

ובת תמן ארום טמעת ליה שמשא וצלי באתרא	Ni 1
ואבית	Ni M
ואבית תמן ארום טמעת ליה שמשא וצלי באתרא	P
וצלי באתר בית מוקדשא ובת תמן ארום טמע שמשא	TJ I
וערע -- -- בית מקדש/ ובת תמן ארום טמע -- - שמשה	Ni M

מן אבנוי דאתרא תמן ונסב	Ni 1
מן כיפי אתרא ונסיב	P
ונסיב ארבעה מאבני אתר קדיש	TJ I
ונסיב ארב/ אבנין מן אבני אתרא קדישא ההוא	Ni M

ושוי תחות אסדי ראשה	Ni 1
ושוי תחות אסודי רישיה	P
איסדוי ושוי	TJ I
ואתעבדון לאבנ/ חדא ביה"א איסדוהי ושרינון	Ni M

זמנא ידע דהוא עתיד למיסב ארבע נשין ומינהון עתידין	Ni M

ודמך לה באתרא ההוא:	Ni 1
ודמך ליה באתרא ההוא:	P
ושכיב באתרא ההוא:	TJ I
למיפק ארבע משירייין ויהון לעם חד ושכיב באתרא ההוא:	Ni M

Ex. 36:16   Ex. 36:16

ודבק ית חמש יריען לבלחודיהון	Ni 1
חמישתי יריעתה	Ni M
ולפיף ית חמש יריען לחוד כל קבל חמשה ספרי	TJ I
ולפף ית חמישתי יריען לחוד - - - קובל חמישתי סיפרי	Ni M

וית שית יריען לבלחודיהון:	Ni 1
אישתתי יריעתה	Ni M
אורייתא וית שית יריען לחוד כל קבל שיתא	TJ I
אורייתה וית שית יריען לחוד - - - קובל שיתה	Ni M

סידרי מתנייתה:	TJ I
סידורי משנה	Ni M

Lev. 9:6   Lev. 9:6

ואמ/ משה דן   פתגמה די   פקד   יי/   תעבדון:
מימריה דיי/
ואמר משה דין פיתגמא   דתעבדון אעברו
דפקיד   יי/   תעבדון אעברו

Lev. 9:6 (cont.)   Lev. 9:6 (cont.)

ותתגלי עליכו/ איקר	Ni 1
ויתגלי יקר	Ni M
ית יצרא בישא מן לבכון ומן יד איתגלי לכון איקר	TJ I
– יצרה בישא מן ליבכון ומן יד יתגלי לכון איקר	Ni M

שכינתיה דיי/:	Ni 1
שכינתא דיי/:	TJ I
שכינתה דיי/	Ni M

Lev. 10:2   Lev. 10:2

ונפקת אשא מן קדם יי/	Ni 1
ונפקת שלהובית אישתא מן קדם יי/ כרגז ואיתפליגת	TJ I
עמודא דאשתה מן קדם יי/ – – ואתפליגת לתרין	Ni M

לארבעתי חוטין ואעלת [ועאלת ,read] בגוא	TJ I
חוטין ומתרין לארבעה – – – ועלת – –	Ni M

אפיהון ואוקידת ית נשמתהון ברם גופיהון לא איתחרכו	TJ I
באפהון – – – – – – – – – – – –	Ni M

ואכלת יתהון ומיתו קדם יי/:	Ni 1
במימר	Ni M
ומיתו קדם יי/:	TJ I
– – – – – – ומיתו בגירין דאשה קדם יי/:	Ni M

Nu. 20:17   Nu. 20:17

נעבר כען בארעך לא נעבר בחקלין	Ni 1
נאנוס אניסן	Ni M
ניעבר כען בארעך לא נינוס אניסן	VB
נעיבר כדון בארעך לא נשרדגה בתולן ולא נאנוס אריסן	TJ I
נשרדגה בתולן ולא נינוס – –	Ni M

ובכרמין ולא נשתי גוברין	Ni 1
– – – ולא נשרדגה בתולן ולא נבעי נשי גוברין	Ni M
ולא נשרדגה*בתולן ולא נבעי נשי גוברין	VB
ולא נבעול נשי גוברין	TJ I
נשי גוברין – – – – – – – – – – – –	Ni M

*
Reading of B.

Nu. 20:17 (cont.)   Nu. 20:17 (cont.)

Ni 1	ארח מלכא	נהלך לא נסטי לא לימינה ולא
Ni M	באסרטא דמלכא	ניזיל לא נסטי|לא לימין ולא
VB	באיסרטא דמלכא	ניזיל לא נסטי לא לימין ולא
TJ I	באורח מלכא דבשמיא ניזיל לא נסטי לימינא	
Ni M	באורחה דמלכא דעלמא ניזיל	

Ni 1	לשמאלה	עד זמן די תחומך נעבר:
Ni M	ליסמיל	
VB	לשמאל	עד זמן די נעבר*
TJ I	ולשמאלא להנזקא בשבילי רשותא עד	דניעיבר

VB	תחומך:
TJ I	תחומך:

Deut. 8:9   Deut. 8:9

Ni 1	ארע די לא במסכנות תאכלון בה לחם	לא תחסרון
Ni M	ומזון	תחסר
TJ I	ארעא דלא בחוסרנא תיכלון בה לחמא	ולא תחסר
Ni M	בחוסרנה	

Ni 1	כל מן דעם בה ארע דאבניה שריין	וברירן היך
Ni M	כל מנדעם בה ארע די אבניה - -	בריריך -
VB	ארעא די אבנייה	בריריך
TJ I	כל מידעם בה ארעא די חכימהא גזרין גזירן בריר2 הי
Ni M	דחכימאה - - - -	תקיפין הי

Ni 1	פרזלה ומן טורייה	חצבין נחשה:
Ni M	כפורזלא - וטורייה	חשמין כנחשה
VB	כפורזלא וטורייה	חסימין* כנחשא:
TJ I	כפרזלא ותלמידהא שאלין שאילן חסימן	כנחשא:
Ni M	כפרזלה ותלמידייהא חסנין הי כנחשה	

*
Reading of B.

Ni 1	ארום לא אתיתון עד כדון לנוווחתא	
Ni M	עלתון ולבית מוקדשה – – – – – – –	
TJ I	ארום לא אתיתון עד כדון לבי מוקדשא דהוא בית נייחא	
Ni M	לבית מוקדשה דמתקרי בית נייחה	

Ni 1	ולאחסנותה דיי/ אלהכון יהב
Ni M	ולאחסנתה – – – – – – – – –
TJ I	ולאחסנת ארעא דיי/ אלקכון יהיב
Ni M	ולארעה דישראל דמתקריי אחסנתה

Ni 1	לכון:
TJ I	לכון:

CHAPTER III

PRELIMINARY LINGUISTIC PROFILES

A.   The Language of Type I Mgg

By the comparative method it was discovered that certain
variants are to be found in Mgg both where comparisons are possible and where no comparisons can be made.   An investigation
of the usage of these variants reveals that they occur repeat-
edly throughout the Ms, sometimes singly, sometimes in context,
sometimes in combinations with one another.   The following
tabulation is an indication of the frequency and distribution
of the words discussed in the preceding chapter.

לייץ [י] אֹ [ה]

Gen.	11:27; 15:1,11; 25:16; 27:46; 28:10; 34:21.
Ex.	1:1; 10:28; 11:10; 17:4; 20:1.
Lev.	4:2; 10:16; 20:5; 22:26; 23:2,4; 24:14; 25:6.
Nu.	1:5,16,17; 3:1,2,3,17,18,20,21,33; 4:15,37,41,45; 5:22,23; 7:19; 11:11,13; 13:18,28; 14:23; 22:15.
Deut.	1:1; 2:4,8,22,29; 3:5; 4:45; 7:20; 12:1; 18:12.

דאית

Gen.	7:19; 8:17; 9:10; 14:23; 18:14; 20:16; 22:17; 23:9,11,17,19,20; 24:1,36; 25:6; 31:1,21; 39:4.
Ex.	4:18; 7:17,21; 9:3,25; 11:8; 12:22,29; 13:20; 16:1,16; 20:11; 23:5; 37:13; 40:9.
Lev.	1:8,12,17; 3:3,4,5,9,10,14; 4:7,8,9,18; 7:3,20; 8:16,26,31; 11:9,10; 19:9; 27:24,28.
Nu.	1:50; 3:26; 4:16,26; 7:89; 8:24; 11:4,20,25; 12:3; 15:14; 16:31,32,34; 18:13; 21:20; 22:5; 31:15.
Deut.	2:36; 3:8,12,25; 4:18,47,48; 5:8,14; 6:14; 11:6; 12:12; 13:8(7); 16:11; 21:2; 28:23,43.

הנון [י] ה

Gen.	7:14; 14:13,24; 15:11; 19:3; 21:29; 25:16; 26:20; 30:2; 40:12.
Ex.	1:10,19; 4:18; 5:5,7,8,16; 7:11; 8:17,22; 12:4, 42; 13:2; 14:3.
Lev.	11:8,13,27,35,42; 17:5,7; 18:10,17; 22:2; 25:42, 55; 26:29.
Nu.	1:16,50; 3:9,13,20,21,33; 4:22; 7:2,3; 11:14,16; 13:3,18,19,20; 14:27; 16:16.

Deut. 1:1,39; 2:11; 4:10; 5:17,18,20; 7:16,26; 9:29;
19:17; 28:65; 29:2(3),17(18).

זרז

Gen. 18:6,7; 19:22; 24:18,20,46; 27:20; 44:11; 45:9.

Ex. 2:18; 10:16; 34:8.

זרעיית בני/

Gen. 9:9; 12:7; 13:15; 15:18; 17:7,9,10,12,19; 24:60;
26:3,4; 28:4,13,14; 35:12.

Ex. 28:43; 32:13; 33:1(30:21, in the text).

Lev. 21:17.

Nu. 14:24; 18:19(25:13, in the text).

Deut. 1:8,36; 4:37; 5:29; 10:15; 11:9; 12:25; 28:46.

טלי[י]תה

Gen. 24:61; 34:3,4,12.

Ex. 2:5,8.

Deut. 22:16,19,20,21,23,25,26,27,28,29.

[מן] בגין כן or כן

Gen. 6:22; 10:9; 18:5; 19:22; 20:6; 29:26,34,35; 30:6;
31:48; 33:17; 34:7; 50:12.

Ex. 1:12; 5:8,17; 6:9; 10:10,14; 14:4; 15:23; 16:29;
20:11; 25:9; 36:22,29.

Lev. 8:35; 10:13; 17:12; 24:19,20; 27:14.

Nu. 2:17,34; 5:4; 6:21; 8:20,22; 9:14,16; 14:28; 15:14;
18:24,28; 21:27; 27:7; 32:31; 36:10.

Deut. 3:21; 4:5; 5:15; 7:19; 8:20; 12:22,30,31; 15:11,15,
17; 20:15; 22:3,26; 24:22.

עוד

Gen. 8:10,12,21; 9:11,15; 17:5; 18:29; 19:12; 24:20;
29:27,30; 30:7,19; 32:29.

Ex. 2:3; 9:29; 10:29; 36:3(14:13 חרב with no M).

Lev. 25:51(עד in text).

Nu. 8:25(עוד in text; עוד in context); 18:5,22; 32:14.

Deut. 3:26; 5:25; 13:17(16);17:13; 18:16; 19:9,20; 28:68.

Gentilic names in אי

Gen. 10:16,18; 12:6; 13:7; 14:6,7,13; 15:21.

Ex. 8:22; 9:4; 10:2,6,19; 11:3; 12:12,23,27,30,33,35,
36,39; 13:11; 14:9,10,12,24,25,27.

Lev. 25:32,33.

Nu. 1:47,50,51,53; 3:32,39,41,45,46; 4:20; 8:10,11,
12,14,18,22; 14:25,43,45; 21:3,21,24,25,26.

Deut. 1:5,7,19,20,27; 2:9,11,18,19,22,37; 7:1; 11:30;
20:17.

כדו

    Gen.   11:6; 20:7; 27:3,8,43; 29:34; 30:30; 31:13,16,28,42;
                   32:5; 44:30; 45:5; 48:5.

    Ex.   18:11; 33:13.

    Nu.   22:6,34.

    Deut. 2:13; 5:25(22); 10:22.

The linguistic elements used in the margin show a very
high degree of agreement with those found in CG E, and, to a
somewhat lesser degree, with those of CG F.　Some other usages, such as מימריה דיי/ and דאית , ally the marginal language
with usages common to all the texts of the CG, which are recognized as ancient and relatively pure witnesses.　Other marginal
language elements, such as כדו and טליחה, are not attested in the
CG Mss but are found in the FT texts.

After a considerable number of observations of consistency
of usage in various parts of the marginal material were made, it
seemed worthwhile to make a complete study of linguistic elements
in order to determine the consistency of their usage as variants
to, and in relation to, the text.　Because the Targums, aside
from expansions and free paraphrase, are basically translations,
it is possible with the aid of a Hebrew concordance to the MT to
learn in each instance of a word's use in the MT the translation
equivalent used in the Targums.[1]　From this information it is
possible, even though allowances must be made for idiosyncracies
in the Mss, to determine the consistency with which a Hebrew word
with a given meaning has been translated by one and the same Aramaic word.

We have made this kind of survey for various elements of
vocabulary and morphology of the texts of TJ II.　A complete
listing was made for all Hebrew words studied which occurred less
than fifty times in the MT, and for some occurring up to 100
times.　For more frequently used words (more than fifty occurrences) a sampling was taken from every chapter of every book of
the Pentateuch where found.　For morphological elements, such as
prefixes or suffixes, various approaches were used, such as use
of English concordances, observations of forms included in vocabulary surveys, and collation of all suffixed forms of a common
noun or verb.[2]　The words listed above were included in the survey.　These words, like others surveyed, proved to be not only
repetitive throughout the Ms but also to be standard translations
of the Hebrew behind them.　We present below some examples of
this regularity of translation.

The repeated M which attracts one's attention upon first examination of Ni 1 is מימריה דייי/, "the word of the Lord," used as a circumlocution for the Tetragrammaton. Of 135 instances in Gen. where the Ni 1 text translates יהוה with /יי alone, the margin has מימריה דייי/ (or slight variations from this) eighty-eight times. This same variant continues to appear throughout the remainder of the Ms. However, because of its theological significance, it is not the best example to use if one seeks to establish a pattern of linguistic variation between text and margin. There are other examples, however, where the pairs of variants not only have no effect on the meaning of the text, but where one cannot even say that one is more "correct" or more "Palestinian" than the other. Frequently, both forms are attested in the various CG texts.

In translating three MT words for "girl," text and margins each employ one word for all three. For the one occurrence of ילדה (Gen. 34:4) in MT, text has רביתה, M, טליתא. For twenty-four instances of נערה (often spelled נער) in MT, the text gives רביתה (with orthographic variations) twenty-two times; Mgg, טליתא (or variations) fifteen times. For two of the twenty-four instances MT has נערה בתולה, for which Ni 1 text has רבי בתולה; Ni Mgg has טלייה in both instances (presumably replacing רבי only). For two instances of MT עלמה, the text has רביתה/א; against one of these the margin has טלייתא. רביתא is found in CG C (Gen. 34:12), while טליתא is attested in the FT (Deut. 22:20, PVBNL; Deut. 22:21, VBN).

The Hebrew words הם and המה (they) appear sixty-three times in the MT text of the Pentateuch. In one instance the Ni 1 text lacks a corresponding word, while the margin has הנון. In the remaining sixty-two instances the Ni 1 text has אינון or אנון. Of these, three occur in a section of Gen. where the Mgg were left undone by the scribes (Gen. 37:16; 42:35, twice). Of the remaining fifty-nine occurrences, הנון or הינון appears in the margin, alone or in context, forty-five times.

In the MT עוד or ע'ד (again, yet, still) is used seventy times in sixty-seven verses. The Ni 1 text has עוד eleven times, תוב forty-three times (plus one interlinear insertion of תוב omitted from the text, Nu. 18:5), the conflated reading עוד/עד תוב three times, and other readings twelve times. Against the forty-four uses of תוב in the text, the margin has עוד twenty-seven times; two of the three conflated readings are countered by marginal עוד. Four of the forty-four uses of תוב

in the text occur in a section where Mgg were not done at all (Gen. Chs. 37-38). The CG texts employ עוד fourteen times (B, C, E; eleven examples in E) and תוב/חובן four times (D, F, two examples each).

MT Pentateuch has כן (so, thus) ninety-six times. The Ni 1 text has כן sixteen times; כדין or כדן seventy-one times; other renditions nine times. Against the seventy-one text usages of כדן/כדין, the margin gives כן thirty-seven times. Three additional instances fall where the Mgg were not done. All three forms are found in the CG texts: כן fifteen times (C,3; E,11; F,1); כדין seven times (C,2; D,4; F,1); כדן eight times (B,1; D,2; E,1; F,4).

In MT Pentateuch forms of the verb מהר (to hurry) occur seventeen times. Ni 1 text uses Aphel forms of יחי (e.g., אוחי) sixteen times, a form of זרז once. Against the sixteen occurrences of forms of יחי in the text, forms of זרז appear thirteen times in the margins; one additional instance in the text falls where Mgg were not done (Gen. 41:32). The CG texts employ זרז once (Gen. 43:30, E) and אוחי once (Lev. 22:27, F, in an expansion; Ni, Ni Mgg, VBNP, also אוחי). FT employs זרז twice (Gen. 24:20, VBNL; Ex. 34:8, VBN (corrupt in form).[3]

The process of tracing translation equivalents serves as a check and refinement upon earlier observations of typical usages and strengthens the case for a single text/language type underlying the majority of Mgg. It is more difficult to determine whether a specific M is clearly Type I when textual evidence is lacking. One Aramaic word frequently translates several Hebrew words, or, conversely, a Hebrew word with several shades of meaning is frequently translated by two or more Aramaic words.[4] The use of שיזי, Shafel of יצא, illustrates this need for caution. Forms of this word appear frequently in the Ni Mgg of Deut. At Deut. 7:10 the verb שיצי is identical with the FT reading. At 7:20 the verb is found in context with אליין, another form typical of the FT vocabulary. The verb is attested as FT vocabulary also at 7:23 and 33:27, the only other extant verses where a verb of this meaning is required by the context. Although it is likely that the great majority of Ni Mgg in Deut. involving שיצי do indeed belong to Type I, it cannot be concluded that שיצי is a "Type I word" which, in itself, justifies identification of a marginal reading with this type. Firstly, consultation of a lexicon quickly reveals that the word is widely used, not only in the TJ II, but in O and TJ I as well. At Gen. 18:23,

for example, some form of this word is used in O, TJ I, Ni 1
text and Ni Mgg (FT and CG are not extant for this verse).
It is necessary, then, to inquire as to the actual nature of
the frequent contrast of text with M in Deut.

A preliminary examination of the Hebrew forms translated by
שיצי in Ni 1 text and Ni Mgg reveals the following:

Forms of שיצי are used at various times to translate the
following Hebrew words: אשביתה (hapax legomenon, Deut. 32:26),
נשמד and (נכה Hiphil of) הכה, אבד, חרם (כרת Hiphil of) הכרת,
הדף, (ירש Hiphil of) הריש, (שמד Niphal and Hiphil of) השמד
כלה and ,ספה ,בער.

In all except two of these instances, no systematic pattern
of marginal use of שיצי is discovered. The first exception is
that in Deut. in particular, the Ni 1 text translates Hebrew
אבד with סוף against שיצי in the margin. Outside of Deut. the
usage of the text is less consistent: שיצי and אבד are also used
to translate Hebrew אבד; סוף and אבד also appear in the margin.
The contrast between סוף in the text and שיצי in the margin in
Deut. is, however, sufficiently regular to justify designating
the translation of Hebrew אבד by שיצי as a Type I marginal usage.

The second exception involves a specific use of the Hebrew
stem בער in the following phrases:

ובערת הרע מקרבך	(Deut. 13:6; 17:7; 19:19; 21:21; 22:21,24; 24:7).
ובערת הרע מישראל	(Deut. 17:12; 22:22).
ובערת דם הנקי מישראל	(Deut. 19:13).

Of the ten occurrences cited here, seven (all except Deut.
13:6; 19:19 and 24:7) give ותבערון in the text against the variant ותישיצון in the margin. Although no external evidence is
available at these places, it is probable that this is also a
Type I variant in view of its repeated and regular occurrences
against the reading of the text.

We are also aware of the "counter examples" which can be
brought forth owing to the failure of Mgg to appear as and when
expected. However, the account of the dedicatory offerings for
the altar (Nu. 7:12-83) provides an illustration of the consistency of the Mgg in spite of minor discrepancies and frequent
lapses. The account repeats a basic three-verse statement
twelve times. Verses 20, 26, 32, 38, 44, 50, 56, 62, 68, 74,
80, repeat v. 14; vv. 21, 27, 33, 39, 45, 51, 57, 63, 69, 75,
81, repeat v. 15; vv. 22, 28, 34, 40, 46, 52, 58, 64, 70, 76,
82, repeat v. 16. In the Appendix (pp. 69-71) following this

chapter we set forth a tabulation of the Mgg to the three sets
of repetitive verses.   From the tabulation discrepancies among
Mgg and lack of expected Mgg are obvious.   Yet, in spite of
the irregularities, there is also a pattern which is easily
discernible.   The consistency of the Mgg is such that we are
able to give for each variant a model M -- the M one could expect were the Ms absolutely consistent in its Mgg -- and to re-
construct the two versions of the account in the margins of
Ni 1.

    None of the words given as examples in this monograph, or
any of the others traced, is present in every instance where it
may be expected.   However, the variants that are present show
a high degree of consistency.   כן, for example, appears only
about half the time expected, but no examples of כדין appear.
While it is too much to say that all irregularities of the Ms
can be explained or understood, nevertheless, from the study of
translation equivalents a "linguistic profile" emerges.   This
profile allies the Type I Mgg linguistically as well as textually with FT and CG E and F.

B.   The Language of Type II Mgg
    No attempt has been made to make a final judgment about
the number of sources involved in the Type II material, or a-
bout the origin of this material and its relationship to other
Targumic sources.   Rather, we have made a preliminary examination of the language of the variants grouped in this category.
We present below significant points which emerged from this examination.   The texts referred to are transcribed in Ch. V.

    1.   The variants display the following typically Palestin-
ian usages, which are shared by both TJ I and TJ II against O:

ארום	(Gen. 28:11; 31:22; Deut. 24:6)
(O ארי)	
אין	(Lev. 14:53; Nu. 16:30; Deut. 25:2)
(O אם)	
כדון[5]	(Gen. 45:28; Nu. 16:30; Deut. 29:14)
(= MT עתה) (O כען)	
חמא	(Gen. 45:28; 49:18; Nu. 12:12)
(O חזא)	

    2.   The variants include a number of elements shared by O
and TJ I against the normal TJ II usage:

נא (first person   (Nu. 12:12; Deut. 29:14, 3 times)
pronominal suffix)   (but cf. ך, Gen. 28:17; Lev. 27:29)
                             (O נא, TJ I נא and ך, TJ II ך)

Attached pronominal   (Gen. 3:9; 27:22,27; 28:11; 33:14;
object suffixes   Lev. 9:22; Deut. 20:6; 25:2)
with verbs   (O and TJ I suffix, TJ II avoids
                             suffixes, uses forms with ית)

Non-Peal infinitives   (Gen. 33:14; Lev. 8:34; 16:8; 21:4)
without prefixed מ   (TJ II uses prefixed מ with all
                             infinitives; O and TJ I with Peal)

למה[6]   (Gen. 25:22)
                       (TJ II למה כען)

    3. The variants include usages distinctive to TJ I against O and TJ II.

כדון[5]   (Nu. 12:12, twice; but also כען,
(= MT נא)   Gen. 33:14)
                   (O and TJ II כען)

הי כ   (Deut. 8:9, twice)
                   (O and TJ II, various usages;
                   הי כ distinctively TJ I)

אמטול   (Lev. 21:4)
                   (O and TJ II, various usages;
                   אמטול, distinctively TJ I)

מטול ד   (Lev. 27:29)
                   (O and TJ II, various usages;
                   מטול ד, distinctively TJ I)

תריסר   (Nu. 33:9)
                   (O and TJ II, תריסר; תרין עש/סר,
                   distinctively TJ I)

    The three classes of evidence all point toward a linguistic relationship between the Type II material and TJ I. The appearance of morphological elements common to O and TJ I, but rare in TJ II texts, is particularly striking. The elimination of pronominal object suffixes and the use of מ with all infinitives are two of the most regular characteristics of TJ II. Although all the medieval Mss of TJ II show corruption to usages of the O type, this corruption is random; TJ II forms

remain dominant.   In the Type II material, however, there
seem to be too many occurrences of usages of the O/TJ I type
in a limited amount of material to be attributed to random
corruption.

In the case of Type I Mgg, we find a strong textual as
well as linguistic relationship to various other Targumic
witnesses.   The relation of Type II Mgg to TJ I is not so
clear.   In its linguistic peculiarities, the Type II material
shows a striking agreement with TJ I against both O and TJ II.
There are also many affinities with individual readings and
words found in TJ I.   The texts surveyed, however, certainly
cannot be identified simply as selections from the TJ I version known to us.   Many of the readings diverge from those of
TJ I; some are unknown elsewhere in the Targumic traditions.
Perhaps the most accurate classification, based on current
knowledge, would be as additional material belonging to a
"TJ I group," which heretofore included only the two versions
of PJ.

A better understanding of the textual and linguistic relationships of the Ni 1 text and Mgg can be gained only by
detailed study of each passage.   It is hoped that the transcriptions of verses with multiple variants in Ch. V will
facilitate such study.

A. Model Reconstruction of the Three Versions of Nu. 7:14-82
    in Ni 1

Neofiti 1 Text

בזן חדה מתקלייה עשר סלעין דכסף הוות עבידה והיא הוות דדהב קרב
יתה מלייה ראשי קטרת בוסמנין טבין מפטמין ודכיין לקטרתה: תור חד
בר תורין בר תלת שנין דכר חד בר תרתין ואמר חד בר שתה תלתיהון
קרב לעלה: צפיר בר עזין חד קרב יתה לחטאתה לשבקות חוביך ולשלוון
למכפרה באדמה דצפירה על חובוי ועל חובי שלות שבטה:

Marginal Version A (= Type I, VB)

בזיך חדה מתקלייה עשרה סלעין די הוות דדהב קרב יתה מלייה ראש
בוסמנין טבין מפטמין ודכיין לקטורת בוסמנייה: תור חד בר תורין
בר תלת שנין דכר חד בר תריין ואמר חד בר שתייה תלתהון הוה רב
שבטה מקרב לעלה: צפיר בר עזין חד קרב רב שבטה לחטאתה:

Marginal Version B (Literal Translation of MT)

בזן חדה מתקלה עשרה דדהב מלייה קטרה: תור חד בר תורין דכר חד
אמר חד בר שתה לעלה: צפיר בר עזין חד קרב יתה לחטאתה:

B. Actual Mgg of Marginal Version A with Model Mgg

First Verse of Sets

			Model
ראש בוסמנין	עשרה סלעין די הוות דדהב	בזיך	Model
בוס	עשרה סלעין די הוות דדהב	--	14
ראש בוס/	עשרה סלע די הוות	בזיך	20
ראש בוס/	עשרה סלעין די הוות דדהב	--	26
ראש בו/	עשרה סלעין די הוות	בזיך	32
--	--	--	38
ראש בוס/	עשרה סלעין די הוות דדה/	--	44
ראש בוסמ/	עשרה סלעין די הוות דדהב	--	50
ראש בוסמני/	עשרה סלעין די הוות דדהב	--	56
ראש בוס/	עשרה סלעין די הוות דד/	--	62
--	עשרה סלעין די הוות דדהת	--	68
ריש בוסמנין	עשרה סלעין דדהב מלייה קטרח*	--	74
--	עשרה סלעין די הוות דדהב	--	80

*Conflation of Versions A and B.

First Verse of Sets (Cont.)

Hebrew	Set
לקטורת בוסמנייה |	Model
לקטורת בוסמנייה |	14
לקטורת בוסמנייה |	20
לקטורת בוס/ |	26
--	32
לקטורת בוסמנייה |	38
לקטורת בוס/ |	44
--	50
לקטורת בוסמנייה |	56
לקטורת בוס/ |	62
לקטורת בוסמנ/י |	68
לקטורת בוסמנייה |	74
--	80

Second Verse of Sets

Hebrew (col 3)	Hebrew (col 2)	Hebrew (col 1)	Set
הוה רב שבטה מקרב לעלה |	שתייה תלתהון |	תריין |	Model
הוה רב שבטה מקרב לעולה |	שתייה תלתהון |	תורתין |	15
הוה רב שבטה מקרב לעלם |	--	תריין |	21
הוה רב שבטה מקרב לעלה |	--	תריין |	27
הוה רב שבטה מקרב לעולה |	--	תריין |	33
רב שבטה לחטאתה* |	--	תריין |	39
הוה רב שבטה קרבן לעלה |	שתייה |	תריין |	45
הוה רב שבטה מקרב לעולה |	שתייה |	--	51
הוה רב שבטה מקרב לעלה |	שתייה |	תריין |	57
--	שתייה |	תריין |	63
הוה רב שבטה מקרב לעלה |	שתייה |	תריין |	69
הווה רב שבטה מקרב לעלה |	--	--	75
הוה רב שבטה מקרב לעלה |	שתייה |	תריין |	81

Third Verse of Sets

Hebrew	Set
קרב רב שבטה לחטאתה |	Model
רב שבטה לחטאתה |	16
רב שבטה לחטאתה |	22
קרב רב שבט/ לחטאתה |	28
קרב רב שבטה לחטאתה |	34
See v. 39.	40
רב שבטה לחטאתה |	46
--	52
--	58
רב שבטה לחטאתה |	64
רב שבטה לחטאתה |	70
רב שבטה לחטאתה |	76
--	82

*Misplaced, M to v. 40.

C. Actual Mgg of Marginal Version B with Model Mgg

First Verse of Sets

	Hebrew	Model
|	מתקלה עשרה דדהב מלייה קטרה	Model
|	--	14
|	מתקלה עשרה דדהב מלייה קטרתה	20
|	מתקלה עשרה דדהב מלייה קטורדה	26
|	--	32
|	עשרה דדהב מלייה קטרה	38
|	לה עשרה דדהב מלייה קטרה	44
|	--	50
|	מתקלה עשרה דדהב מלייה קטרתה	56
|	מתקלה עשרה דדהב מלייה קטרה	62
|	מתקלה עשרה דדהב מלייה קטרה	68
|	עשרה סלעין דדהב מלייה קטרתה*	74
|	מתקלה עשרה דדהב מלייה קטרה	80

Second and Third Verses of Sets

					Model
| קרב יתה לחסאתה		|	דכר חד חד אמר חד בר שתה לעלה	|	Model
| --	16	|	--		15
| --	22	|	דכר חד חד אמר חד בר שתה לעלה		21
| קרב יתה לחסאתה	28	|	דכר חד חד אמר חד בר שתה לעלה		27
| קרב יתיה לחטא/	34	|	דכר חד חד אמר חד בר שתה לעלתה		33
| --	40	|	דכר חד חד אמר חד בר שתה לעלתה		39
| --	46	|	דכר חד חד אמר חד בר שתה לעלה		45
| --	52	|	דכר חד חד אמר חד בר שתה לעלה		51
| --	58	|	דכר חד חד אמר חד בר שתה לעלה		57
| לחטאתה	64	|	--		63
| לחטאתה	70	|	דכר חד חד אימר בר שתה לעלה		69
| --	76	|	דכר חד חד אמר חד בר שתה לעלה		75
| --	82	|	דכר חד חד אימר חד בר שתה לעלה		81

*Conflation of Versions A and B.

CHAPTER IV

VARIANT VERSIONS WITHIN THE Ni 1 TEXT

While much the greater part of the text of Ni 1 seems to
represent a single basic recension, in Gen. 1:1-3:4 and Deut.
29:17(18)-34:12 changes in the character of both text and Mgg
are sufficiently marked to indicate that several additional
distinct recensions were used to complete the text.[1] A pre-
sentation of the evidence for the positing of these several
recensions follows.

A.   Gen. 1:1-3:4

Studies of the vocabulary and morphology of Ni 1 reveal a
concentration of atypical forms in text and margin at the beginning and end of the manuscript, and a scarcity of Mgg in these
sections. In addition, another unexplained phenomenon draws
attention to the beginning of Gen. Between Gen. 1:1 and 3:4
there are sixty-six Mgg, and fifty-nine of these are marked
with א"ס or א"נ. After 3:4 sigla are not used.[2] The usual
assumption has been that these sigla were discontinued after a
few chapters because the system of indicating variant readings
had by this time become self-evident.[3] This assumption, however, does not account for the seemingly inexplicable alter-
nations between the sigla in the margins. An unmarked M appears beside Gen. 1:1, but the variant at 1:2 and all subsequent ones to and including the one at 1:20 have the siglum,
א"ס (eight Mgg).[4] Verses 21-23 have no Mgg. Verse 24, with
which a new page of the Ms is begun, has three Mgg, each with
the siglum, א"נ. This siglum is then employed with all Mgg
from this verse to and including verse 2:5a (twenty-four Mgg).
At 2:5b two Mgg with siglum, א"ס, appear, and this siglum is
employed for all but five Mgg from verse 2:5b to 3:4 (twenty-
seven of thirty-two Mgg). It can be noted also that four of
the five unmarked Mgg between 2:5b and 3:4 are to verses 1 and
2 of Ch. 3; in other words, from 2:5b to, but not including,
3:1, there is only one unmarked variant amid twenty-four marked
variants.

The first indication that these shifts in sigla might sig-
nify something more than scribal inconsistency came during examination of Gen. 1:24. This verse stands out from the preceding verses for many reasons. In the first place, it is the
first verse with the siglum, א"נ, instead of א"ס, in the margin.

72

Secondly, this verse differs from vv. 1-23 in the morphology of the circumlocution for the divine name, "word," in the text. This difference is shown below:

Text

Gen. 1:1-23   ממרא/ה   (1:3,4,5,6,8,9,10,11,16,20,22, ממרה
only at 1:9)

Gen. 1:24   ממריה

Thirdly, this verse (1:24) differs noticeably from vv. 1-20 in the orthography of the circumlocution for the divine name in the margins. This difference is shown below:

Margin

Gen. 1:1-23   ס"א ממרה   (1:3,4,10)
Gen. 1:24   נ"א ממרא

Fourthly, this verse differs from vv. 1-23 in writing "Lord" as ה rather than as יי.[5]

Finally, there are two Mgg to the verse of types not found in parallel instances in vv. 1-23. This difference is shown below:

	Text		Margin
Gen. 1:21	דרחשא	(RSV: that moves)	---
Gen. 1:24	ורחש	(RSV: creeping things)	נ"א ורמש
Gen. 1:3	כגזירת ממריה		---
Gen. 1:7,9 11,15	כממריה		---
Gen. 1:24	כממריה		נ"א כגזירת ממרי/

This juxtaposition of so many new elements in one verse suggests that the verse may be the beginning of a new version of the text. An examination of the text and Mgg of the succeeding verses marked by the siglum, נ"א, confirms this hypothesis. Although ממריה proves not to be the typical usage of the text of succeeding verses of this section, and in fact now appears consistently in the margin", the usage for "word" throughout the section differs from that of the previous section. The difference is shown below:

	Text	Margin
Gen. 1:3,4,5,6,8, 10,11,16,20,22	ממרא	ס"א ממרה (1:3,4,10)
Gen. 1:9	ממרה	---
Gen. 1:1,7,14,21	יי/	---
Gen. 1:17	איקהי (for איקריה)	---
Gen. 1:24	ממריה	נ"א ממרא
Gen. 1:25,27	ממרה	---
Gen. 1:26	יי/	נ"א ממריה

	Text	Margin
Gen. 1:28,29; 2:3 (twice)	איקריה	ממריה נ"א
Gen. 2:2	ממריה	---
Gen. 2:4	יי / אלהים	/ ממריה דיי נ"א

It can be seen that the usage for "word" in the second section differs noticeably from that of the first section, where, in fact, there was consistency in the text in the use of ממרא/ה. Of sixteen occurrences, ממרא is found ten times, ממרה once. The most frequently used circumlocution for the divine name in the second section is איקריה, which appears only once in the first section. So far as the Mgg are concerned, ממרָה is the reading consistently in the first section and ממריה in the second. No instance of the orthography, ממרָה, so distinctive in the margin in the previous section, is found in the second section.

Also, the M רמש for the text רחש is a consistent variant in the second section, but does not appear in the first section. This can be seen from the tabulation below:

	Text	Margin
Gen. 1:21	רחש	---
Gen. 1:24,25,26,28,30	רחש	רמש נ"א

The clues to a change of manuscript between 1:23 and 1:24 are to be found primarily in the Mgg. Thus, ממרָה is found before 1:24; ממרא at 1:24 and ממריה after 1:24. Both יי/ and איקריה appear without Mgg in 1:1-1:23 but with the M ממריה in 1:25-2:3. כממריה appears in 1:1-1:23 without M, but with the M כגזירת ממרי/ at 1:24. (This is the last occurrence of this expression in the Creation Account.) רחש appears in 1:1-1:23 without M, but in 1:25-2:5a with the M רמש. That these significant Mgg occur within different <u>sigla</u> suggests that the <u>siglum</u> itself indicates a distinct manuscript.[6]

Mgg in 1:1-1:20 are marked by the siglum, ס"א; Mgg in 1:24-2:5a are marked by the <u>siglum</u>, נ"א; Mgg in 2:5b to 3:4 are marked by the <u>siglum</u>, ס"א. Inasmuch as differences in text and Mgg between 1:1-1:20 and 1:24-2:5a can be construed as evidence for two different recensions of TJ II, 1:24 is distinctive enough to suggest a break at 1:23, and Mgg to each section have their own distinctive <u>siglum</u>; it seems reasonable to hypothesize that 2:5b to 3:4, with its <u>siglum</u> of ס"א also represents a recension distinct from the preceding section or sections.

We will now discuss each of the three proposed sections in more detail.

1. <u>Gen. 1:1-1:23</u>. The frequent usage of the circumlocu-

tion, "word," for the divine name in this section distinguishes
it not only from the following section but from the major part
of the Ni l text.   The most common usage for the greater part
of Ni l is the abbreviation, /יי, with the variant, ממריה דיי/,
frequently given in the margin.   Again, the word כן is used
consistently (1:7,9,11,15) in this section, whereas the main
text most often uses כדן/כדין (frequently with כן given as the
M).

Textually, this section agrees most closely with P; it is
closer to P than to the V 440 group.   Nevertheless, the Ni l
text does differ from P consistently in its use of ממרא P) ממריה),
שפר וחקן (1:10,12,18,21, but 1:4 טוב; P טב וחקין 1:10,12,18,21,
but 1:4 טב), and כן (P כדין; 1:7 כדנן), and כמימריה (1:7,9,11,15;
P במימריה). בגזירת ממריה P, כגזירת ממריה Ni l 1:3 but ;בגזירת מימריה P.   Because of these variations as well as many minor differences in
orthography, this text is certainly not a copy of, nor the original of, P.   Also, since P contains a complete text for this
section of Gen., it cannot be determined whether the text used
here was a "FT" paralleling P or a complete recension of the
Pentateuch.

2. Gen. 1:24-2:5a.   This section, like the first, uses
circumlocutions in translating the Tetragrammaton more consistently than the main Ni l text.   The combination of איקריה
with the M ממריה (1:28,29; 2:3 twice) is found only in this
section.   For the use of כן (1:24,30), see the discussion above.
דאית, used to translate אשר before a preposition (1:29,30), is
infrequent in the Ni l text, and is one of the most consistently
supplied Mgg against די of the text.

A particularly interesting relationship of text to Mgg is
shown in the translation of the Hebrew רמש in this section.   The
root, in verb and noun forms, is translated throughout the Ni l
text, including the first two sections, with רחש.   It appears
at Gen. 1:21 with no M, and five times in the second section
with M רמש (1:24,25,26,28,30).   In the remainder of the Codex
the M continues to appear regularly (twelve times out of thirteen), but it is consistently spelled רמס.   This is evidence
that the source for the Mgg in this section is not identical with
the source used for the greater part of the Ms.

This section, like the first one, resembles P (as well as
the one verse from the V 440 group available for the section,
1:27).   The text revised by the Mgg approaches more closely
that of P, but the Mgg do not account for all the variations of

P from the Ni 1 text. Also, P does not follow the marginal
text in the use of רמש. As in Section 1, our text uses כן
where P has כדין (1:24,30), and כמימריה where P has בגזירת
מימריה (1:24; at 1:30 P has a divergent reading without an
equivalent phrase).[7] For the first time here, however, Ni 1
gives the marginal reading, כגזירת ממרי/ (1:24). As in Section
1, Ni 1 gives שפר ותקין where P has טב ותקין at 1:25; at 1:31
both have שפר ותקין. Ni 1 has בר נש[א] for Hebrew אדם at 1:26
and 1:27; P agrees with Ni 1 at 1:26 but has אדם at 1:27. בר
נש is also employed in the expansion of Gen. 1:2 by Ni 1; P employs בני נשא. P employs דאית twice in 1:29 where Ni 1 uses די
for the first occurrence.

   To complete the discussion of Sections 1 and 2 in relation
to P, a few other points may be mentioned. Gen. 1:1 in Ni 1
begins, בחוכמתא ברא יי/, with מלקדמין, with a M, בחכמה ברא דיי/, without siglum and in a different hand. P begins, בחכמה ברא יי/
with a M, marked נ"א, מן לקדמין. At Gen. 2:2, Ni 1 begins the
verse with ואשלם. P reads וחמיד, again with a M, marked with
נ"א, ואשלים.[8]

   3. <u>Gen. 2:5b-3:4</u>. The translation of this section seems
to show linguistic accommodation to the MT. For example, one
finds אדם as the regular translation of Hebrew אדם (2:5b, 7
twice, 8,15,16,19 twice, 20 twice, 21,22 twice, 23 once, 25), but
בר נשא at 2:18 (cf. בר נש[א] at 1:2,26,27). בר נש or בני אנשא
are also the usual translations for אדם later in the Ni 1 text.[9]
One also finds אדמתא (2:7,9,19; but ארעא 2:5b,6) for Hebrew האדמה,
which is translated elsewhere in Ni 1 by ארעא.

   Also, one finds in the text, יי/ אלהים, paralleling the
Hebrew text, with ממריה דיי/ in the margins. (Note that this
terminology begins at 2:4 in the preceding section where the
Hebrew usage begins.) This accommodation is shown below:

	Text	Margin	
Gen. 2:5b,7,8,15,16,18,19,21,22	יי/ אלהים	/ממריה דיי	ס"א
Gen. 2:9	יי/ אלהים	---	
Gen. 3:1, first occurrence	יי/ אלהים	/ממריה דיי	
Gen. 3:1, second occurrence	יי/	/ממריה דיי	
Gen. 3:3	יי/	/ממריה דיי	ס"א

However, examination of all available Targum witnesses to this
section (O, TJ I, P, VBNL) reveals that all show accommodation
to the MT forms in Ch. 2. It can be easily understood that the
theological importance of the Hebrew words in this section might
cause the Targums to be rendered with the equivalent forms. For

the use of כן in the phrase בגין כן (2:24), see the discussion
under Section 1 above.

The text and Mgg of this section remain closely related
to both V 440 group and P, where these are extant. The inter-
relationships are well illustrated by collating the Ni 1 text
and Mgg against P and V for Gen. 2:15, the only verse complete
in the FT for this section.

Ni 1	ונסיב	יי / אלהים ית אדם ואשרי	יתיה בגנתא דעדן
Ni M	ממריה דיי /	ית אדם ואצנע	יתיה בגינתה - -
P	ונסיב מימריה דיי /	ית אדם **ואצנע**	**יתיה** בגינתא דעדן
V	ונסב	יי / אלהים ית אדם ואשרייה	בגינתא דעדן

Ni 1	למהוי פלח באורית/ ולמטור פקודיה:
Ni M	למהורי ולמיטר
P	למיהוי פלח באוריתיה ולמיטר פיקודוי:
V	ואצנע יתיה למיהוי פלח באורייתא ולמטור:

B. Deut. 29:17(18)-34:12

At Deut. 29:17(18) the number of Mgg diminish sharply
until they end at 33:12. No strong correlation between the
Mgg from 29:17 to 33:11 and the V 440 group and the CG E and F
can be made. Readings found in the Ni Mgg prior to 29:17 now
begin to appear in the text; other textual usages remain con-
stant, but the expected Mgg against them cease to appear.
Also, it would seem that there are at least two distinct sections in this latter part of Deut. We now discuss these two
sections in greater detail.

1. Deut. 29:17(18)-33:29. When a very detailed study
of this long section has been made, it may be found to be
composed of several versions, rather than one. At any rate,
one is immediately struck by the scarcity and changed character of the Mgg. From 29:17-33:12, there are sixty-eight Mgg.[10]
Of these, sixteen effect a change in the construction of the
genitive case. This grammatical change accounts for nearly
one-third of all the Mgg to Chs. 31, 32, 33. Sixteen Mgg
differ from the text in orthography only. Further, the Mgg
which have been conspicuously present, such as, מימריה דיי/,
זרעיית בני /, עוד, חנון, are conspicuously absent. Although
יי/ appears in this section thirteen times, the M מימריה
דיי/ appears only twice; although א[י]נון appears ten times,
there is no M, ה[י]נון; תוב appears at 31:2 without the M עוד.
מדייניי, ליוויי, אומריי appear without the usual variant in
אי (but אימוראי at 33:17).

If the Mgg in this section are collations from another
text, then that text must have been closer to the text of Ni 1
than the text from which the principal Mgg were collated was
to the text of the main body of Ni 1. It is also possible
that the Mgg in this section do not represent collations but
notations. If so, either the text being collated with Ni 1
ended at 29:16, or the work of collating was left unfinished at
29:16. In any case, one is ill-advised to use indiscriminately
the Ni Mgg in this section with those in the main body of the
text.

This also can be said about the text of this section. It
is in many respects like the main text of Ni 1; for example, in
the use of אינון, /יי, חוב, generic ending יי. At the same time
readings which formerly appeared in the margins now appear in the
text. For example, /יי זרעיית בני appears as M for the last time
at 28:46 and appears in the text at 30:19 and 31:21; דאית, a
familiar M for די before a preposition, now appears in the text
at 31:12, 16. This section of the text needs to be used cau-
tiously as representative of the Ni 1 text proper until further
study of it is made.

2. <u>Deut</u>. <u>34:1-12</u>. The final chapter of Deut., unlike the
section just discussed, exhibits a striking similarity to the
text of V insofar as that text is extant; i.e., vv. 1-7. Although V is not extant for comparison with the last five verses
of the chapter (vv. 8-12), these verses also appear to belong to
a text type within the FT tradition more like that of VL than
like that of BN. The chief single piece of evidence supporting
this conclusion is the use in this chapter of /יי מימריה די, the
usual reading throughout the text of VL, against /יי מימרא/ה די,
the usual reading of BN.[11] /יי מימריה די appears at 34:1,4,9,10,
11; /יי מימרה די is found at 34:5.

A collation was made of the text in question against the
texts of VBN for vv. 1-7, BN for vv. 8-12, and CG F for vv. 5-
12. The FT Mss L and P, which were also examined, are present
only fragmentarily for this chapter and contribute nothing additional to the evidence. Since the readings of BN are identical
here, we have in effect three TJ II texts with which to compare
this text.

A comparison of significant textual variants (differing
vocabulary or syntax, additions or omissions) yields the following results:

Where VBN and CG F are extant (5-7), this text of Ni 1

agrees with VBN four times and with VF twice; and disagrees
with all twice.

Where BNF are extant (8-12), this text agrees with BN
six times, and with F twice; and disagrees with all twice.

Where VBN only are extant (1-4), this text agrees with V
against BN five times, with BN against V once; and disagrees
with all three times.

We find, then, for vv. 5-12, a total of twelve agreements
with FT witnesses against four agreements with F. It would
seem that this text is more closely allied to the FT tradition
than to that of F. Two of the agreements with F, in v. 6, also
agree with V against BN.

Where VBN are extant in vv. 1-7, the text agrees with V
against BN seven times and agrees with BN against V only once.
Thus the initial impression that this text is very similar to
that of V is strengthened.

On the other hand, the text shows sufficient divergence
from V to rule out a direct dependence of one Ms upon the other.
The one agreement with BN against V in v. 4 involves a reading
of לי, followed by an insertion, אמר משה, in Ni 1 and אמר משה
נבייא in BN.

Of the seven disagreements of Ni 1 with all others, two
involve inclusion of waw (vv. 1,2), and two involve omissions,
which are probably scribal errors (vv. 4,5). The remaining
three involve three-way variations among the available witnesses.
In vv. 6 and 10, the Ni 1 text employs כל וקבל, VBN ל[י]בל[ו]קכל,
and F לקבל. In v. 9 Ni 1 has a more literal rendition than either of the others.

The Ni 1 text here also shows many minor orthographic and
morphological variations from V (and from BN where V is not extant). These include use of abbreviations (more common in VBN),
use of double waw and double yodh to indicate consonantal value
(more common in the Ni 1 text), and variations of די vs. ד (VBN,
די twice; Ni 1, די once). Internal vowels are used more frequently in nouns in VBN; other orthographic variants are ראש in
Ni 1 against ריש in VBN and מואביי in Ni 1 against מואבאי in VBN.

There are five instances in which VBN include an internal
yodh in a verb form whereas Ni 1 does not. These are: 34:1,
פקיד|פקד 34:9, הכים|החכם 34:6,10, איתין|אתן; 34:4, סליד/סלק.

Finally, the most common variant involves final ה vs. א
for feminine nouns and the definite article. Ni 1 has ה against
א in the FT witnesses 20 times; no examples of the reverse are

found.   The text of Ni 1 here agrees with the FT in use of א
eight times, six of which are occurrences of אראע.

In summary, it would seem that at the beginning and end
of the Ni 1 Ms there are at least four, possibly five, distinct
texts, each different from the principal text.   Each section,
both text and variants, must be considered as if it were a separate Ms.   For this reason, all Mgg from Gen. 1:1-3:4 and Deut.
29:17(18)-34:12 have been excluded from consideration in this
monograph.

CHAPTER V

VARIANT VERSIONS IN THE Ni 1 MGG:

TEXTS AND TRANSLATIONS

A. Classification of Texts

1. **Two Sets of Variants: Dissimilar.** Variants in this
category exhibit a clear contrast between Type I Mgg and Type
II Mgg. Those designated "I" are in good agreement with the
text(s) of FT (V 440 group and/or P) and/or CG E or F, and/or
exhibit typical Type I linguistic elements. Those Mgg designated "II" are so designated because of the significant differences from Type I Mgg which they exhibit. These differences
may involve one or all, and frequently more than one, of the
following characteristics. They have elements of vocabulary
or morphology like those of TJ I and/or O (e.g., attached pronominal suffixes; TJ I and O), or in agreement with the Ni 1
text against Type I usage (e.g., חוב vs. עוד). They approximate
the text, or, more often, a portion of the text, of TJ I (e.g.,
Gen. 14:14). They tell a different "story" from that of Type I
Mgg (e.g., Gen. 28:11, Ex. 3:14, Lev. 9:6, Deut. 8:9). This
different "story" may be found in TJ I (e.g., Lev. 9:6); or it
may be unique among the Targumic witnesses (e.g., Gen. 28:11).
Gen. 28:11 exhibits all three differences from Type I Mgg. It
has an attached pronominal suffix (ושרינון), shows textual affinity with TJ I, and continues the narrative even further than
TJ I.

2. **Two Sets of Variants: Similar.** No significant contrast between Type I Mgg and Type II Mgg could be discerned
for this group. Those variants designated as "I" are in good
agreement with FT and/or CG E or F text(s) extant. Other Mgg,
however, exhibit linguistic elements typical of Type I and/or
a reading not different from that of the Ni 1 text or the corresponding Mgg. At Gen. 29:22, for example, the Mgg in the
right margin are in agreement with CG E; the FT are not represented; the M in the left margin cannot be assigned to Type II,
for its language is that of Type I and its reading is not that
of TJ I, or, indeed, "different." At Nu. 21:15 the first
three Mgg agree with P most closely; the fourth M, with V 440
group. Both sets of Mgg appear to be Type I Mgg.

3. **Two Sets of Variants: Unclassified.** We have placed
in this group those verses with dual Mgg the identities and

relationships of which are not readily discernible on the basis
of present knowledge.   Except for Gen. 9:21, 32:25; Ex. 9:30;
Lev. 10:1; Nu. 21:28; Deut. 15:14, all the verses included in
this group are extant for TJ II in Ni 1 text only.   For those
verses for which there are texts extant in the FT and/or CG a
comparison of texts is not materially helpful in making distinctions between sets of variants.   Many Mgg (or sets of Mgg) are
too brief to allow an effective study of the language and/or too
similar to make distinctions.   Studies are needed to determine
whether "story" is a factor in any of these verses.

4. Variants Marked, ס"א.   The common denominator for verses in this group is that all have a M with the siglum, ס"א.
Of the Mgg, ס"א, those at Gen. 34:31 and Nu. 34:8 may be distinguished from the others.   The M at Gen. 34:31 is a two-word
M which may be a notation distinct from the Ni Mgg in general.
The M at Nu. 34:8 is written in a different hand from the surrounding Mgg and is obviously a notation distinct from the Ni
Mgg in general (cf., Mgg at Gen. 1:1,10,14; see also editio
princeps, IV, 317, at Nu. 34:8).   The siglum, which appears before the remaining verses -- all in Gen. -- , seems to be meant
as an indicator that these Mgg are from "another source;" that
is, from a source distinct from that of the surrounding Mgg or
from that of Mgg to the book of Gen.   More study of these Mgg
is needed to determine their relationship to Type I and Type II
Mgg.

5. Three Sets of Variants: Unclassified.   Only eight
sets of three Mgg were discovered.   Members of the group present difficulties in understanding the relationship of the Mgg
to the text.   For example, at both Gen. 47:21 and 50:1 two fair-
ly extensive readings are written in the LM in close proximity
but with a clearly discernible separation.   It is not clear
whether the two represent one continuous M, two separate Mgg
from one source, or two separate Mgg from two sources.   At
Gen. 48:22 it is possible that the second M in the RM is a variant to the other M in the RM rather than to the text.   At Gen.
44:18, there are numerous Mgg, but no lemmata.   The M, די נמלו
כל אר/, may be a variant to the M, עד זמן דימלו כל ארעא דמצרים
קטילין, or, as we have interpreted, to די ימלי כל ארעא of the
text, rather than to that text close to which it is located,
עד זמן דקטיל אנה כל מצראי.

B.   Transcribed Texts

1. Two Sets of Variants: Dissimilar

Gen. 3:9   Extant: VBNL, P   Gen. 3:9

וקרא יי/ אלהים לאדם ואמר ליה הא כל עלמא דברית גלי קדמי חשוכה
ונהורה גלי קדמי ואת חשב דלא גלי קדמי אתר דאת גבויה אן היא
מצוותה דפקדת יתך:

I   LM   יי/ [/] ממריה דיי/

I   LM   ואת חשב...דפקדת יתך] ואך את סביר דלית גלי קודמוי
[קודמיי ,read] אתרא די את גבווה היך אינון פיקודייה
די פקדת יתך

II RM   היא מצוותה דפקדת יתך] פיקודיה די פקדיתך

Gen. 4:8   Extant: VBN, P, CG B   Gen. 4:8

ואמר קין להבל אחוי איחה ונפק תרינן לאפי ברא והוה כיוון דנפקו
תריהון באפי ברא ענה קין ואמר להבל מסתכל אנה דלא ברחמי/ איתברי
עלמא ולא על פירי עובדין טבין הוה מדבר ומיסב אפין אית בדינא מן
בגלל מה איתקבל קרבנך ברעוא וקרבני מני לא אתקב/ ברעוא: ענה הבל
ואמר לקין מסתכל אנא די ברחמין איתברי עלמא ועל פירי עובדין
טבין הו/ מדבר ועל דהוו עובדיי טבין מן דידך אתקביל קרבני מני
ברעוא קרבנך מינך לא אתקביל ברעוא: ענה קין ואמר להבל לית דין
ולית דיין ולית עולם חורן לית מתן אגר טב לעדיקיא ולית מתפרעה
מן רשיעיא עני הבל ואמר לקין אית דין ואית דיין ואית עלם אוחרן
ואית מתן אגר טב לצדיקיא ואית מתפרעה מן רשעי/ לעלמא דאתי על
עסק פתגמא הדין הוון תריהון מדייניין באפי ברא וקם קין אל [,read
על] הבל אחוי וקטל יתיה:

I   RM   ונפק...וקטל יתיה] ונפוק תרינן באפי ברא וקם קין על הבל
אחוי וקטל יתיה

II LM   כיוון דנפקו] כד נפ/

II LM   דלא ברחמי/] דברחמין

II RM   מסתכל אנא די (2)...]ועל] אפעלגב די ברחמ/ אתברי עלמא
כפרי עובדין [טבין הו/ מדבר]¹ ומסב אפין לית בדינא ועל

II LM   אתקביל קרבני מני ברעוא קרבנך] וקדמין לדידך אתקביל
ברעוא קרבני וקרב/

II RM   מתן(1)[] למיחן

II RM   מתפרעה(1)[] למ/ [למתפרעה ,read]

II RM   מתן(2)[] למ/ [למתן ,read]

II LM   מתפרעה(2)[] למ [למתפרעה ,read]

II RM   מדיינין] מתיצין

¹Omitted in error? Cf., TJ I.

Gen. 9:27   Gen. 9:27

יפת יי/ תחומא דיפת וישרי יקר שכינתי/ בגו משכוני דשם ויהווי
כנען עבד משתעבד להון:

     I   RM   יי/ תחומא] ממריה דיי/ ית תח/

   II   LM   וישרי...להון] וכד מתגיירין בנוי ישדון במדרשי/ דשם והי
                      כנען משתע/ להון

     I   RM   בגו משכוני דשם ויהווי] בבית מדרשוי דשם רבה ויהווי

Gen. 14:14   Extant: VBNL; Arûk,   עד קיסריון   Gen. 14:14

ושמע אברם ארום אשתבי לוט בר אחוי וזאין ית עלמוי ית תורבבות ביתיה
תלת מאה עשר ורדף בתריהון עד קיסריון:

     I   LM   עלמוי...ביתיה] עולמוי מרביוני ביותה

   II   RM   תורבבות...עד קיסריון] מרבייניי ביתיה ולא צבו למהלכה
                     עימיה ואיתבחר מניהון אליעזר דהוות: מן   דן: שקיל קבל
                                        דקי/
                       מאה: ותמנת עשר:

     I   LM   מאה] מאות ותמנת

Gen. 24:60   Extant: P   Gen. 24:60

וברריכו ית רבקה ואמרין לה כרם עד כדון אחתן הויית כרם מן הכא
ולהלא את אזלה ומדבקה לה לגברא חסידא ומניך יקומון אלפין
וריבוון וירתון בניך ית קרי בעלי דבביהון:

   II   RM   ואמרין...וריבוון] אמרו לה עד כדון הויית אחת/ כדון את
                    אזלה מזדווגה בההי/ צדיק/ יהי רעווא דמניך יפקון/ אלפין
                    ורבבן אוכלסין צדיקין

     I   LM   וריבוון...בעלי] ורבבי דמלאכן צדיקין וירתון זרעיית
                    בניך ית קורוי דבע/

Gen. 25:22   Extant: VBNL, P   Gen. 25:22

ואדחקו בניא במעהא ואמרת אן כדין היא צערהון דבניא למה כען לי
בנין ואזלת לבית מדרשא דשם רבה למתבע רחמין מן קדם יי/:

   II   LM   אן כדין...קדם יי/] א"כ הוא צערא דילדותא למה דין אנא
                    מעדייא ואזלית לבית מדרשא דשם רבא בעייא ומצלייי/ קדם ה
     I   LM   לי בנין...קדם יי/] אית לי חיין למהוי לי בנין ואזלת
                    למתבוע רחמין מן קדם ה בבית מדרשו של[1] שם רבה

[1]Probably scribal error.

Gen. 26:35   Extant: VBNL, P   Gen. 26:35

והוון סורכנין ומפחן רוח ומגחכן בפולחנא נוכראה הוון ולא
[ולא הוון, read] מקבלן אולפן לא מן יצחק ולא מן רבקה:

          RM   והוון] והוראה

     I   LM   סורכנין...מקבלן] סרהוונייין ומפחת רוח פלחן בפולחנא
                    נכרייה ולא הוון מפכ/

   II   RM   ולא הוון...רבקה] ומררו חייהון דיצח/ ודרבקה

Gen. 27:22   Extant: VBNL   Gen. 27:22

 וקרב יעקב לוות יצחק אבוי ומשש יתה ואמר הא קלה קלה דיעקב ומוש
ידיה מוש ידוי דעשו:

I   RM   ומשש] ומשמש

II   LM   הא קלה..דעשו] כד משתמע קלא דיעקב בצלותא לית רשו לעשו
למנזקיה וכד מחרשל בפתגמי אוריתא שלטין ביה ידוי דעשו

I   RM   ומוש ידיה מוש ידוי] ברם ממוש ידיה ממוש ידוי

Gen. 27:27   Extant: VBNL, P   Gen. 27:27

וקרב לוותיה ונשק יתה ואריח ית ריח לבושוי וברך יתיה ואמר חמון
ריחה דברי כריח קטרת בסמניה טביה דעתיד למתקרבא על גבי מדבחא
בטור בית מקדשא הוא טורא ברך יתיה חי וקיים כל עלמיא יי/:

RM   לוותיה ונשק] ונש

RM   חמון] אתון חמון

II   RM   כריח קטרת..כל עלמיא יי/] כריחה דגינתא די נציבא בחקלא
דעדן דברכיה יי/

I   LM   בסמניה...יי/] בסמנין טבין דעתידין למתקרבה בטור בית
מקדשה די ברך יתיה ממריה דיי/

Gen. 28:11   Extant: P   Gen. 28:11

וצלי באתרא ובת תמן ארום טמעת ליה שמשא תמן ונסב מן אבנוי
דאתרא ושוי תחות אסדי ראשה ודמך לה באתרא ההוא:

II   RM   וצלי...באתרא ההוא] וערע בית מקדש/ ובת תמן ארום טמע
שמשה ונסיב ארב/ אבנין מן אבני אתרא קדישא ההוא ושוינון
איסדוהי ואתעבדן לאבנ/ חדא כיהיא זמנא ידע דהוא עתיד
למיסב ארבע נשין ומינהון עתידין למיפק ארבע משיריין
ויהון לעם חד ושכיב באתרא ההוא:

I   RM   ובת] ואבית

Gen. 28:17   Extant: P, CG E   Gen. 28:17

ודחל ואמר מה דחיל הוא אתרא הדין [¹לית אתרא הדין¹] אתר הדיוט
ארום אתר מזומן מן קדם יי/ והדן תרעא תרעא דצלו מזומן עד צית
שמיא:

II   RM   לית אתרא...עד צית שמיא] לית דין אתר חול אילהן אתר בית
מקדשא דיי/ ודין היכלא מכוון תרע בית מקדש/ די בשמייא

I   LM   לית אתרא..עד...] ולית דין אתרה אתר הדיוט ברם אלאהן אתר
מזמן לבית צלו הוא והדן תרעא דמכוון עד

¹···¹Omitted from text; supplied interlinearly in square script.

Gen. 31:22   **Extant: BN, P, CG E**   Gen. 31:22

והוה כיון דאזלו רעוי דלבן למשקיה ענה מן בארה ולא יכלו

ואמחינו תריך תלתא יומין סבריך דלמה דהיא טיפה ולא טפת בכדן

אתני ללבן ביומא תליתייא ארום ערק יעקב:

I LM   והוה כיון...ערק יעקב] ואתני ללבן ביומא תליתאה ארום

ערק יעקב

LM   רעוי] רעיא בתר[1]

II RM   מן בארה...ערק יעקב] יעקב תמן על בארה ולא אשכחו מיא

ואמחינו תלתא יומין דלמה יהא טיפה ולא ספת ובכן אתני

ביומא תליתאה ארום אזל יעקב חסידא דבזכו/ הורן מיא

טיפין מיא על בירא עשרין שנין

[1]Error for /בעי?   Cf. FT.

Gen. 33:14   Gen. 33:14

יעבר כען רבוני קדם עבדה ואנא אדבר יתהון להוני לרגל עבידתא

די בידי ולרגל טלייא עד זמן די אזל לוות רבוני לגבלה:

II RM   יעבר...רבוני לגבלה] יקדם כען רבוני ויקבל חולקיה ואגר

בירכתא רברבתא דברכיה אבא בעלמא הדין קדם עבדיה ואנא

אדבר לבלחודוי לאולפן אוריתא די קרמיי ולסוברה בזכותיה

ית בני גלותא עד זמן דיסתפון גלותא ורבין אעול לות

רבוני לאגחא קרבא כגבולא

I LM   די בידי] דאית קרמי

Gen. 45:28   **Extant: VBNL, P**   Gen. 45:28

ואמר ישראל סגי טבין ונחמן סכיית למיחמי ולדא לא סכיית דעד

כדון יוסף בחייך איזיל כען ואיחמי יתיה קדם עד לא אימות:

I RM   סגי] סגין

II RM   טבין...איזיל] טבותא וסגי נחמתא אסתכיתי למחמי והדא

ניחמותא לא סברית טוב [תוב, read] למחמי ומן דעד כדון

יוסף ברי קיים איזיל

I LM   איזיל...ואיחמי] ניזל ונחמי

I RM   אימות] נמות

Gen. 49:1   **Extant VBNL, P**   Gen. 49:1

וקרא יעקב לבנוי ואמר להון אתכנשון וחווי לכון רזייא סתימייא

קיצייא גניזייא מתן אגריהון דצדקייא ופורענותהון דרשיעיא

ושלוותה דעדן מה היא כחדא מתכנשין תרי עשר שבטייא ומקפן לדרגשה

דדהבא דהוה אבונן יעקב רביע בגוויה מן דאתגלי לי קיצא ולאיתני

להון קץ ברכתא וניחמתא מן דאתגלי ליה קיצא אתכסא מינה סברין

דהוא מתני להון קץ פורקנא וניחמתא מן דאתגלי ליה רזא אתכסי מנה

ומן דאתפתח ליה תרעא אסדר מנה ענה אבונן יעקב וברך יתהון גבר

לפם עבדוי טבייא ברך יתהון:

I LM   וחווי לכון...מתן] ואתנו לכון ניסייא גניזייי/ רזייי/

טמירת/ מתן

Gen. 49:1 (cont.)   Extant: VBNL, P   Gen. 49:1 (cont.)

I   RM   מתכנשין תרי...לדרגשה] מתכנשא תרי/ עשתרי שבטיי/ מקפין
         לדרגשה

I   LM   מן דאתגלי לי קיצא...ברך יתהון] בעא לאיתן/ להון קץ
         ברכתא וניחמתא ואתכסי מיניה וכיון דאיתכסי מיני/ ברך
         יתהון לפום עובדי/ טביא

II RM   מינה סברין דהוא...ברך יתהון] עלי/ סיברון דהוי מתני
         להון כל מה דאתערע דיערא להון בסוף יומא מן דאתגלי להו
         ליה [read, רזא אתגנז מיניה חזר וברך יתה/ גבר כמפתר
         ברכתיה ברך אותם

Gen. 49:18   Extant: VBN, P, Tosefta   Gen. 49:18

אמר אבונן יעקב לא לפורקנא דגדעון בר יואש סכיית נפשי דהוא
פורקן שעה ולא לפורקניה דשמשן בר מנוח סכיית נפשי דהוא פורקן
עבור אלא לפורקניה סכיית נפשי דאמרת למיתייה לעמך בית ישראל לך
לפורקנך יי/:

II RM   לא לפורקנא...סכיית יי/] כד חמא ית גדעון בר יואש וית
         שמשון בר מנוח לא אנה מסכי דפורקניה פורקן דשעתא ולא אנה
         מודי/ דפורקנא פורק/ דריגעה לפורקנך סכיית ואודיקת רבון
         כל עלמיא דפורקנך פורקן עלמא

I   RM   דאמרת] די אמרית

I   RM   לך לפורקנך] ליה לפרקנה

I   LM   יי/] דהו יי/

Ex. 3:14   Extant: VB, P   Ex. 3:14

ואמר יי/ למשה אהיה אשר אהיה ואמר כדין תאמר לבני ישראל מן
דאמר והוה עלמא מן שדויא ועתיד למימר ליה הוי ויהוי הוא שלח
יתי לוותכון:

I   LM   יי/ למשה...הוא שלח] מימריה דה למשה דן דאמ/ לעלמ/ הורי
         והורה ועתיד למימ/ ליה הוי והורי ואמ/ כדן תימ/ לבני
         ישראל אהיה שלח

II RM   אהיה אשר...לוותכון] אנא הוויתי עד לא איתברא עלמ/ ואנא
         הוריתי מן דאיתבריה עלמ/ אנא הוא דהוויתי בסעדבון בגלותא
         דמצראי ואנא הוא דעתיד למהוי בסעדכו/ בכל דד ודד ואמ/
         כדנא תימר לבני ישראל אהיה שלח יתי לוותכון

Ex. 4:13   Extant: VB   Ex. 4:13

ואמר בבעו ברחמין מן קדמיך יי/ שלח כען ביד דן דחמי ליה
למשתלחא:

I   RM   ברחמין...שלח] מנך רבוני שלח

I   LM   ביד...למשתלחא] ביד דן דחמי ליה לאשתלחא

II RM   ביד...למשתלחא] ביד מלאכא משיחה דעביד למשתלחא

Ex. 9:14   Ex. 9:14

ארום בזמנא הדא הא אנה משלח ית כל מחוותיי עֿל לבך ובשלטונך
ובעמר מן בגלל די תדע ארום לית כוותֿי בכל ארעא:

  I LM משלח...על לבך] מגרי לכולהון מחתי וימטון עד לבבך

  II RM מחוותיי...ובשלטונך] מחת פרענותי על ליביה דפרעה ובעבדך

  I LM כוותי] כוות ממריה דיי/

Ex. 9:20   Extant: P   Ex. 9:20

מן דחֿל מן קדם יי/ מן שֿליטוי דפרעה ערק ית עבדוי וית בעיריה לגֿו
ביתא:

  I RM דחל] דן דהוה דחל

  II LM מן דחל...יי/] איוב דהוה דחיל מן פתגמ/ דיי/

      RM שליטוי] עבדוי

  II RM בעיריה לגו ביתא] נכסוי לגו בייתיה

Ex. 10:28   Extant: VB, P   Ex. 10:28

ואמר ליה פרעה אזיל מעלוי [מעלי, read,] לֿא תוסיף לממללה קדמ/
תוב חד מאילן מלייה קשייתא ברם צבי אנה לממות ולא למהוי שמע מי[1]
מֿליר אזדהר לך דלא יתקף רוגזי בך ואמסר יתר בידיהון דעמא דהון
תבעין נפשך ויקטלון יתר:

  I LM לא תוסיף לממללה...אזדהר לך] אזדהר לך[2]

  I LM ואמסר יתר...ויקטלון יתר] למימ/ דלא [הלא, read,] מלייא
קשייתא האלן דאת אמ/ לי כרם בעי אנא למימות ולא למיהווי
שמע למיליר איזדהר לך דלא יתקף רוגזי בך ואמסור יתר בין
ידיהון דעמה אליין די תבעו ית נפשר למקטול יתר

  II LM מליר אזדהר] מליא האליך לכן אמר ליה אזדהר

[1]Scribal error.

[2]The first and second Mgg as here interpreted in relation to
the text produce the reading of B. The text is close to that
of P. However, P includes אזדהר לך after מעלוי, so that it
is difficult to decide whether by the first M is meant the
omission of part of the verse (cf., VB) or the addition of the
M (cf., P). Inasmuch as Ni Mgg can be shown to give VB readings, rather than P readings, we have so interpreted this M.

Ex. 13:8   Ex. 13:8

ותחנון לבניכון ביומא ההוא למימר מן בגלל מצוותה דפטיריא עבד
יי/ לן נצחני קרבינן באפקותן פריקין מן מצרים:

  II LM בגלל...מן מצרים] בגין מצוותה דפטיריא דא ומרורא ובשר
פיסחא דין עבד יי/ ניסין לי במפק/ ממצרים

  I RM יי/ לן...באפקותן] לן מימרי דיי/ ניסים במפקיהון

Ex. 14:3   Extant: VBN, P   Ex. 14:3

[ויימר]¹ פרעה על עמא עסק עמא הבני ישראל טעיין אינון באורחא טרד
עליהון בעל צפון טעותי נגדוי דמדברא:

RM II   [ויימר] פרעה...ישראל...בעל צפון טעותי] עתיד דיימר פרעה
        לדתן ואבירם דמשתיירן במצרים על עסק בני ישרא/...²
        טעוותי פעור ורב

RM II   טעיין אינון באורחא] אחידין הנון בארעא

RM I   טעיין...דמדברא] טעיין הינון באורחא טרד עליהון טעותא
        דצפון נגהו [read, נגדוי] דמדברא

¹Missing from text.   Cf., P.
²See following M. In Ms this M follows immediately after ורב.

Ex. 14:20   Extant: VBN, P   Ex. 14:20

ועל בין משרייתהון דמצריי וביני משרייתיהון דישראל והוה עננא
[פלגא]¹ חשוך ופלגא נהורא חשוכא מחשך למצרייה ונהורא לישראל כל
ליליא ולא קרבו אליין לאליין לסדר קרבא כל ליליא:

LM I   [פלגא] חשוך...ולא] [פלגא] נהור ופלגא חשך נהורא מנהר על
        ישראל וחשוך/ מחשך על מצראי ולא

LM II   לישראל...לסדר קרבא כל ליליא] ישראל אנהר לליא לא קריבו
        משרה אל משרה ברם מלאכי שירותא לא אמרו שירתא כל ליליא

RM   לליא or לליא] לילותא

LM I   לסדר קרבא] למסדרה סדרי קרבא

¹Missing from text.   Cf., FT.

Ex. 15:25   Extant: VBN, P   Ex. 15:25

וצלי קדם יי/ וחוי ליה יי/ אילן ונסב מיניה מימריה דיי/ מלה
האוריתא וטלק לגו מיא ואתחלון מיא תמן שוי ליה קיימין וסדרי
דינין וחמן נסי יתיה:

RM I   וצלי] + משה

RM I   יי/ (2)](2) מימרי/ דיי/

LM II   אילן ונסב...לגו מיא] אילן דארדופני וכתב ביה שמא מפרשא
        וטלק במיא

LM I   ונסב...ואתחלון] דארדופני וקלק בגו מיא ואת

LM I   שוי ליה] חווי לי [ליה [read, מימרי/ דיי/

RM   נסי יתיה] ניסין יתי/ בנסיוני/ עשדיה

Ex. 17:7   Ex. 17:7

וקרא שמה דאתרא נסייוניה ודיינוותיה על דאדיינון בני ישראל ועל
די נסון קדם יי/ למימר הא מן קושטא איקר שכינתה דיי/ שדייא
ביניהון¹ ביניגן אי לא:

LM II   נסייוניה...קדם יי/] בית נסיון/ ומצוותא על דאתנצון בני
        ישראל ועל דנסי דנסי יתהון יי/

RM I   דאדיינון] דאדיינן

RM I   די נסון] דנסון

RM I   איקר] אית יקר

¹Scribal error.

Ex. 19:3   Extant: VBN, P, CG F   Ex. 19:3
ומשה סלק למתבע אולפן מן קדם יי/ וקרא ליה דבירה דיי/ מן טורא
למימר כדין תימר לדבית יעקב ותתני לשבטא דבני ישראל:
RM I   למתבע] למתבוע
LM I   לדבית יעקב] לאנשי בייתיה דיעקב
RM II לדבית יעקב...דבני ישראל] לנשיא דבית יעקב ותתני לגברי
       דבית ישראל

Ex. 19:18   Extant: VBN, P, CG F   Ex. 19:18
וטורא דסיני הוה תנן כוליה מן בגלל דאתגליית עלוי איקר שכינת/
דיי/ באשתא וסלקת תננא כתננא דאתונא ואזדעזע כל טורא לחדא:
RM II הוה תנן or מן בגלל דאתגליית...דאתונא] אתרגיף ואתמלי מזיו
       יקר שכינתיה דיי/ וסלק קוטרי/ היך קלטרא [קוטרא ,read]
       דאתונ/
LM I   באשתא...לחדא] כשלהובא דאשא וסלק תננא כקטון [כקטור ,read]
       תנן[1] אתונה וזער כל עמא דאית במשדית/

[1]Conflation? Cf., CG F.

Ex. 20:25   Ex. 20:25
ואם מדבח דאבנין תבנון לשמי לא תבנון יתהון חציבין ארום פרזלא
[1]ארום פרזלא[1] דחרבא מתעברא עברת עליהון ואפסת יתהון:
RM I   חציבין...יתהון] חציב ארום פרזלא חרבא מתעבד מיני/ אין
       עברת פרזלא עלוי אפיסת יתיה
LM II דחרבא...יתהון] מינה אתבדו [אתעבדו ,read] קרב/ מותא
       לכולא אסטמר דלא תריק/ סייפר עלי ולא תפיס יתיה
[1]...[1]Dittography

Ex. 22:12(13)   Extant: VBN, P, CG A   Ex. 22:12(13)
ואין מטרפה ויטרף [יטרף ,read] ייתון סהדין קטילא לא ישלם:
RM I   מטרפה...סהדין] מתקטלה יתקטל יתיה [יתי ,read] ליה מן
       אברוי שהד
RM II ייתון...ישלם] ימטינ/ עד גושמת חיובא דתבירא ולא ישלם

Ex. 24:11   Extant: P   Ex. 24:11
ולות עולימיהון דבני ישראל לא פשט ידיה וחמון ית איקר שכינתה
דיי/ והוון חדיין על קרבניהון דאתקבלון היך אכלון והיך שתין:
LM I   ולות עולימיהון] ולות רברבניי/
RM II ולות...ישראל] ולנדב ואביהו עולמייא שפירא דהוון מתמנן
       על בני ישרא/
RM   איקר שכינתה דיי/] אלהא דישראל
LM I חדיין...היך] מתחמיין היך

Ex. 32:5   Extant: VBN, P   Ex. 32:5

וחמא אהרן ית חור נביא קדמוי ודחל ובנה מדבח קדמוי ואכרז אהרן
ואמר חגא קדם יי/ למחר:

I   RM   וחמא...נביא קדמוי] וחזא אהרן ית חור נכיס קדמוי

II   RM   ואכרז...למחר] ואכרז אהרן ואמר יהא רעוה דייהי נכסא בי[1]
כחגה מן רשיעיה קדם יי/ מחר

I   LM   ואכרז] וקרא

[1]Probably scribal error.

Ex. 33:11   Extant: VBN, P   Ex. 33:11

וממלל יי/ עם משה ממלל לקבל ממלל היך מה דממלל גבר עם חבריה וחזר
למשריחה ושמשיה יהושע בן נון טלי לא יזייע מגו משדיתא:

I   LM   יי/] מימריה דיי/

I   LM   לקבל] כל וקבל

I   LM   מה דממלל] מה די ים

I   LM   לא יזייע מגו] זעיר לא הווה פסק מגו

II   LM   לא יזייע...משדיתא] מתרבי לא עדי מגו משכן בית אלפנה

Ex. 36:16   Ex. 36:16

ודבק ית חמש יריען לבלחודיהון [1]וית שית יריען לבלחודיהון[1]:

II   RM   ודבק...לבלחודיהון (2)] ולפף ית חמישתי יריען לחוד קובל
חמישתי סיפרי אורייתה וית שית יריען לחוד קובל שיתה
סידורי משנה

I   LM   חמש יריען] חמישתי יריעתה

I   LM   שית יריען] אישתתי יריעתה

[1]...[1]Omitted from text; in margin in square script.

Lev. 4:22   Lev. 4:22

אין [read, אין] כהנא דמתרבי יחטא ויעבד חדא מן כל מצוותה דיי/
אלהה דלא כשרין למתעבדה בשלו ויתחייב:

II   LM   אין...יחטא] בזמן דרבה יחוב

I   RM   דמתרבי...ויעבד] דירבה יתחייב ויע/

        LM   מצוותה] פיקודוי

I   RM   דלא] די לא

Lev. 8:34   Lev. 8:34

היך מה דעבד ביומא הדין פקד יי/ למעבד למכפרה עליכון:

II   LM   היך...עליכון] היך כמה דעבד הדין: הכדין פקד יי/ למעבד
שבעה יומין קומי יומא דכיפורי מטול לכפרה עליכון

I   LM   דעבד] די עבד

I   RM   יי/] ממרא דיי/

Lev. 9:6   Lev. 9:6

ואמ/ משה דן פתגמה די פקד ייי/ תעבדון ותתגלי עליכו/ איקר

שכינתיה דייי/:

I   RM   ייי /[/ ממריה דייי/

II   RM   [read די פקד ייי/.../שכינתיה דייי/] דפקיד ייי/ תעבדון ואערו

לכון איקר שכינתה דייי/ [מן ליבכון ומן יד יתגלי read ,כישא] אעברו] יצרה בושא

I   LM   ותתגלי] ויתגלי

I   RM   איקר] יקר

Lev. 9:22   Lev. 9:22

וזקף אהרן ית ידוהי בצלו על עמה וברך יתהון ונחת מן דקרב חטאתה

ועלתה ונכסת קודשיה:

II   RM   וזקף.../מן דקרב] וקם אהרן על דוכנה וזקף ידוי קבל עמה

וברייכינון ופסק מלמעבד

I   LM   דקרב חטאתה] למקרבה חט/

Lev. 10:2   Lev. 10:2

ונפקת אשא מן קדם ייי/ ואכלת יתהון ומיתו קדם ייי/:

II   RM   אשא מן.../קדם ייי/ (2)] עמודא דאשתא מן קדם ייי/ ואתפליגת

לתרין חוטין ומתרין לארבעה ועלת באפהון ומיתו בגירין

ראשה קדם ייי/:

I   LM   קדם] במימר

Lev. 14:40   Lev. 14:40

ויפקד כהנא וישמטרון ית אבניה די בהן מכתשה ויטלקון יתהון לבר מן

קרתה לאתר מסאב:

II   RM   וישמטרון.../לאתר מסאב] ויטלקון ית אבנייה דבהון מכתשה

למברה לקרתה דאיהוא בנה ביתה באונס/ וטלומא יתרמון לאתר

מסאב

I   LM   די] דאית

Lev. 14:53   Lev. 14:53

וישלח ית צפרה חייתה לבר מן קרתה לאפי ברה ויכפר על ביתיה וידכי:

II   RM   וישלח.../וידכי] ויפטור ית ציפורא חייתה למברא לקרתה לאפי

ברא ויהי אין יטיניוס [טימוס read,] הוא למלקי תוב

בצרעתה תויבה ציפורה לוותיה ויכפר כהנא על ביתיה וידכי

I   LM   צפרה.../לבר] ציפורתה דבחיין לב/

Lev. 16:3   Lev. 16:3

כהדן סדרא יהוי אהרן עלל לֹשמשה לגו בית משׁדיתא בתור בר תורין
לחטאתה ודכר ֹלעלתה:

II   LM   כהדן...משׁדיתא] כהדא מצוותה יעול אהרן בי[ומא]‎[1] דכיפורי
/לקודשׁ

I   LM   ודכר] + חד

I   RM   לשמשה...משׁדיתא] ומשמש לבית קֹדשׁה

‎[1]Letters in brackets are illegible in microfilm owing to their
closeness to book binding.

Lev. 16:8   Lev. 16:8

ויתן אהרן על תרין צפיריה עדוין עֹדיו חד לשם ממרי/ דיי/ ועדיו
חדֹ לעזאזל:

I   RM   עדיו] עדיוו

II   LM   עדיו...לעזאזל] עדב חד לשמה דיי/ לכפרה על עמא ועדב חד
למפטור למדכר צוק לעזזל

I   LM   ועדיו] ועדיוו

Lev. 16:34   Lev. 16:34

ותיהוי דא לכון לקיֹם עלם למכפר/ על בני ישׂראל מן כל חוביהון חֹדא
זמן בשתה ועבד היך מה די פקד יי/ ית משֹׁה:

I   LM   עלם] דעלם

I   RM   חדא...בשׁתה] חד זמן בכל שׁתה

II   LM   זמן בשתה] זמנה בשתה בעשׂרתי יומין לירח תשׂרי

I   LM   יי/] ממריה דיי/

Lev. 18:29   Lev. 18:29

ארום כל מן דיעבד מן כל מרחקתה האליין וישתיצון נפשׁתה דעבדן מן
גו עמהון:

I   RM   מן דיעבד] די יעב/

I   RM   נפשׁתה...עמהון] נפשׁה דעבדה מן גו עמהון

II   LM   דעבדן...עמהון] די יעבדן הי כאליין ביאורייא [read,
באוריתא] מן חיי עלמא דאתי ולא יהי להון חולק בגו עמהן?

Lev. 19:14   Extant: P   Lev. 19:14

לא תלו/ ית מה דלא שמע וקרם ֹמן דלא חמי לא תתן תקלה ותדחלון מן
אלהכון כדן אמר יי/:

I   RM   לא תלו/...ותדחלון] ולא תלוטון חרשׁה בגין דלא שׁמע לקדם
אכסנייה דהוא מדמי לסמייה לא תשׂרון קללה ות/

II   LM   וקדם מן...תקלה] ולקדם אכסנייה דדמי לסמיא לא תשׂרון תקלה

Lev. 21:4   Lev. 21:4

לֹא יסתאב רבה דְּבעמה דלא יפס ית כהנתא:

II   RM   יסתאב...כהנתא] יסתאב כהנא רבה ואפילו בעמיה לאפסה
                       כהונתה רבה אמטולליה

I   LM   דְּבעמה...כהנתא] דְּבעמכון למפסה כלול כה

Lev. 23:29   Extant: VBN, P, CG F   Lev. 23:29

ארום כל נְפש גבֹ[1] די תֹאכל למצום ולא [2]צֹיימה[2] בזמן יום צומה
דכיפורייה ותשֹתיצא מן גו עמֹא:

II   RM   נפֹש...ולא ציימה] בר נש דלא תצום

I   LM   תֹאכל למצום] כמסת למצ

I   RM   בזמן...דכיפורייה] כיום צום כפו/

[1]Scribal error.

[2]...[2]Omitted from text; in margin in square script.

Lev. 27:29   Extant: VBN   Lev. 27:29

כֹל אפרשו די יתאפרש מן בר נשה לא יתפרק ממת ימות:

II   RM   כֹל...ימות] כל חרמה דמתחרם מן בר נשא לא יתפרק בכספא
          אלהן בעלוון ובכסת קודשין ובמבעי רחמין מן קדם יי/ מטול
          דדין קטול מתחייב איתקטלא איתקטיל

I   LM   בר נשה...ימות] בני אנשא לא יתפרק מת[קטלא][1] יתקטל

[1]Letters in brackets are illegible in microfilm owing to their
closeness to book binding.

Nu. 4:20   Extant: VBN, P   Nu. 4:20

ולא ייעלון למיחמי כד מֹשקע כהנה רבה ית כל מני בית קודֹשה דלא
ימותון:

I   RM   ייעלון] + לויאי

I   LM   מֹשקע...ימותון] יהורן כהנייא מֹשקעין מאני בית קודשא דלא
          ימר/

II   RM   כד מֹשקע...קודֹשה] כד מכסן כהנייא ית מאני קרשא

Nu. 10:29   Nu. 10:29

ואמר מֹשה לחובב בר רעואל מדיניה חמוי דמֹשה נטלין אנן לאתרה די
אמר יי/ יתה אתן לכון אזל עמן ונוטב לך ארום יי/ במימריה אמר
למיתיה טבה ונחמן על ישֹראל:

I   RM   יי/ יתה...על ישֹראל] מימריה דיי/ יתיה אתן לכון אתה עימן
          ונייטבה לך ארום מימריה דיי/ מלל טב על ישֹראל

II   LM   יי/ במימריה...ישֹראל] מן קדם יי/ איתמר מן יומי עלמא
          לאיתי/ טבתה על ישֹראל

Nu. 12:12   Extant: VBNL, P   Nu. 12:12

לא כען תיהוי מרים מסאבה באהילה כמיתייה והא מדמיא[1] לוולדה דעבד
[דעבר, read] במעיה דאמיה תשעה ירחין במיא ובאשתא ולא מתנזק
וכיון דמטא קצה למפוק לגו עלמ/ אתאכל פלגות בשריה כדין כד הוינא
משתעבדין במצרים וחזרין ומטרפין במדבר/ הוות אחתן חמייה בשעבודן
וכיון דמטה קצה למחסנה ית ארעא למה היא מתמנעה מנן צלי על בשרה
מיתה רנה ויחי למה[2] עבד ית[2] זכותה:

II RM לא כען...מתמנעה] לא כדון תיהווי מרים אחתן כאיתתה מעברה
דמצטרעה בעיברה וכד מטה זימנא למילד מית וולדה במעיה
[במעיה, read] הלא מרים אחתן איצטרערת [איצטערת, read]
עימנה וכדי מטת זימנא[3] למיטת[3] למיחמי בנחמותה לא כדון
תתרחק דא/

I   LM מסאבה...במעיה] מצרעה באהילה כמיתה ארום [היר]4 מה דהדין
וולד דהוי במע/

I   LM לגו עלמ/...אתאכל] מן מעוי דאימיה את/

I   RM כדין כד הוינא...וכיון] כן הוות מרים אחתן מטרפה עמן
במדברה והווי עמך בעקנ/ וכיון

I   RM קצה...למה] קצן למיעול לארעא דישראל למ/

I   RM צלי] + כען

I   RM דנה ויחי...זכותה] הדין וייחי דלא נובד זכותה

[1]Originally, מחמיא. Corrected by scribe.
[2]...[2]Probably corrupt. Cf., FT, TJ I. We have read, עבר.
[3]Scribal error.
4Emendation. Cf., FT.

Nu. 12:16   Extant: VBNL   Nu. 12:16

אוף על גב דאתחייבת מרים נבייתה למצטרעה אית אלולפן [read
אולפן] סגי לחכימי[1] ולנטדי אוריתה דמצוה זעירה דאנש עבד הוא
מקבל עילוי אגר סגיא לפם דקמת לה מרים על גיף נהרא למידע מה
יהוי בסופיה דמשה[2] הוון ישראל[2] אשתין רבוון דאנון פמום [read
סכום]תמנייןליגויניין ועננני איקרה וביירה לא הוון זייעין ולא
נטלין מן אתריהון עד זמן דאתסיאת מרים נבייתה מן צרעתה נטלו עמה
מן חצרות ושרון במדברה דפארן:

I   LM אוף] אף

II LM אוף על גב...אתריהון or מן צרעתה] ומן בגלל דאימתינת
למשה על נהרא שעה חדה אמתינת לה שכינתה דמרי עלמא ומשכנה
וכל ישראל שבעה יומין

I   LM הוא מקבל] מק

I   LM דאנון] דהנון

I   LM מן צרעתה נטלו] מצרעתה ומן בתר דאתסיית נביאתיה מן
מצרעתה מן בתר כן נט/

I   RM ולא נטלין] ולא נטלו

[1]Originally לחידימי. Corrected by scribe.
[2]...[2]Words transposed; noted by scribe.

Nu. 16:1   Extant: VBNL, P   Nu. 16:1

ופליג קרח בר יצהר בר קהת בר לוי דתן [ודתן, read,][1] ואבירם
בנוי דאליאב ואון בר פלת בנוי דראובן:

    I   LM   ופליג] ונסיב עיצה ופלג

    II   RM   ופליג קרח] ונסיבו עיצה בישתה ואיתקוטטו קרח

        LM   בנוי (2)] מן שבטה דבנוי

[1]Error noted by scribe.

Nu. 16:30   Nu. 16:30

ואן ברייה חדתה יברא יי/ ותפתח ארעא ית פמה ותבלע יתהון וית
כל מה דלהון ויחתון חיין לשאול ותדעון ארום ארגיזו גברייה
האליין קדם יי/:

    II   RM   ואן...ותפתח] אן מן יומי עלמא איתברי את מיתותה בעלמא
            לעלמא הדין הא טב ואין לא תתברי כדון ותפתח

    I   LM   יי/ ותפתח] מימריה דיי/ ותפתוח

    I   LM   ותבלע] ותבלוע

    I   RM   חיין לשאול] כחיין לשילו/ [לשיול/, read,]

Nu. 20:17   Extant: VBN   Nu. 20:17

נעבר כען בארעך לא נעבר בחקלין ובכרמין ולא נשתי מי[1] גובין ארח
מלכא נהלך לא נסטי לא לימינה ולא לשמאלה עד זמן די תחומך נעבר:

    I   RM   נעבר בחקלין...לא נסטי] נאנוס אניסן ולא נשדגה בתולן
           ולא נבעי נשי גוברין באסרטא דמלכא ניזיל לא נסטי/

    II   RM   נעבר בחקלין...נהלך] נשדגה בתולן ולא נינוס נשי גוברין
           באורחה דמלכא דעלמא ניזיל

    I   RM   לא לימינה ולא לשמאלה] לא לימין ולא ליסמיל

[1]Scribal error.

Nu. 33:9   Extant: VBN   Nu. 33:9

ונטלו מן מרה ואתון לאילם ובאילם תרתין עשרי פיגיין דמיין כל
קבל תרי עשרתי שבטיה דישראל ושבעין דקלין דתמרין כל קבל
שבעתי[1] חכימי דבני ישראל ושרון תמן:

    I   RM   לאילם] מה [לאילמה, read,]

    I   LM   תרתין...כל קבל] תרי עשרי עיינוון דמיין כל וקבל

    I   RM   תרי] תרתי

    II   RM   תרתין...שבטיה] תריסר מבועין דמיין כל וקבל תריסר
           שבטין

    I   LM   חכימי דבני] סבייה דבני

    II   RM   תמן] + על ימא

[1]Read, שבעיתי? But cf., FT.

Deut. 7:7   Deut. 7:7

לא מן ¹סוגי̇ יתכון¹ מן כל אומייה אתרעי יי/ בכון ארום אתון עׄם
קלילין מן כל אומייה:

       LM סורבי יתכון] סוגייכון

   II   LM סוגי...קלילין] בגלל דבכורכון² צבא מימריה דיי/ בכון
ואיתרעי בכון ארום מן בגלל דאתון ענוותנין

       I   RM יי/] מימריה דיי/

       RM קלילין מן] זערין מ/

¹...¹Error for סוגייכון? See first M.
²Conjectural reading.

Deut. 8:9   Extant: VBN   Deut. 8:9

ארע די לא במסכנוׄת תאכלון בה לחם̇ לא תחׄסדון כל מן דׄעם בה ארע
דׄאבניה שׄדיין וברירן היך פרזלה ומן טורייה חצבין נחשׄה:

   II   RM במסכנות] בחוסרנה

   I   LM לחם] + ומזון

   I   RM תחסדון...נחשא] תחסד כל מנדעם בה ארע די אבניה בריירן
כפורזלא וטורנייה [וטורייה read,] חשמין כנחשה:

   II   LM דאבניה...נחשה] דחכימיאה תקיפין הי כפרזלא ותלמידייהא
חסינין הי כנחשה

Deut. 10:20   Deut. 10:20̇

מׄן קדם יי/ אלהכון̇ תהוון דׄחלין וקדמוי תהוון מצליין ובאולפן
אורייתה תתבקון ובשמיה קדישה תהוון משתבעין ומקיימין:

   II   RM מן קדם...ומקיימין] קדם אלה אלהכון תצלון ויתיה תפלחון
בקרבנה ובמימרה תתבקון ובשמיה תימון [תימרון read,
בקושט/

   I   LM תהוון דחליז...קדישה] תדחלון וקדמוי תפלחון ובשם ממר/
Deut. 12:9   ̇   .Deut. 12:9̇

ארום לא אתיתון עד כדון לנווחתה ולאחסנותה דיי/ אלהכון יהב
לכון:

   I   LM אתיתון] עלתון̇

   II   RM לנווחתה...ולאחסנותה] לבית מוקדשה דמתקרי בית נייחה
ולארעה דישראל דמתקריי אחסנתה

   I   LM לנווחתה...ולאחסנותה] ולבית מוקדשה ולאחסנתה

Deut. 14:1   Extant: VBN   ̇   Deut. 14:1

חביבין אתון קדם יי/ אלהכון לא תעבדון חבורן חבורן בפׄולחנה
נכרייה ולא תשוון רשׄום על בית אפיכון על נפׄש דמית:

   II   LM תעבדון...נכרייה] תתגייסון חבורן חבורן לאבאשא

   I   RM בפולחנה] לפ

   I   LM רשום על] קרחה על

   I   RM על (2)] לטמא/

Deut. 17:8　　　Extant: VBN, P　　　　　　　Deut. 17:8

ארום יתכסי מנכון פתגם בדינה בין אדם דכתולון [דכתולין ,read[[1]
לאדם דקטולין בין דיני ממון לדיני נפשן בין מכתש צרעותה למכתש
נתקה מילי דיוניין בקורייכון ותקומון ותסקון לאתרה די יתרעי יי/
אלהכון ביה:

I　　RM בדינה...מכתש] לסדר דדין בין אדם דקטולין בין אדם
דכתולא בין מכתש

II　　LM אדם...בקורייכון] דם דכי לדם מסאב בין דיני נפשא לדיני
ממונא בין מכתש סגיר למכתש חליט מילוי/ פלוגתא כבית
מדרשיך

I　　RM דיוניין] דמצות

[1]Error noted by scribe. Cf., FT.

Deut. 20:6　　　Extant: VBN　　　　　　　Deut. 20:6

ומן הוא גברא די נצב כרם ולא אפריק פירוי יזיל ויחזור לבייתיה
דלא ימות בסדרי קרבא וגבר אחרן יפרק יתיה:

LM הוא] + דן

I　　LM אפריק...ויחזור] פרק יתיה יזל ויח/

II　　LM אפריק פירוי] פרקיה מן כהנה

I　　RM יפרק] פרק

II　　RM יפרק יתיה] פרקינה

Deut. 22:3　　　Extant: VBNL　　　　　　　Deut. 22:3

וכדן תעבד לחמרא וכדן תעבד ללבושה וכדן תעבד לכל אבידתה די יאבד
מניה ותשכח יתיה לית רשיי למכסייה עיינך עיינך[1] מניה:

I　　LM וכדן] כן

I　　RM וכדן (2)] וכן

I　　RM ללבושה] לאסטליתא

II　　RM אבידתה] ייכירת אחור

I　　RM די יאבד] דייב/

II　　LM יאבד מניה] תיכד מנה

I　　RM יתיה] יתה

I　　RM רשיי...מניה] לך רשו למטמרה יתיה

[1]Dittography.

Deut. 22:12　　　Extant: VBNL, P　　　　　　　Deut. 22:12

צניפן תעבדון לכון על ארבעתי זבית גוליכון די תתעטפון בהון:

I　　RM צניפן תעבדון] גדילן דציצית תעב/

II　　RM צניפן...תתעטפון בהון] צניפן ציצייתה תעבד לך ארבע גדפי
טליתה דטתתעטף [דתתעטף ,read[בה

I　　LM זבית גוליכון] צניפת גול/

I　　LM תתעטפון בהון] תכסון ביה

Deut. 23:2(1)   Deut. 23:2(1)

לא ייעול דפסיק ודמסרס בקהל כנשתה דיי/:

II RM   ודמסרס] גידה ודמחבל בהתייה

I LM   דפסיק ודמסרס] כל דפסיק וכל דמסרס

Deut. 24:6   Extant: VBNL, P   Deut. 24:6

עמי בני ישראל לא תהוון אסורי חתנין וכלין ולא תמשכנון ריחייה
ארום כל דעבד כדן בחובי נפשן הוא חביל:

I LM   עמי בני...הוא חביל] לא תמשכנון ריחייה ורכבה ארום צרכי
        הוא[1] נפשא הוא ממשכן ולא תהוון אסור חתנין וכלין ארום
        כל דעביד אלין כפר בחיוורייה דעלמא דאתי

II LM   לא תהוון...הוא חביל] לא תהוון: לית אתון רשיי למיסב
        משכנתה ריחייה ורכבה גרם לית אתון רשאי למיהווי אסרין
        חתנין וכלתין מלמקרב ארום כאשדיות אדם וזכיי ,read]
        זכיי] הוא מתחשב ונפשתה הוא ממשכן

[1]Scribal error.

Deut. 24:14   Extant: VBN   Deut. 24:14

לא תעצי אגירה דאגירה דמסכינה וצריכה מן אחיכון או מן גיוריכון
די בארעכון בקורייכון:

II RM   תעצי] תטלום

I RM   תעצי] תעצום (sic)

I RM   די] דאית

Deut. 25:2   Extant: VBNL   Deut. 25:2

ויהווי אין מרדו אתחייב למלקה חייבא וירבע יתיה דיינה וימחי
יתיה קדמוי: כמסת: חובתיה במניין:

II RM   אין...וירבע יתיה] אין מין דינה למלקי רשיעה ויכפתיניה

I RM   מרדו...וירבע] צורך [צריך ,read] חייבא למלקי וירב/

Deut. 29:14(15) Extant: VBN   Deut. 29:14(15)

ארום כל דרייה דקמו קדמינן מן עלמא ועד כדון עמן אנון קיימין
הכה יומא הדין קדם יי/ אלהן וית כל דרייה דעתידין למקום מן
בתרן עמן קיימין הכה יומא הדין:

I RM   דקמו...עלמא] דקמו מן יומת עלמא

II LM   דקמו...יומא דין] דקיימין הכא עמנא קיימין יומא הדין קדם
        יי/ אלהנה וית כל דריה דהוו מן יומי עלמא ודלא אתבריו עד
        כדון כולהון קיימין עמנא יומא דין:

I RM   מן בתרן] מבתרן

I LM   קיימין (2)] קיימה

2. Two Sets of Variants: Similar

Gen. 29:22   Extant: VBNL, CG E   Gen. 29:22

וכנש לבן ית כל עמה דאתרא ועבד שירו שירו ענה לבן ואמר להון הא שבע
שנין גברא חסידא הדין שרי ביניין בארנן[1] לא חסרו ובית שקוותן
סגון וכדון מה אתון יהבין עצה וניישרי יתה ביניין הכה עוד שבע
שנין ויהבו לה עצה דרמיו למסבה יתה ללאה חלף רחל:

I   RM   שבע שנין (1)...ויהבו] גברא הדין שרי ביניין שבע שנין
דיומין מבועינין אתברכו ועדרי ענינן סגון וכדו היבו לי
עצה מה נעבד בה וישרי גבן ושב [שובע read,] שנין[2]
אוחראין וקמו עמה דארעא ויהבו

LM   מה אתון יהבין...הכה עוד] הבו עצה דתשרי ביניין הכא עוד
I   RM   דרמיו למסבה יתה] דרמיו ואסיבו לה

[1] With scribal notation; probably to be read, בארניין.
[2] Cf., CG E.

Gen. 35:9   Extant: VBNL, P, CG C   Gen. 35:9

אלהא דעלמא יהא שמיה מבורך לעלם ולעלמי עלמין ענוותנותיך [read,
ענוותנותיך] וישרותך וצדיקותך ותוקפך והדרך והדרך[1] לא פסקין
לעלמי עלמין אלפת/ יתן למברכה לחתנה ולכלתה מן אדם וזוגיה ועוד
אלפת/ יתן למבקרא ית בישיא מן אבונן אברהם צדיקא כד אתגליתא
עלוי במשרה חזווה ועד כען הווה צער מן גזרתא ועוד אלפא יתן
למנחמה ית אבליה מן אבונן יעקב צדיקא אורחיה דעלמא ארעת לדבורה
מרבעותא [מרבניתא read,] דרבקה אמיה ומיתת רחל עלוי באורחיה
ויתב ליה צווח ובכה ומלל ואמר [ומילל ומאך read,] ואת ברחמך
טביא אתגליתא עלוי וברכת יתה ברכת האבילה ונחמת יתיה
דכן כתבת [כתבא/ה read,] מפרש ואמר ואתגלי יי/ על יעקב זמן
תנינות במיתיה מן פדן ארם וברך יתיה:

LM   אלהא] אלהא כול

I   LM   ענוותנותיך...למברכה] אלפת ית [יתן read,] פקודין יאיין
וקיימיך שפירין אלפת יתן למברכה כול

I   LM   ועוד אלפת] דכן כתבה מפרש ובריך יתהון ממריה דיי/ ואמ/
להון מימריה דיי/ תקופו וסגון ומלון ית ארעא וכבשו יתה
ועוד אלפת

I   LM   ועד כען הווה...דכן כתבא מפרש ואמר] ופקהת יתיה למגזור
עורלתיה ויתב ליה בתרע משכניה במחום יומא דכו [דכן read,]
כתבא מפרש ואמר ואיתגלי עלוי ממריה דיי/ במשרי חזווה
ועוד אלפת יתן למיברכה ית אבליה מן אבונן יעקב צדיקא כד
איתגליון עלוי במתייה מן פדן ארם אורחיה דעלמא כד ארעת
לדבורה מרבית/ דדבק/ אימיה ומיתת עלוי רחל באורחא ויתב
ליה אבונן יעקב צווח ומיילל ומספד ובכי ואת רבון כל עלמא
יי/ במכלת רחמיך טביה איתגלייית עלוי ונחמת יתיה וברכתה
דאבלייה ברכת יתיה על אימיה בגין כדין כתב/ מפרש ואמ/

Gen. 35:9 (cont.)　　　　　　　　　　　Gen. 35:9 (cont.)

RM ‏וברכת יתה ברכת...ואמר ואתגלי] וברכת/ דאבילא ברכת יתיה‏
‏ונחמת יתיה וכן כתבא מפר/ ואמ/ דאיתגלי‏

RM ‏זמן תנינות...וברך יתיה‏[add to verse, or] ‏ועוד אלפתא יתן‏
‏למיקבר מיתיא מרבנא משה דקבר יתיה רבון עלמיא יי/ יהיא‏
‏שמיה מברך לעלמיא‏

I　BM ‏יי/...במיתייה] מימריה דיי/ [זמן]‏[2]‏תנינות על יעקב‏
‏במיתייה‏

[1]Dittography.
[2]Conjectural. Cf., FT, CG C.

Gen. 49:22　　　　Extant: VBN, P　　　　　Gen. 49:22

‏ברי דרבית יוסף ברי דרבית ותקפית ותוב הוי חמי לך למתקף מדמי‏
‏אנה לך יוסף ברי לגפן שתילה על מבועין דמיין ושלחת שרשי/ לארעא‏
‏ופגרת שיני כל סיפי [כיפי,‏[1] ‏ועוברתא שלחת לרומה וכבשת כל‏
‏אילנייא כן כבשת יוסף ברי בחכמתך כל חהשיהון דמצראי רית כל‏
‏חכימיהון כד ארכבו יתך בארתכא תינייתא הפרעה והוון מקלסין‏
‏קדמיך יחי אבוי דמלכא דרב בחכמתא וזעירא כשנייא והוון בנחהון‏
‏דמלכייא ושלטנייא מדיקין‏[2] ‏עליך על כוותיה ומצוותך [read,‏
‏ומצוותך‏[3] ‏עליך מן חרכייא והוון מזרקן קדמיך שירין עזקין קטלין‏
‏מעוכין וכל מיני דהב סברין דאת תליית עיינך ומסתכלין [read,‏
‏ומסתכיל] בחדא מנהון חס לך יוסף ברי ולא תליית עיינך ואסתכלת‏
‏בחד [בחדא ,read] מנהון והוון בנתהון דמלכייא ושולטנייא אמרין‏
‏אלין לאלין ארום דין הוא יוסף גברא חסידא דלא אזל בתר חיזוי‏
‏עייניה ולא בתר הרהורי לבוי אינון דמובדין לבר נשא מן עלמא בגין‏
‏כדין יקום מנך תרין שבטין מנשה ואפרים ויקבלון חולק ואחסנון עם‏
‏אחיהון בפלג ארעא:‏

LM ‏ותוב הוי...למתקף] ואוף חמי הוה לך למתקוף‏

LM ‏דמיין] דמים‏

LM ‏ופגרת] ופגרת::‏

I　LM ‏ופגרת שיני כל] ופכרת שני כל‏

RM ‏כבשת] מלף [מלפת ,read]‏

LM ‏רית כל חכימיהון] וכל חרשהון‏[4]

I　LM ‏דפרעה] דאית לפרעה‏

LM ‏וזעירא] ורכיך‏

LM ‏ומצוותך...בחדא מנהון] ומן חרכיי/ ומסתכל [ומסתכלן,read]‏
‏בך בך‏[5] ‏מן שירוויאה והוון מטלקין עלך שירין קטלין‏
‏ומעוכין דלמ/ תתלי אפר ותסתכל בחד/ מנהון‏

RM ‏תליית עיינך ואסתכלת] תליית אפיר ולא אסתכלת‏

LM ‏מנהון והוון בנתהון] מנהון דלא תיהוי שתוף שרתף עמה‏
‏בגיהנם לעלם/ דאתי והוויין בנתיהון‏

Gen. 49:22 (cont.)　　　　　　　　　　　　Gen. 49:22 (cont.)

RM I　דלא] די לא

RM　אינון דמובדין...בגין] דאינון טרדין לאינש מהדין עלמא
בגין

LM I　אינון דמובדין...מן עלמא] הנון מובדין ית בר נשא מן גו
עלמ/

[1] In text, line drawn through word; corrected in LM: כֵיפֵי.

[2] So VP; BN: מדיקן.

[3] But cf., VBN. Note masculine forms predominate in passage.

[4] Cf., P: כל חכימיא ... וכל חרשיהון.

[5] Dittography.

Gen. 50:16　　　　　Extant: VB, P　　　　　Gen. 50:16
ופקידו שבטי/ ית כלהה למרביתה דיוסף למימר לה אבוך פקיד קרם עד
לא ימות למימר:

RM I　למרביתה...אבוך] אמהתא דדחל למימ/ ליוסף אבוך
LM　ית כלהה...אבוך] לוות בלהה למימ/ ליוסף אבוך
LM I　ימות] איתכנש

Ex. 2:12　　　　　Extant: VB, P　　　　　Ex. 2:12
ואסתכיל להכא ולהכא וחמא ארום לא הורה תמן גבר וקטל ית מצרייה
וטמריה בחלא:

RM I　להכא ולהכא...בחלא] ברוח נבואה בעלמא הדין ובעלמא דאתי
וחמא והא לית גבר זכאי נפיק מיניה ומחא ית מיצראה וטמע
יתיה בחלא

LM I　להכא ולהכא...בחלא] משה ברוח קודשא בתרין עלמיא וחמא והא
לית גיורא עתיד למקום מן ההוא מצראה ומחא ית מצראה וטמע
יתיה בחלא

Ex. 12:30　　　　　　　　　　　　Ex. 12:30
וקם פרעה בליליא הוא וכל שלטונוי וכל מצריי והות צוותחת רבה
במצרים ארום לא הוה תמן בית די לא הוה תמן מיתין:

RM　שלטונוי] עבדוי
LM　מצריי] מצראי
LM　בית...מיתין] ביית מן מצרים די לא הוה ביה מית מצרים
RM　בית...מיתין] בייתא די לא הוה ביה מיתא מן מצראי

Ex. 13:17　　　　Extant: P　　　　Ex. 13:17
והוה כד שלח פרעה ית עמא ולא דבר יתהון יי/ ארח ארעהון
דפלישתי ארום קריבה הוא ארום אמר יי/ דלא יתבר לבהון דעמא כד
יחמון סדרי קרבא ויחזרון למצרים:

LM　כד שלח] בזמן דשלח
RM　יי/ ארח] מימריה דיי/ מהלך

Ex. 13:17 (cont.)   Ex. 13:17 (cont.)

RM הוא] הוות

RM יי/] מימרי/ דיי/

LM יי/ דלא] מימרי/ דיי/ במחשבת דלא

Ex. 15:7   Extant: P   Ex. 15:7

ובסגי גיוותנותך תפגר בעלי דבביהון דעמך תשלח בהון תקוף רוגזך

תתכל יתהון היך מה דנורא בער בקשא:

RM ובסגי...בעלי] ובסוגי תוקפך תברת שורי בעלי

LM תפגר בעלי] תברת שורי בעלי

LM תתכל יתהון] ותחבל בהון

Ex. 31:2   Extant: VBN   Ex. 31:2

חמי משה דמנית וקראת בשם טב דרבן בצלאל בר אורי בר חור מן שבטא

דבנוי דיהודה:

I   LM דמנית וקראת] הא רביית וקריית

LM דמנית...דרבן] דרברית וקריית בשום טב מן יומי עלמא

Lev. 17:10   Lev. 17:10

וגבר גבר מן דבית ישראל ומן גיוריה דמתגיירין ביניהון די יאכל
כל אדם ואשוי תקוף רוגזי בנפש [בנפשא ,read] די תאוכל[1] ית

אדמה ואישיצא יתה מן גו עמה:

RM דבית] ני [בני ,probably read][2]

LM ביניהון] בניכון [ביניכון ,read]

RM יאכל כל אדם...ית אדמה] [יא]כול כל [א]דם ואשו[,read]

ואשוי] אפי רוגזי בנפשה דאכלה ית ארמ/[3]

LM כל אדם...רוגזי] כל אדם ואשוי אפי רוגזי

[1]Omitted from text; supplied in margin. M ends with /א ית.
[2]Cf., v. 8.
[3]Letters in brackets are conjectural. M is close to edge of page and illegible on microfilm.

Nu. 11:7   Nu. 11:7

ומנה כזרע כסבר הוא ועינה כחזיו בדולחה:

LM כסבר הוא] דכסב [דכסבר ,read] חוור הוא

LM כזרע כסבר] כבר זרע כוסבר חיור

RM ועינה כחזיו בדולחה] וחזויה כחזוו בדו/

Nu. 21:15   Extant: VBN, P   Nu. 21:15

כד הוון ישראל עברין בנחלי ארנונה אטמרו אמוריי בגו מעריה דנחלי
ארנונה אמרין כד יהוון בני ישראל עברין אנן נפקין לקבליהון
ומקטלין יתהון ורמז רבון כל עלמיא יי/ דידע מה בלבביה וגלי
קדמוי מה בכוליתה רמז לטוריה ואקפו רישיהון אלין לאלין ורציצו
רישי גיבריהון ושטפו נחליה מן אדמיהון ולא הוון ידעין נסיה
וגבורתה דעבד יי/ עמהון בנחלי[1] ומן בתר כדן אתפרשו ואזלו להון[2]
לאתריהון לחוות קרתה די לא הוות בעצתהון אשתיזיבת והא היא סמיכה
לתחומיהון דמואביי:

RM   אטמרו אמוריי...ישראל] אטמרי אמוראי במערייה אמרין אלין
     לאלין כד יהוון ישראל

RM   לקבליהון...רישיהון] לקדמותהון ומשיצין יתהון ומקטלין
     מלכין עם שלטנין בהא בשעתה רמה [read ,רמז] יי/ לטוריה
     ואקפו ראשי[3]

LM   ושטפו...לחיית קרתה] ונגרו נחלייה מן אדמהון ולחיית
     קרתה[4] (erasure)

LM I מן אדמיהון...נסיה] מדם קטולהון והוו ישראל מהלכין על
     רישי טוריה מלעיל ולא ידעו נסיה

LM I בנחלי...קרתה] בנחלי ארנון ולחיית קרתה

LM I דמואביי] דמואבאי

[1]Supply, ארנונה.

[2]Probably scribal error.

[3]Cf., P. As interpreted clause found in both VBN and P is
omitted by the M.

[4]Cf., P. As interpreted expansion in P is omitted by the M.

Deut. 18:14   Extant: VBN   Deut. 18:14

ארום אומיה האיליין די אתון משצי יתהון לחדודי עייניו ולקסמי
קסמין אינון שמעין ואתון עמי בני ישראל לא כוותהון יהב לכון יי/
אלהכון:

RM   משצי] ירתין

LM I עייניו] עינייה

RM I קסמין אינון] קסמייה

RM   ואתון...לא כוותהון] ואת לא כוותהון

LM   עמי...אלהכון] לא כן יהב בחולקך יי/ אלהך

Deut. 20:8   Deut. 20:8

ויוספון סרכייה לממללה עם עמא ויימרון מן היא גברא דדחל מן
חובוי וליביה תביר על עבידתיה יזיל ויחזור לביתיה ולא יימסי
ית לבהון דאחוי כלבביה:

LM   עם] לוות

Deut. 20:8 (cont.)   Deut. 20:8 (cont.)

LM מ[ן...כלבביה] מן גברא דדחלה ותביר ליבה מן חובה די
    בידיה יהך ויחזור לביתיה ולא יגרום לאחוי לתברא לבהון
    היך לביה

RM יימסי] ית [יתמסי read,]

RM כלבביה] כליביה

Deut. 24:15   Extant: VBNL   Deut. 24:15
    ביומיה תתן אגריה ולא יטמע עלוי שמשא ארום מסכן הוא ולאגר
    פעליה הוא מסר קדמר ית נפשיה אזדהר לך דלא יצוח עלך קדם יי/
    דלא יהווי בתרך חובה:

RM I ביומיה...עלוי] ביומה תתן לה אגריה לא תטמוע ע/

LM יטמע...קדם יי/] יטמרע שמשא דיקבול עלך קדם יי/

RM I ולאגר...חובה] ומן כגין אגריה [אגירה read,] הוא סבל לך
    ית נפש/ דלא יצורח עליכון קדם יי/ אזדהרו דלא יהווי
    בכון חובה

    3. Two Sets of Variants: Unclassified

Gen. 9:21   Extant: CG E   Gen. 9:21
    ושתה מן חמרא ורווה ואתגלי כגו משכנה:

LM חמרא] יינא

LM ורווה] ורבה

RM ואתגלי] ואתרשל

LM ואתגלי כגו משכנה] ירוש/ ואתפרסם במצע משכניה דסוראי
    ואתבזי במ/ מש/

Gen. 21:6   Gen. 21:6
    ואמרת שרה חדו רבה אתעבד לי מן קדם יי/ כל דשמע יחדי עמי:

RM חדו רבה...יי/] סגי לי חדוה עבד לי יי/

LM חדו רבה...יחדו עמי] חדה רבה עבד לי ממריה דיי/ כל דשמע
    בקלי וחדי לי יתי[1] ויחדי עמי

[1]Probably scribal error.

Gen. 25:1   Extant: VBNL, P   Gen. 25:1
    ואוסף אברהם ונסב אתה ושמה קטורה:

RM קטורה] + היא הות הגר דהות אסירה לה מן שירויה

LM קטורה] + היא הגר דהות קטירא ליה מלקדמין

Gen. 27:8   Gen. 27:8

וּכדוּן בּרי שׁמע בקלי וׂאזל לאן דאנׂה מפקדה יתך:

RM   וכדון] וכדו

LM   ואזל לאן דאנה] כמה די אנא

RM   דאנה] די אנא

Gen. 32:25(24)   Extant: CG C   Gen. 32:25(24)

ואשׁתייר יעקב לבלחדוׂי ואתפגש מלאך שׂדיאל בדמות גבר וגפף עמיה עד זמן די סליק עמודׂ שׁחרא:

RM   ואשׁתייר...ואתפגש or ואתפגש] ואשׁתדר[1]

LM   ואתפגש...עד זמן] ואישׁתדר עמה מלאך בדמות גבר עד מסק

RM   עד זמן...שׁחרא] עד מסק קריצתא

[1]M indicates either incomplete verse and vocabulary change, or
a vocabulary change.

Ex. 8:17(21)   Ex. 8:17(21)

ארוׂם אן ליתך משׁלח ית עמי הא אנא מגרׂי בך וׂבשׁלטונך ובעמך ובאנשׁי ביתך ית עׂרברובא ויתמלון בתיהון דמצרא [דמצראי read, מן ערבובא וית ארעא די אנון שׁׂריין בה:

LM   אן ליתך] לית את

LM   מגרי] משׁלח

RM   ובשׁלטונך] בעבדיך

RM   עׂרברובא] ערובא ולחוד

LM   די אנון שׁריין] די הינון שׁריין

LM   די אנון שׁריין בה] די אינון יתבין עלה

Ex. 9:30   Extant: CG D   Ex. 9:30

ואתׂ ושׁלטונך ידע אנה ארום על דקדם אתוׂן דחלין מן קדם יי/ אלהׂן:

LM   ואת...ידע] ואת פרעה ועבדיך ידע

RM   ארום...קדם] ארום על לא ימטון עליכון מחוותא לית אתון מתכנעין מן קדם

RM   ארום...דחלין] דעד לא דחלון [דחלין ,read]

LM   יי/] מימריה דיי/

Ex. 16:17   Ex. 16:17

ועבדו כדן בני ישׂראל ולקטו מן דאסגו ומן דזער:

RM   מן דאסגו ומן דזער] שׁבט/ דאסגי ושׁבט/ דאצער[1]

LM   מן דעסגו ומן דזער] דן ודן ודן דאצער[1] [,read
דן ודן דן דאסגי ודן דאצער]

[1]Cf., editio princeps, II, 107, where it is suggested that
דאצער be read דאזער.

Ex. 32:22   Ex. 32:22

ואמר אהרן למשה לא יתקף רוגזא דריבותי את חכם ית עמא ארום
בישין אינון:

LM   ‏ארום..אינון] ארום דברא בישה שלטה ‎¹בישה שלטה¹ ביה והוא
     גרם ליה למעבד

RM   ‏בישין] מבעשין

‎¹...¹So Ms.

Ex. 33:8   Ex. 33:8

‏והוה כד הוה משה נפק למשכנה קיימין כל עמא ומתעתדין גבר בתרע
משכניה ומסתכלין בתר משה עד דהוה עליל למשכניה:

RM   ‏והוה כד...ומתעתדין] ויהוי כד יפוק משה למשכנה הוון
     קיימין כל עמא ומעתדין

LM   ‏נפק] יפוק

RM   ‏ומסתכלין] והוון מס/

RM   ‏עד דהוה עליל למשכניה] למעלה למ/

Lev. 11:10   Lev. 11:10

‏וכל די לית ליה סנפירין וקסקסין בימיא ובנחליא מן כל שרצא דמיא
ומן כל נפש חיתה די במי/ מרחקה אנון לכון:

LM   ‏וקסקסין] וקסקסיין

RM   ‏חיתה...לכון] דחייה דאית במיא שקץ הנון לכון

RM   ‏ומן...מרחקה] ומן כל נפש חייתה די במיא מר/

Lev. 20:6   Lev. 20:6

‏ונפש/ די תסטי בתר שאלי אובה ומסקי זכורן [למטעי]‎¹ בתריהון
ואשוי תקוף רגזי בנפש/ ההוא ואצישי [ואשיצי ‎²[read, יתיה מן
גו עמיה:

RM   ‏ונפש/...מן גו עמיה] ובר נש די יסתכל בתר בידין וגרם
     ידוע [למטעי]‎¹ תבריהון ואחל [ואתז ‎³[read, רוגזי בבר
     נשא ההוא [ואשיצי]‎¹ יתיה מן חיי עלמא דאתי ולא יהיא
     יהוא [read, ליה חולק ביני עמיה

LM   ‏זכורן...בתריהון] דכורון למזנייה מן בתר

LM   ‏תקוף רגזי] אפי רוגזי

‎¹Text erased; conjectural reading.
‎²Error noted by scribe.
‎³Cf., TJ I.

Nu. 11:22

הא עמיה [ענייה ,read] ותורייה אין מתנכס להון הא ספק להון אן
ית כל נוני דימא אן מתכנש להון הא ספק להון:

RM   הא ענייה...ספק להון (2)[אין ענה ותורייה דימה רבה אין
מתכנשין להון הא מלא יספק להון:

RM   אן מתכנש...להון (4)[רבה אין מתכנישין להון הא מלא יספק
להון

Nu. 17:3(16:38)   Extant: VBN,P   Nu. 17:3(16:38)

ית מחתיתהון דחייביה האליין דחכו בנפשתהון ויעבדון יתהון טסין
מרדדין חפיי למדבחה ארום קרבו יתהון קדם יי/ אתקדשו ויהויין
לסימן לבני ישראל:

RM   מחתיתהון] מחתייתה [מחתייתהון ,read]
LM   האליין...בנפשתהון] בנפש [בנפשתהון?[[read,
LM   דחכו בנפשתהון] יקידת אשתה בנפש [בנפשתהון?[[read,
LM   ויעבדון...חפיי] ועבדו יתהון רדודי טסין ח/
LM   ויהויין] ויהוון

Nu. 21:28   Extant: VBN, P   Nu. 21:28

ארום עם גיברין בעריך היך אשתא נפקו מן חשבון עבדי קרב כשלהביתה
נפקו מן קרתא דסיחון שיצון לחוות מואביי (censored) [דהוון ,read]
דהוון] מדבחין קדם במתה דארנונה:

LM   עם גיברין...לחית מואביי] מלך חציף הי/ אשא נפק מן
חשבון וליגיונין עבדי קרבא כשלהובית גהינם נפקו מן קרתה
דסי/ לחית מואבאי

RM   היך אשתה] כאש
LM   כשלהביתה] כשלהביתה
LM   לחוות מואביי] לחית מואבאי
LM   במתה] טעוותה

Deut. 3:16   Deut. 3:16

ולשבטה דבנוי דראובני ודבנוי דגדי יהבית מן גלעדה ועד נחל
ארנונה אמצע נחלה ותחומה ועד נחל יבקה תחומיהון דבני עמוניי:

RM   ולשבטה...דגדי] ולראובני ולגדי
LM   אמצע נחלה] מצעית נח
LM   עמצע...ותחומה] קרתא דהא [דהיא ,read] מתבנייה בימצע
נחלא והוא תחומה
RM   יבקה] יבוק
RM   עמוניי] עמונאי

Deut. 15:14   Extant: VBN   Deut. 15:14

מזודא תזודיד ליה מן ענך מן אדרך ומן מעצרתך מן מה די ברך יתך
יי/ אלהך תתן לה:

LM   מזודא תזודיד ליה] מזדרזה תזדרז לה

RM   תזודיד] תזוודון

LM   יתך...לה] יתכון יי/ אלהכון תתנון לה

Deut. 23:6(5)   Deut. 23:6(5)

ולא צבא יי/ אלהכון למשמע ללווטוי דבלעם והפך יי/ אלהכון לכון
ית קללה לברכה ארום רחמכון יי/ אלהכון:

RM   למשמע...דבלעם] מוע לב [למשמוע לבלעם ,read]

LM   קללה לברכה] לווטייה לברכן

RM   קללה] הק/]הקלל, read[

RM   רחמכון] רחם יתכון

Deut. 25:9   Deut. 25:9

ותקרב יבומתיה לוותיה לעיני חכימיה ותשלף סנדלה מעילווי רגלה
ותירוק קדמוי ותיעני ותימר כהדן סידרא יתעבד לגברא די לא צבה
למיבני ית ביתה דאחוי:

LM   ותקרב...ותשלף] ותקרוב יבמתה לוותיה קדם חכימייה ותשלוף

RM   ותשלף סנדלה] ותשלף (sic) סנדליה

RM   רגלה] רגליה ומינה [ימינה ,read]

LM   כהדן..דאחוי] ככה יעשה לאיש אשר לא יבנה את בית אחיו:

RM   לגברא] לגבר

4. Variants Marked, ס"א

Gen. 12:3   Extant: VBNL   Gen. 12:3

ואברך ית מן דמברכך [דמברך ,read[יתך ומן דלאיט יתך יהוי ליט
ויתברכון בזכותך כל זעזר[1] זערֹיותא [זרעיותא ,read[דארעא:

LM   ית מן...יהוי ליט] ס"א מברכך כאהרן כהנא ומללטך [,read
       ומללטך] אלוט כבלעם רשיעיא

RM   זרעיותא] זרעייות

[1]Scribal error; noted by scribe.
[2]Error noted by scribe by two vertical dots over ע.

Gen. 15:12   Extant: VBNL, P   Gen. 15:12

והורת שמשה אישון למטמע ושנה בסימה נפלת על אברם והא אברם חזי
ארבעה מלכוון קיימא עלוהי אימה דא היא בכל חשכה דא היא מדי גדולה
דא היא ירון נפלת עלוהי דא (censored)

RM   והורת שמשה... [to end of verse ס"א ויהי השמש לבוא:

והוה שמשא קריב למטמוע ושנתא עמיקתא איתרמית על אברם והא
ארב/ מלכוון קיימן למשעברא ית בנוי אימתא דא היא בכל

Gen. 15:12 (cont.)   Gen. 15:12 (cont.)

קיבלא דא היא מידי סגיאת דא היא ייוון נפלת עלוהי דא היא

(censored) ומן בתר כדין תהדר מלכוותא לעמא בית ישראל

I   LM   אישון למטמע] אזלה למטמוע

I   LM   ושנה] + עמוקה [עמיקה ,read]

I   LM   מלכוון קיימא...חשכה] מלכוותה דעתידי/ למקום ומשעבדה
         בכנוי אימה חשכה

Gen. 15:17   Extant: VBNL, P   Gen. 15:17

והא שמשא טמע וחומטה הורה והא אברם חזי עד די סאבסלין אסתדרו
וכורסוון רמיו והא גהינם דמתילה באתונה בתנורא מקפה שביבין די
נור שלהין [שלהבין ,read] דאשה דבגוה נפלו רשיעי/ על דמרדו
רשיעיא על אורייתא בחייהון בעלמ/ הדין וצדיקיא על דנטרו יתה מן
עקתא אשתיזבון כל כדין אתחוי לאברם כד הוה עבד כיני גזרייא
האילין:

LM   והא שמשא...בגזרייא האילין] והרות שמשא אזלה למיסוק
     וקטמת/ [וחמטא ,read] הורת והא אברם חזו [חזי ,read]
     על די ספסלין אתעותדו וכרסוון רמיו וגהינם דמתילה באתונה
     דמעתדא לרשיעיא לעלמא דאתי על די לא עסקו אולפן אורייתא
     בעלמא הדין ולא נטרו פקודייא כל כדן הוה הוה אברם חזי כד
     הוה אברם עבד כיני בתרייא האליין:

RM   דאשה דבגוה...על אורייתא] דאשיה ובגי/ רשעין די כפרו
     באורייתא

RM   וצדיקיא על דנטרו...כל כדין] וצדיקין די קיימו אורייתא
     מן עקתא אשתיזבו כל כדן   "   "   "

BM   והא שמשא...בגזרייא האילין] ס"א ויהי השמש באה: והוה
     שמשא טמעה וחומטא הורת: הוה[1] אברם והא גהינם דכערה כאתונה
     כשביכין די'נור [די נור ,read] וגומרין דאשתה ומסקה תננה
     ורשיעי/ לגווה אתמריין [אתרמיין ,read] על די מרדו
     בחייהון באולפן אורייתא בעלמא הדין ולא קיימו פקודייה
     וצדיקייא מן דינה אישתיזבו על די פלחו בחייהון בעלמא הדין
     וקיימו פיקודייה ובזכוותהון עתיד דאישתרי בסוף יומיא גומרא
     די נור מן כורסי יקרא יתוקיד ותצרי כל מלכותא איליין חזויא
     רברביא חזא אברם בזמן דעבר כין פסגייא האיליין

[1]Supply חזה.

Gen. 18:2   Gen. 18:2

ונטל עיינוהי וחמא והא תלתא מלאכין בדמות גברין קיימין עלוי וחמא
ורהט לקדמותהון מן תרע משכנה ושאל בשלמהון כנימוס ארעא:

RM   קיימין עלוי] ס"א קיימין קודמוי חד מניהון הוה אזל
     למבשרא ית שרה דילידה בר דכר וחד מניהון הוה אזל למהפך ית

Gen. 18:2 (cont.)   Gen. 18:2 (cont.)

סדום וחד מניהון הוה אזל למישזבא ית לוט מן גוא הפיכתא

LM קיימין...ורהט] מעתדין מעלווי וחמה יתהון ורהט

Gen. 27:41   Extant: P   Gen. 27:41

ושטם ית[1] עשו ית יעקב על ברכתא די ברך יתה אבוי ואמר עשו בלבא
לית אנא עבד היך מה דעבד קין די קטל להבל בחיובי[2] דאבוי וחזר
אפוי ואוליד ית שת וקרא ית שמיה על שמיה הא אנא ממתין עד זמן
דיקרבון יומי אבלא דאבא ואקטול ית יעקב אחוי ואנא מתקרי קטול
וירות:

LM ושטם...יעקב (1)] ונטר עשו סנה על יעקב

LM אבוי ואמר עשו] יצחק אבוי עני עשו

RM בלבא לית] לית

LM היך מה] היכמה

RM די קטל...דאבוי] להבל אחוי די קטל יתיה בחיי אבוי

RM וחזר] והדר

LM הא אנא...דיקרבון] דקטילה ארום ממתן עד זמן יקרב/

LM הא אנא...וירות] ס"א דהבל כרם מתעכב אנא עד זמן די ימטון
יומי אבלא דמיתת אבא ובכן אנא קטל ית יעקב אחי ואנא
משתכח קטול וירית

[1] Scribal error. Not noted by scribe.

[2] Read, בחיווי (so <u>editio princeps</u>)?; בחיי?; בהיייני? From first
<u>yodh</u> letters may be scribal errors from confusion with follow-
ing word.

Gen. 34:31   Extant: VBNL, P   Gen. 34:31

עניין תרין בנוי דיעקב שמעון ולוי ואמרין ליעקב אבוהון לא יאה
יאי] [read, הוא דיהוון אמרין בכנישתיהון ובמדרשיהון (censored)[1]
סאיבו בתולן ופלחו [ופלחי] [read, (censored)[2] לברתיה דיעקב כרם
יאי הוא דיהוון אמרין בכנישתיהון דישראל ובבית מדרשהון ערלין
אתקטלו על עסק בתולה (censored)[3] על די סאבו לדינה ברתיה דיעקב
כלא מן כל כדין דלא יהוון [יהווי] [read, שכם בר חמור מלגלג בנפשיה
ומתגאי בלביה ויאמר באתה דלית לה כר נש תבע עלבנה כדון אתעבד
לדינא אחתן היך אתה טעיא נפקת ברא:

LM II הוא דיהוון אמרין] למהוי מית [מיתאמר [read,

LM I   דיהוון אמרין] דהוי [דיהוי [read, מתאמר

RM I   ובמדרשיהון] ובבתי מד

LM   בתולן] ס"א בתולן לבתולתא

LM II לברתיה] טניפו ית ברתא

RM II ברם יאי הוא דיהוון] אלא כדן יאי דיהוון

LM I   דיהוון אמרין בכנישתיהון (2)] דיתאמר בכני/

RM   ובכית] ובבתי

Gen. 34:31 (cont.)   Gen. 34:31 (cont.)

II LM על עסק בתולה] בגין בתולה

II RM על די סאבו...דלא] בגין ברתיה דיעקב ולא עוד אלא דלא

I LM כלא מן...שכם] דא מן דא לא יאי לשי/

I RM מלגלג...ומתגאי] מתג [מתגאי ,read]

II LM בנפשיה...בלביה] במיליה

II RM דלית לה...נפקת ברא] מטעיה נפקת ברא דלית ליה תביע
איתעביד בדינה אחתי [אחתן ,read] בגין כן עבדינן פתגמ/
הדין

I LM בר נש⁴...נפקת ברא] תבוע אדם ולא תבוע עלבן כן הוה לדינה
ברתיה דיעקב ואמר [ואמרין ,read] היך אתה זני ונפקת ברא⁵
ית אחת/

.ערלין¹

.צלמין²

.ופלהי צלמין³

⁴But cf., FT.

⁵FT: + [ן]מחשב

Nu. 34:8   Extant: VBN, P   Nu. 34:8

מן טוורוס מינוס [מנוס ,read]¹ תכוונון למעלני אנטוכייה ויהוון
מפנוקי [מפקנוי ,read], דתחומה לאולס דקילקי:

LM טוורוס מנוס] ס"א טורי יסמינוס²

RM למעלני] מעלך

I RM למעלני] למעלה

I RM דתחומה...דקילקי] בתחומה דא/ דקלקאי

¹Error noted by scribe.

²In a foreign hand. Obviously a notation distinct from surrounding Mgg. See <u>editio</u> <u>princeps</u>, IV, 317.

---

5. <u>Three</u> <u>Sets</u> <u>of</u> <u>Variants</u>: <u>Unclassified</u>

Gen. 15:11   Extant: VBNL, P   Gen. 15:11

ונחת עופה על פסגייה ואשבת יתה זכוותה דאברם כד נחת טייסא הוה
שכין על פסגיי/ היידין¹ הוא טייסא דן [דין ,read]² הוא טייסא
מסאבה די [היי ,read]¹ דין הוא עופא מסאבא אילין אינון¹ מלכוותא
דארעא כד יהוון עייצין עצן בישן על דבית ישראל בזכוותיה דאברם
אבוהון משיזבה להון:

RM ונחת...משיזבה להון] ונחתו אומיא דמתיליין לעופא מסאבא
למיכז נכסיהון דישראל והות זכותא דאברהם מגנא עליהון

RM טייסא (2)] עופא

RM טייסא (2) or (3)] עייטא

LM היי דין] והיידן

Gen. 15:11 (cont.)   Gen. 15:11 (cont.)

LM היי דין..אילין אינון] אליין הנון

RM אילין אינון...משיזבה לכון] אליין הנון ארבעתי מלכוותא
דעתידין.משעבדה לבנוי דאברם וזכותא דאברם צדיקה משיזבה
להון

[1]...[1]Cf., **FT**. Ni 1, corrupt text?

[2]We read supralinear notation as a <u>yodh</u>. Cf., <u>editio prin-
ceps</u>, I, 81, where it is read as a lemma.

Gen. 44:18   Extant: VBNL, P, CG D   Gen. 44:18

וקרב לוותיה יהודה זעף במלין ומדכדך בלישנא נהם כאריה ואמר בבעו
מינך רבוני ימלל כען עבדך פתגם ורבוני לא יתקוף רוגזך בעבדך הלא
מן זמנא קדמייא דאמינן לוותך הוויית אמר לן מן קדם יי / אנה דחיל
וכדון חזרו דינך למהווי מדמיין לדינוי דפרעה רבך: ואמר הא כען
רבונן הא בזמנא קדמאה דאתינא אמדת לן מן קדם יי / דחיל וכדו את
אמדת מן פרעה אנה דחיל דילמא לא אתאמר לך או דילמא לא אשתמע לך
מה דעבדו שמעון ולוי תרין אחיי בכרכה דשכם דעלו בגווה וקטלו בה
כל דכורא מן בגלל דסאיבו בגווה ית דינה דלית היא ממניין
שבטיא ולית לך [לה, read,] חולקא ואחסנא בפילוג ארעא כל דכן בגלל
בנימן אחונן דהוא ממניין שבטיא ואית ליה חולק ואחסנא בפיליג
[בפילוג, read,] ארעא ואנא חיליה תקיף מן חילהון דשמעון ולוי
בשבועתא אם אשלוף סייפי מן תיקא לא אתיבנא לגווה עד זמן דקטיל
אנה כל מצראי מינך אנה משרי ובפרעה רבך אנה מסיים ארום יקיר אנה
כוותך ואנה [ואבא, read,] כוות פרעה רבך ארום [דאת ימה מה,[1]read,]
בה] משתבע[1] ים [ימה, read,] בה את[1] משתבע אנה לך בחיי רישיה דאבא
היך מה דאת משתבע בחיי רישיה דפרעה רבך דאן שלף אנה חרבי מן גווה
תיקא לית אנה מחזר יתה לתיקה עד זמן די ימלי כל ארעא דמצרים
קטילין לית אנה מחזר יתה לתיקה עד זמן דנעבד כל ארעא דמצרים צדי
מן דיור מנך אנה משרי ומן פרעה רבך דאת ימי ביה אנה מחסל על מנת
למעבד מעבד על כורחיה דאבא הא לא אשתמע לך ולא אתני לך מה עבדו
תדין אחיי שמעון ולוי בכרכא דשכם דהוו בשלווה ועלו בגווה וקטלו
כל דכורא לפתגם דחרב על די סאבו לדינה אחתן דלא הוו / מתמניי
עמן מן שבטיא ולא מקבלה עמן אחסנייה על חד כמה וכמה על אחונן
דהוא מתמני עמין [עמן, read,] מן שבטיא ומקבל חולק ואחסנא עמן
בפלוג ארעא ועל חד כמה וכמה דאנה קשה מינהון ועל חד כמה דחילי
קשי מן דידהון וערבת ית טליא מן לוות אבה ואמרי [ואמרית, read,
ליה למימר אין לא אייתת יתי [יתיה, read,] לוותיך ואקמית יתיה
קדמך נהוי מדחק מן שאלת שלמה דאבה דאבה כל יומיא או דלמא דלא אשתמע
לך ולא אתני לך ארום מלכין ושליטין אנן כוותך בארעא דכנען היך מה
דאת ופרעה רבך שליטין בארעא דמצרים כן אנה ויעקב אבה שליטין
בארעא דכנען:

114

Gen. 44:18 (cont.)   Gen. 44:18 (cont.)

RM   זעף...ואמר בבעו] ואמר בבעו

RM   ואמר בבעו...אנה מסיים] ואמר בבעו רבנן הא בזמנא קדמא
דאתינא אמרת לך מן קדם יי/ אנא דחיל וכדו את אמרת מן
קדם פרעה אנה דחיל דילמא לא אתמר לך או דילמא לא אשתמע
לך מה דעבדו שמעון ולוי תרין אחיי בכרכה דשכם דעלו בגוה
וקטלה בה כל דכור/ מן בגלל דסאיבו בגווה ית דינה אחתן
דלית היא ממניך שבטייא ולית לה חולק ואחסנא בפילוג ארעא
כל דכן בגלל בנימין אחונן/ דהא [דהוא read,] ממניך שבטיי/
ואית ליה חולק ואחסנא בפילוג² ואנה חילי תקיף מן חיליהון
דשמעון ולוי בשבועתא אם אשלוף סייפי מן תיק/ לא אתביני/
לגוה עד זמן דקטל אנה כל מצראי מנך אנה משרי ובפרעה רבך
אנה מסיים

RM   ורבוני לא] במשמועה דדרבנן ולא

RM   למהווי] למהוון

LM   ואמר הא כען...ארום [יקיר]] ארום [יקיר]

LM   משתבע [אנה] or [דאת] משתבע] אשתבע [אנה] or [דאת] אשתבע

LM   לדינה] ית דינה

RM   ק"? [at extreme right edge

RM   דחילי] בחיי [בחיילי read,]

RM   עד זמן דקטיל אנה כל מצראי] עד זמן די נעבד כל ארעיה
דמצרי/ צדי

LM   עד זמן דקטיל אנה כל מצראי] עד זמן דימלו כל ארעא דמצרים
קטילין

LM   די ימלי   כל ארעא] די נמלו [נמלי read,] כל אר/

LM   ובפרעה רבך אנה מסיים...הא לא אשתמע] ובפרעה רבך אנה
מסיי/ הלא לא אשתמע

RM   דלא הוו/ מתמניי/ עמן...על חד כמה וכמה (1)] ולא הוה
מתמניא עמנן לא בפלגא [?מקבלה read,] עמן חולק ואחסנ/
בפילוג ארעא עד חד כמ/ וכמ/

RM   מן שאלת שלמה] למשאל בשלמא

LM   ושליטין] + אוף

1...1Versions are corrupt here. Cf., FT.
²Supply ארעא.

Gen. 47:21   Extant: VBNL   Gen. 47:21

וית עמא מלשנה לשנה בישא עבר יתהון יוסף ואגלי יתהון וטלטל
יתהון מן קרייה לקריה ומן סיפא תחומיהון דמיצראי ועד סייפא ועמא
דבקריית [דבקרייתא read,] אשרי במדינתא ועמא דמדינתא אשרי
בקרייתא מן סייפי דארעא דמצרים ועד סייפיה דלא יהוון מצראי
מוניין לאחוי דיוסף ואמרין להון אכסניא גלוליא:

Gen. 47:21 (cont.) Gen. 47:21 (cont.)

LM רית עמא...אכסניא גלוליא[רית עמא טלטל יתהון מן קרי
לקרי מן בגלל דלא יהוון קריין לאחוי מטלטליא וגילוליא
כנישיכפן מן בגלל כן טלטילינון מן סוף תחום מצרים ועד
סופיה:

LM רית עמא...אכסניא גלוליא[רית עמא דהורון שדין במדינתא
אעבד בקורייתא רית עמא דהורון שריין בקורייתא אעבר
במדינתא דלא יהוו]יהוון ,read[מונייך לבנוי דיעקוב
ואמרין להון אכסנאי גלולאי:

RM סיפא...אכסניא גלוליא[סיפא תחום/ דמצריים עד תחומא
סיפא מן בגלל לחו]לאחוי ,read[דיוסף דלא קריין להון
אכסניי גלוליי

Gen. 48:22 Gen. 48:22

ואנא יהבית לך חולק חד יתיר על אחך לבושיה דאדם קדמי נסב יתיה
אברהם אבוי דאבה מן ידוי דנמרוד רשיעא ויהב יתיה ליצחק אבה
ויצחק אבה יהב יתיה לעשׂו אחוי ואנה נסבת יתיה מן ידוי דעשׂו אחוי
לא בחרבי ולא בקשׂתי ארום אלהן בזכוותי ובעובדי טביא דאינון
טבין לי מן חרבי ומן קשׂתי ועוד יהבית לך חולק חד יתיר על אחיך
שכם דנסבית בזכוותי ובעובדיי טביא מן ידיהון דאמוראי דטבין לי
מן חרבי וקשׂתי:

RM לך חולק חד (1)...חרבי וקשׂתי[לכון חולק חד יתיר על אחוך
]אחיך ,read[[1] דנסבית בזכותי ובעבדיי/ טביא דהוויי[2] מן
ידיהן דאמוראי טבין לי מן חרבי ומן קשׂתי

RM לך (1)...דאמוראי דטבין[לך]חולק חד יתיר על[אחיך]שכם
דנסבית[מן ידיהון דאמורﺍﺉ בזכותי ובעבדיי/ טביי/ דהוי
טביי/

LM קדמי...לעשׂו...מן חרבי ומן קשׂתי[קדמאה דנסיב אברהם מן
ידי נמדרד ויהיבנון ליצחק ויצחק יהיבן/]יהיבנון ,read[
ליעקב[3] לעשׂו דהלך בנימוס דאמוראי...בגבורתי: ו?[4] עבריה/
]עבריי/ read[, רב/ דברירין...בין]?מן reac,[סייפין[5]
ומן קשׂת/[5]

[1]Supply שכם.

[2]Transposed. Read after דאמוראי.

[3]Scribal error; noted by scribe.

[4]Waw and at least one illegible letter close to binding.

[5]In Ms the M is one continuous variant, including the
colon. Suggested breaks in the reading are ours.

Gen. 50:1   Extant: VBN, P   Gen. 50:1

ונפל יוסף על אפוי דאבוי ובכה עלוי ונשק ליה וארבע יוסף ית אבוי
בערס דשנדפין מחפיא דהב מבקעא [מקבעא read,] מרגליין מליא ומחזקא
באבנא [?כמאני read,]¹ בועה² כוצה וארגוונא שפיכין תמן חמדנין
וריחנין טבין מוקדן תמן בוסמנין טבין קיימן תמן מלכוון ושולטנן
[ושולטנין read,] מן בנוי דישמעל קיימין תמן שולטנין מן בנוי
דעשר קיימין תמן שולטנין מן בנוי דקטורה תמן קאים יהודה אריה
גוברין דאחוי ענה יהודה ואמר לאחוי איתון נבני לאבונן ארזא רמא
לרישיה מטי עד צית שמיא ושרשוי מטיין עד דרי עלמא די נפקו מיניה
תרי עשר שבטיא דבני ישראל די נפקו מיניה כהנייא בחצצרותיהון
ולוייא בכינוריהון בכדן אתרכן יוסף על צווריה דאבוי ובכא עלוי
יוסף ונשק יתיה:

LM   דשנדפין] די ש

RM   דשנדפין] רשינד פין [דשין דפין or דשינדפין read,]

LM   מבקעא...וארגוונא] טב ומבקבעין [ומקבעין read,] באבנין
      טבין ומרגליין ומחזקין באבנ/³ דבו/ וארגוונה

LM   שפיכין תמן...אריה] תמן שפכן שפכן⁴ חמד ני/ [חמדנין read,]
      ריחנין תמן קיימין גיברין מן דבית עשו תמן קיימין שליטין
      מן דבית יעקב תמן קאים אריה

LM   שפיכין תמן...אריה] תמן הוו [הווו read,] שפכן תמריין
      [חמדריין read,]⁵ רתחנין [ריחנין read,] ותמן מוקדן ⁶ותמן
      הווו קיימין⁶ בוסמנין עבין תמן הווו קיימין מדבית עשו תמן
      הוו [הווו read,] קאמין גיברין מדבית יעקב מדבי/ ישמעל
      הווו קיימין אריה

RM   מן בנוי דקטורה] מבני קטורה

RM   מן בנוי דעשו] מבני עשו

RM   נבני לאבונן] ונבני על [אבונן]

RM   נבני לאבונן] ובנון על אבונן

RM   ושרשוי] כרם שרש/

LM   ושרשוי...אתרכן] ענפוי מטיין על כל דיירי ארעא ושרשוי
      מטיין עד ארעית תהום/ מנה קמו בישראל תריסר שבטין מיני/
      לקרבא קרבנ/ ומני/ קמו ליואי במחלוקתיהון לזמרא הא בכין
      אתרכין

¹So FT; but cf., second M in LM.
²Scribal error.
³See n. 1. Also see <u>editio princeps</u>, I, 341, where reading, באטניא, is suggested.
⁴Dittography.
⁵But cf., TJ I.
⁶...⁶Error. Probably in text.

Ex. 20:2   Extant: P, CG F   Ex. 20:2

דבורייא קדמיא דהוה נפיק מן פום קודשא יהא שמה מבורך היך זיקין
והיך ברקין והיך למפדין רנזר [דנור read,] למפד דנור מן ימיניה
ולמפד דאשא מן שמאליה פרח וטייס באויר שמיא וחזר וכל ישראל
חמיין יתיה ודחלין והוה חזר ומתחקק על תדין לוחי קיימא ואמר עמא
בני וחזר ומקף על משרייותיהון דישראל וחזר ומתחקק על לוחי קיימא
וכל ישראל חזיין יתיה בכן הוה צווח ואמר עמי בני ישראל אנה הוא
יי/ אלהכון די פרקת ואפקת יתכון פריקין מן ארעא דמצרים מן בית
עבדי:

LM   וחזר וכל ישראל...בני ישראל] וכל ישרא/ חמיין יתיה ודחלן
     והוה חזר ומתחקק על תרין לוחי קיימו [קיימא read,][1] ואמר
     עמי בני דישרא/

RM   [reads as follows:] וכן הוי [הוא read,] צר[2] צווח ואמר
     וכל ישרא/ חזין יתיה כד הוה צוח ואמ/ עמי בני ישרא/

LM   [reads as follows:] וכן הוה צוח ואמר וכל ישרא/ חזיין
     יתיה

[1]Scribal error; noted by scribe.
[2]Scribal error.

Ex. 22:14(15)   Extant: V, P, CG A   Ex. 22:14(15)
אם מריה עמי/ לא ישלם אין אגיר הוא אתקבל באגרא:

RM   אתקבל באגרא] מקבל אגרא/
RM   אתקבל באגרא] אעל כל פסיד/ אגריה
LM   אתקבל באגרא] יזל אגרי/ בפסדי/

118

C. Translation of Texts
    1. Two Sets of Variants: Dissimilar
Gen. 3:9

And the Lord God called to Adam and said to him: Behold,
the whole world which I created is revealed before me. Darkness and light are revealed before me. And do you think that
the place where you are is not revealed before me? Where is
the commandment which I commanded you?
 I LM the Lord]   the Word of the Lord
 I LM And do you think...which I commanded you?] And how do
       you think that the place where you are is not revealed
       before me? Where are the precepts which I commanded
       you?
II RM   the commandment which I commanded you?] the precepts
       which I commanded you?

Gen. 4:8

And Cain said to Abel his brother: Come, let the two of us
go out to the open field. And when the two of them had gone
into the open field, Cain answered and said to Abel: I see that
the world was not created by love and is not governed according
to the fruits of good works and that there is respect of persons
in the judgment. Why has your offering been received with favor and my offering has not been received from me with favor?
Abel answered and said to Cain: I see that the world was created by love and is governed according to the fruits of good works;
and because my works were better than yours my offering was received from me with favor (and) your offering was not received
from you with favor. Cain answered and said to Abel: There is
no judgment and there is no judge and there is no other world;
there is no giving of a good reward to the righteous and there
is no retribution (exacted) from the wicked. Abel answered and
said to Cain: There is a judgment and there is a judge and there
is another world and there is giving of a good reward to the
righteous and there is retribution (exacted) from the wicked in the
world to come. Concerning this matter the two of them were ar-
guing in the open field, and Cain rose up against Abel his brother and killed him.
 I RM let [the two of us] go out...and   killed him.]   let
       the two of us go out into the open field. And Cain rose
       up against Abel his brother and killed him.

Gen. 4:8 (cont.)

II LM   when/had gone]   synonym for "when"

  LM   that [the world was not created] by love]   that [the world was created] by love

II RM   I see that (2)...and because]   Even if the world was created by love, (still) it is governed according to the fruits of (good?) works and there is no respect of persons in the judgment and because

II LM   my offering was received from me with favor (and) your offering]   and preceded yours my offering was received with favor and your offering

II RM   giving (1,2)]   grammatical change

II RM   retribution]   grammatical change

II LM   retribution]   grammatical change

  RM   arguing]   disputing

Gen 9:27

    May the Lord enlarge the borders of Japheth and make the glory of his Shekinah dwell in the midst of the tents of Shem, and may Canaan be a servant enslaved to them.

 I RM   the Lord/the borders]   the Word of the Lord [enlarge] the borders

II LM   and make...to them]   and when his sons become proselytes have them dwell in the schools of Shem, and may Canaan be enslaved to them.

 I RM   in the midst of the tents of Shem, and may]   in the schoolhouses of Shem the Great, and may

Gen. 14:14

    And Abram heard that Lot the son of his brother had been taken captive, and he armed his young men (youths) grown up in his house, three hundred ten, and he pursued them as far as Caesarea.

 I LM   his young men...his house]   his young men raised in his house

II RM   grown up...as far as Caesarea]   raised in his house, and they did not want to go with him; and he chose from them Eleazar who: from (or, after them [supplying בחריהון]) ...Dan: ...as far as [supplying עד] Caesarea.   equivalent to one hundred: and eighteen

 I LM   hundred]   hundred and eight [teen]

Gen. 24:60

    And they blessed Rebekah and said to her: Truly, until now,
you have been our sister. But henceforth you will go and join
him, the pious man. And from you shall arise thousands and myriads. Your sons will inherit the cities of their enemies.

II RM   and said...and myriads.]   they said to her: Until now
        you have been our sister. Now you will go (and) be
        joined with that righteous (man). May it be (God's) will
        that from you will go forth thousands and myriads, righ-
        teous multitudes.

 I LM   and myriads...enemies.]   and myriads of righteous angels,
        and may your descendents inherit the cities of their ene-
        mies.

Gen. 25:22

    And the children struggled in the womb and she said: If
such is the tribulation of the children, why, pray, do I have
children? And she went to the schoolhouse of Shem the Great to
ask for mercies from before the Lord.

II LM   If such...before the Lord.]   If the pain of childbirth
        is like this why should I be with child? And she went
        to the schoolhouse of Shem the Great, beseeching and
        praying before the Lord.

 I LM   do I have children?...before the Lord.]   is my life to
        have sons? And she went to seek mercies from before
        the Lord in the schoolhouse of Shem the Great.

Gen. 26:35

    And they were rebellious and overbearing of spirit and they
played in idol worship and they did not receive instruction from
either Isaac or Rebekah.

  RM   and they were]   orthographic change

 I LM   rebellious...receive]   rebellious and
        overbearing of spirit, worshipping idols, and they did
        not receive

II RM   and they did not...Rebekah]   and they made the life of
        Isaac and Rebekah bitter.

Gen. 27:22

    And Jacob drew near to Isaac his father, and he felt him
and said: Now, the voice is the voice of Jacob but the touch of
his hand is the touch of the hands of Esau.

Gen. 27:22 (cont.)

  I RM and he felt]   and he felt   (metathesis)

 II LM Now, the voice...of Esau.]   When the voice of Jacob
       is heard in supplication Esau has no power to harm
       him, but when he is negligent in the commandments of
       the Law the hands of Esau will rule over him.

  I RM but the touch of his hand is the touch of the hands
       of]   but the touch of his hand is the touch of the
       hands of   (changes in morphology and vocabulary

Gen. 27:27

     And he (Jacob) drew near to him (Isaac) and kissed him;
and he (Isaac) smelled the odor of his clothing and blessed
him and said: See, the smell of my son is like the smell of
incense of good perfumes which are destined to be offered upon the altar on the mountain of the sanctuary, that is, the
mountain which the one who lives and exists for all ages has
blessed, the Lord.

   RM to him and kissed]   and kissed

   RM See]   Come and see

 II RM like the smell of incense...for all ages/ the Lord.]
       like the smell of the garden which was planted in the
       field of Eden which the Lord blessed.

  I LM of good perfumes...the Lord.]   of good perfumes which
       are destined to be offered on the mountain of the
       sanctuary which the Word of the Lord blessed.

Gen. 28:11

     And he prayed in the place and spent the night there,
because the sun had set on him there; and he took some of the
stones of the place and put (them) as a pillow for his head
and fell asleep in that place.

 II RM And he prayed...in that place.]   And he reached the
       sanctuary and spent the night there, because the sun
       had set; and he took four stones from the stones of
       that holy place and put them as his pillow, and they
       became one stone. At that time he knew that he was
       destined to take four wives and from them were des-
       tined to arise four hosts and they would be as one
       people. And he lay down in that place.

  I RM and spent the night]   grammatical change

Gen. 28:17

     And he was afraid and said: How awesome is this place.

Gen. 28:17 (cont.)

This place is not an ordinary place, but a place set aside
from before the Lord; and this gate is the gate of prayer
set aside up to (which opens upon?) the height of heaven.

II RM place is not...to the height of heaven.]   This is
       not a profane place, but the place of the sanctuary
       of the Lord; and this sanctuary corresponds to the
       gate of the sanctuary which is in heaven.

 I LM [This] place is not...up to]   And this place is
       not an ordinary place, but it is a place set aside
       for the house of prayer; and this is the gate which
       corresponds to

Gen. 31:22

     And it happened that when the shepherds of Laban went to
water the flock from the well they were not able to.   And
they waited two, three days hoping that perhaps it would
overflow, but it did not overflow.   Then it was told to
Laban, on the third day, that Jacob had fled.

 I LM And it happened...Jacob had fled.]   And it was told
       to Laban on the third day that Jacob had fled.
    LM shepherds]   the shepherd(s) after

II RM from the well...Jacob had fled.]   ...Jacob there by
       the well; and they did not find water and waited
       three days for it to overflow, but it did not over-
       flow -- and then it was told on the third day that the
       pious Jacob, for whose merits the waters had over-
       flowed from the well for twenty years, had gone.

Gen. 33:14

     Let my master pass, I pray, before his servant.   And I
will lead them in a suitable manner, according to the pace of
the animals which are in my hand and according to the pace of
the children, until the time that I have reached my master at
Gabla.

II RM Let/pass...my master at Gabla.]   Let my lord, I pray,
       go ahead; and let him receive his portion and the re-
       ward of the great blessing with which my father
       blessed him*in this world before his servant.   And I,
       alone, will lead, according to the instruction of the
       Law which is before me and according to the hope in
       its justice, the exiled community until the time that
       exiles will end, and (with) many I shall meet my master
       to wage war at Gabla.

 I LM which are in my hand]   which are before me

Gen. 45:28

And Israel said: Many good and consoling things have I
expected to see, but this I did not expect -- that Joseph should
still be alive.   I shall go now and see him before I die.
   I RM Many]   morphological change
  II RM good...I shall go]   [Many] pleasures and many consola-
         tions have I expected to see, but this consolation I no
         longer expected to see, but, since Joseph, my son, still
         lives, I shall go
   I LM I shall go/and see]   I (lit., we) shall go and see
   I RM I die.]   I (lit., we) die.

Gen. 49:1

And Jacob called his sons and said to them: Gather together and I will tell you the hidden mysteries, the concealed ends,
the giving of the rewards of the just and the punishment of the
wicked, and what the happiness of Eden is.   The twelve tribes
gathered together simultaneously (like one) and surrounded the
bed of gold in which our father Jacob was lying after the (pre-
determined) end was revealed to him so that the (pre-determined)
end of the blessing and the consolation might be told to them.
After the end was revealed to him, the mystery was concealed
from him.   They expected that he was going to tell them the
(pre-determined) end of the redemption and the consolation.
After the mystery was revealed to him it was concealed from him;
and after the gate was opened for him it was closed to him.   Our
father Jacob answered and blessed them; according to his good
words he blessed each one of them.
   I LM and I will tell you...giving]   and I will tell you (a-
         bout) the hidden signs, the secret mysteries, the giving
   I RM The twelve [tribes] gathered...bed]   The twelve tribes
         gathered together all around the bed
   I LM after the end was revealed...he blessed/ them]
         He asked that the (pre-determined) end of the blessing
         and the consolation be told to them, but it was concealed
         from him; and since it was concealed from him, he blessed
         them according to their good work.
  II RM from him. They expected that he... blessed [each one of]
         them.]   from him.   They expected that he was going to
         tell them everything that was destined to happen to them
         in the end of days.   After the mystery was revealed to
         him it was hidden from him.   He turned and blessed them;

Gen. 49:1 (cont.)

> he blessed each one of them according to the interpre-
> tation of his blessing.

Gen. 49:18

> Our father Jacob said: Not to the redemption of Gideon,
> son of Joash, does my soul look, which was a redemption of an
> hour; and not to the redemption of Samson, son of Manoah,
> does my soul look, which was a transitory redemption; but my
> soul looks to his redemption, which you said you would bring
> to your people, the house of Israel. To you, to your redemp-
> tion do I look, O Lord.

> II RM Not to the redemption...do I look, O Lord.] [said]
> when he saw Gideon the son of Joash and Samson the son
> of Manoah: I do not look...because his redemption is
> the redemption of an hour; and I do not yearn...be-
> cause (his) redemption is the redemption of an instant.
> For your redemption do I look and yearn, Lord of all
> the worlds, because your redemption is an eternal re-
> demption.[1]

> I RM which you said]   morphological change
> I RM To you, to your redemption]   To him, to his redemption
> I LM O Lord.]   who is the Lord.

[1]M is a continuous reading.

Ex. 3:14

> And the Lord said to Moses: I am who I am (Hebrew). And
> he said: Thus shall you say to the children of Israel: The
> one who spoke and the world was created (lit., was from the
> beginning) and shall yet say to it: Be, and it will be -- he
> sent me to you.

> I LM the Lord/to Moses...he sent]   the Word of the Lord
> [said] to Moses: He who said to the world: Be, and it
> was; and shall yet say to it: Be, and it will be; --
> and he said: Thus shall you say to the children of
> Israel: I AM sent

> II RM I am who...to you.]   I existed before the world was
> created and I have existed since the world was created.
> I am he who was your help in the Egyptian captivity,
> and I am he who shall be your help in every generation.
> And he said: Thus shall you say to the children of
> Israel: I AM sent me to you.

Ex. 4:13

> And he said: I beseech by mercies from before you,

Ex. 4:13 (cont.)
O Lord, send, I pray, by the hand of the one for whom it is
fitting to be sent.

  I RM by mercies...send]   from you, my Lord, send

  I LM by the hand...to be sent.] by the hand of the one for
         whom it is fitting to be sent. (grammatical change)

 II RM by the hand...to be sent.] by the hand of the King
         Messiah who is destined to be sent. (Reading ˙ over א
         as sign to ignore the א.)

Ex. 9:14
    For this time I am sending all my plagues against you
(lit., upon your heart) and against your ruler(s) and your
people, so that you may know that there is none like me in all
the earth.

  I LM am sending...against you] am letting loose my plagues
         against all of them, and they will reach to your heart

 II RM my plagues...and against your ruler(s)] the plague of
         my punishment upon the heart of Pharaoh and against
         your servant(s)

  I LM like me] like the Word of the Lord

Ex. 9:20
    Whoever feared from before the Lord among the rulers of
Pharaoh made his servants and his cattle take refuge within
the house.

  I RM [Whoever] feared] He who feared

 II LM Whoever feared...the Lord] Job, who feared the com-
         mandments of the Lord

    RM the rulers] the servants

 II RM his cattle/within the house.] his flocks [take
         refuge] within his house.

Ex. 10:28
    And Pharaoh said to him: Go from beside me (text, him).
Do not speak one of these harsh words before me again. Truly,
I prefer to die than hear your words. Take heed that my
anger does not become strong against you, and I deliver you
into the hands of the people who sought your life and they
kill you.

  I LM Do not speak...Take heed] Take heed

  I LM and I deliver you...and they kill you.] saying, are
         not these harsh words which you say to me? Truly, I
         prefer to die than listen to your words. Take heed
         that my anger does not become strong against you, and
         I deliver you into the hands of these people who seek

Ex. 10:28 (cont.)
    your life in order to kill you.
II LM your words. Take heed]   these words. So, he said to
       him: Take heed

Ex. 13:8
    And you shall tell your sons on that day, saying: Be-
cause of the commandment of unleavened bread the Lord made us
victorious in battle when he brought us, redeemed, from Egypt.
II LM Because...from Egypt.]   Because of this commandment of
       unleavened bread and bitter herbs and this flesh of the
       Passover the Lord worked signs for me when I came out
       from Egypt.
 I RM the Lord/us...when he brought us]   the Word of the
       Lord [worked] signs for us when he brought them

Ex. 14:3
    And Pharaoh will say concerning the people, the children
of Israel: They have gone astray on the way; Baal Zephon, my
idol, has barred against them the passes of the wilderness.
II RM And Pharaoh will say...Israel...Baal Zephon, my idol]
       Pharaoh is surely going to say to Dathan and Abiram,
       who remained in Egypt, concerning the children of Is-
       rael: [They have gone astray on the way;][1] my idol,
       Peor, etc.
II RM They have gone astray on the way]   They are locked up
       on the land
 I RM [They] have gone astray...of the wilderness.]   They
       have gone astray on the way; the idol of Zephon has
       barred against them the passes of the wilderness.
[1]See following M, which, in the Ms, follows "etc.".

Ex. 14:20
    And it went in between the camp of the Egyptians and the
camps of Israel, and the cloud was half dark and half light,
the dark casting darkness upon the Egyptians and the light
(casting light) upon Israel all night; and neither one approached the other to fight all night.
 I LM half dark...and neither]   half light and half dark,
       the light casting light upon Israel and the dark cast-
       ing darkness upon the Egyptians and neither
II RM upon Israel...to fight all night.]   illumined Israel
       (through) the night. Neither camp approached the
       other, but the ministering angels (lit., the angels of
       the service) did not say the service all night.

Ex. 14:20 (cont.)
   RM night]   the night
 I LM to fight]   to engage in battle

Ex. 15:25
   And he prayed before the Lord, and the Lord showed him a
tree; and the Word of the Lord took from it a word of the Law
and threw (it) into the midst of the water, and the water was
made sweet.   There he gave him statutes and judgments and there
he tested him.
 I RM And he prayed]   and Moses prayed
 I RM the Lord(2)]   the Word of the Lord
II LM a tree; and/ took...into the midst of the water]   an
           oleander tree; and he wrote on it the distinguished name
           and threw (it) into the water
 I LM [a tree] and/took...and/was made sweet.]   an oleander
           [tree]; and he cast (it) into the midst of the water and
           [the water] was made sweet.
 I LM he gave him]   the Word of the Lord showed him
   RM he tested him.]   he tested him with his tenth trial.

Ex. 17:7
   And he called the name of the place His Temptation and His
Contentions, because the children of Israel had contended, and
because they had tested the Lord, saying: Does the glory of the
Shekinah of the Lord truly dwell among us, or not?
II LM His Temptation...the Lord]   House of Temptation and Con-
           tention, because the children of Israel [contended] and
           because the Lord tempted them
 I RM had contended]   orthographic change
 I RM because they had tested]   morphological change
 I RM glory]   grammatical change

Ex. 19:3
   And Moses went up to seek instruction from before the Lord,
and the Word (dibberah) of the Lord called to him from the moun-
tain, saying: Thus shall you say to those of the house of Jacob
and (thus) shall you tell the tribe(s) of the children of Israel.
 I RM to seek]   orthographic change
 I LM to those of the house of Jacob]   to the men of the house
           of Jacob
II RM to those of the house of Jacob...of the children of Isra-
           el.]   to the women of the house of Jacob and (thus)

Ex. 19:3 (cont.)
>   shall you tell the men of the house of Israel.

Ex. 19:18

>   And Mount Sinai, all of it, was smoking because the glory
of the Shekinah of the Lord was revealed upon it in fire; and
the smoke went up like the smoke of a furnace and the whole
mountain shook violently.

II RM   was smoking; or because/ was revealed...of a furnace]
>   was shaken and was filled with the splendor of the glory
of the Shekinah of the Lord; and the smoke went up, rising and circling, like the smoke of a furnace

 I LM   in fire...violently.]   in a flame of fire; and the smoke
>   went up like the rising and circling of the smoke of a
furnace, and all the people who were in the camp trembled.

Ex. 20:25

>   And if you build an altar of stones to my name you shall
not build them of hewn stones, because you pass over them iron
(of) which a sword is made and defile them.

 I RM   of hewn stones...them.]   of hewn stone because from it,
>   iron, a sword is made.   If you pass iron over it you de-
file it.

II LM   (of) which a sword...them.]   from it the wars of death
>   are waged toward all.   Take care that you do not un-
sheath your sword upon it lest you (that you may not) defile it.

Ex. 22:12(13)

>   If it has truly been torn in pieces, let witnesses bring
(it); he shall not make restitution for what has been killed.

 I RM   [it has been] truly...witnesses]   it has truly been
>   slain, let him bring some of its parts as evidence

II RM   let/bring ... make restitution]   let him take him to the body
>   of the animal which has been cut in pieces; he shall not
make restitution

Ex. 24:11

>   And he did not stretch out his hand to the young men of the
children of Israel, and they saw the glory of the Shekinah of
the Lord; and they rejoiced over their sacrifices which were received as if they ate and drank.

 I LM   to the young men]   to the lords

Ex. 24:11 (cont.)

II RM to...Israel]   to Nadab and Abihu, the handsome young
          men who had been appointed over the children of Israel
    RM the glory of the Shekinah of the Lord]   the God of
          Israel
  I LM they rejoiced...as if]   they appeared as if

Ex. 32:5

    And Aaron saw Hur, the prophet, before it and was afraid;
and he built an altar before it.   And Aaron uttered a procla-
mation and said: A feast before the Lord tomorrow.
  I RM And [Aaron] saw...the prophet, before it]   And Aaron
          saw Hur sacrificing before it
 II RM And [Aaron] uttered a proclamation...tomorrow.]   And
          Aaron uttered a proclamation and said: May it be the
          will (of God) that the sacrifice be like the feast of
          evildoers before the Lord tomorrow.
  I LM uttered a proclamation]   called out

Ex. 33:11

    And the Lord spoke with Moses, speech opposite speech (in
dialogue), as one speaks with his friend.   And he returned to
the camp; but his attendant, Joshua, son of Nun, a youth, did
not go out from the midst of the camp.
  I LM the Lord]   the Word of the Lord
  I LM opposite]   morphological change
  I LM [as] one speaks] [as] one will speak
  I LM did not go out from the midst of]   a boy, did not move
          from the midst of
 II LM did not go out...the camp.]   an adolescent, did not
          leave the interior of the tent of the house of instruc-
          tion.

Ex. 36:16

    And he joined five curtains by themselves and six cur-
tains by themselves.
 II RM And he joined...by themselves.] And he joined five
          curtains together to correspond to the five books of
          the Law, and six curtains together to correspond to the
          six orders of the Mishnah.
  I LM five curtains]   the five curtains
  I LM six curtains]   the six curtains

Lev. 4:22

    If the priest who is in office sins and does carelessly anything of all the commandments of the Lord his God which are not permitted to be done, then he becomes guilty.

II LM If...sins]   At the time that the master sins

 I RM who is in office...and does]   who rules becomes guilty
      and does

   LM commandments]   synonym

 I RM which are not]   morphological change

Lev. 8:34

    As one has done this day, the Lord has commanded that you do (lit., to do) to make atonement for you.

II LM As...for you.]   As one has done this (day), even so the Lord has commanded that you do (lit., to do) for seven days before the Day of Atonement in order to make atonement for you.

 I LM has done]   morphological change

 I RM the Lord]   the Word of the Lord

Lev. 9:6

    And Moses said: This is the thing which the Lord commanded that you should do, and the glory of the Shekinah of the Lord will be revealed to you.

 I RM the Lord]   the Word of the Lord

II RM which the Lord commanded...the Shekinah of the Lord/[you.]]
    which the Lord commanded that you should do: Remove the evil inclination from your hearts, and at once the glory of the Shekinah of the Lord will be revealed to you.

 I LM and/ will be revealed]   grammatical change

 I RM glory]   morphological change

Lev. 9:22

    And Aaron raised his hands in prayer over the people and blessed them, and he came down after offering the sin offering and the burnt offering and the offering of holy things.

II RM and [Aaron] raised...after offering] And Aaron stood upon the platform and raised his hands towards the people and blessed them, and he finished making

 I LM offering the sin offering]   grammatical change

Lev. 10:2

    And fire came forth from before the Lord and devoured them,
and they died before the Lord.

II RM fire/ from...before the Lord.] a column of fire [came
       forth] from before the Lord, and it was divided into two
       threads, and from two into four; and it went up into
       their nostrils, and they died by arrows of fire before
       the Lord.

 I LM before (2)] by the Word (of)

Lev. 14:40

    And then the priest shall command that they take out the
stones in which the disease is and throw them outside the city
into an unclean place.

II RM that they take out...to an unclean place.] that they
       throw the stones in which the disease is outside the city;
       because he himself built the house with violence and op-
       pression, they shall be thrown into an unclean place.

 I LM which [the disease is]] which there is [the disease]

Lev. 14:53

    And he shall send the living bird outside the city to the
open (lit., face of the) field, and he shall make atonement for
the house and it shall be clean.

II RM And he shall send...and it shall be clean.] And he
       shall send forth the living bird outside the city to the
       open field, and it shall be (that) if it is liable to be
       struck again with leprosy, the bird will return to him.
       And the priest shall make atonement for the house and it
       shall be clean.

 I LM the/bird outside] the bird which is alive outside

Lev. 16:3

    According to this order, Aaron shall enter to serve within
the house of dwelling, with a young bull for the sin offering
and a ram for the burnt offering.

II LM According...dwelling] According to this commandment
       Aaron shall enter on the Day of Atonement into the holy
       place

 I LM ram] one ram

 I RM to serve...dwelling] and he shall serve in the sanc-
       tuary

Lev. 16:8

And Aaron shall cast lots upon the two goats; one lot
for the Name of the Word of the Lord, and one lot for Azazel.

I RM   lot]   orthographic change

I LM   and/ lot] orthographic change

II LM one lot...for Azazel.]   one lot for the Name of the Lord,
      to atone for the people, and one lot to let go to the
      desert of Tsok (or, the precipitous desert) for Azazel.

Lev. 16:34

And this shall be an everlasting statute for you, to atone
for the children of Israel from all their sins one time in the
year.   And he did as the Lord commanded Moses.

I LM   everlasting]   grammatical change

I RM   one...year]   one time in every year

II LM time in the year]   time in the year on the tenth day of
      the month of Tishri.

I LM   the Lord]   the Word of the Lord

Lev. 18:29

As for everyone who does any of these abominations, the
persons who do (them) shall be destroyed from the midst of
their people.

I RM   [everyone] who does]   [all] who do

II LM who does...their people.]   who do such things against the
      Law [shall be destroyed] from the life of the world to
      come and there will be no portion for them in the midst
      of their people.

I RM   persons...their people.]   the person who does (them)
      [shall be destroyed] from the midst of their people.

Lev. 19:14

Do not curse one who does not hear and before one who does
not see do not put a stumbling block,   but fear your God;
thus says the Lord.

I RM   Do not curse...but fear]   And do not curse the deaf
      person because he does not hear; do not place a curse
      before the stranger who is like the blind man, but fear

II LM and before one...stumbling block]   and before the
      stranger who is like the blind man do not put a stum-
      bling block

Lev. 21:4

The leader who is among his people shall not defile himself lest he desecrate the priesthood.

II RM   [The leader/] defile himself...the priesthood.] The high priest
         shall [not] defile himself even for his own people, to
         desecrate the high priesthood on his account (on their
         account?).

 I LM   who is among his people...the priesthood.] who is
         among your people [shall not defile himself] to dese-
         crate the crown of the priesthood.

Lev. 23:29

For any person who eats on a fast day and does not fast
at the time of the fast day of atonement shall be destroyed
from the midst of the people.

II RM   person...and does not fast]   person (lit., son of
         man) who does not fast

 I LM   eats on a fast day]   is able to fast

 I RM   at the time...of atonement]   on the fast day of atone-
         ment

Lev. 27:29

No one consecrated, who has been separated from men (lit.,
son of man), shall be redeemed; he shall surely die.

II RM   No one...die.]   No one set apart to be destroyed from
         men (lit., son of man) shall be redeemed with money,
         but with burnt offerings, and with sacrifices of holy
         things and with supplications for mercy before the
         Lord; because such a one is deserving of death. He
         shall surely be killed.

 I LM   men...shall/die.]   the sons of men shall not be re-
         deemed; he shall surely be killed.

Nu. 4:20

But they shall not go in to look when the High Priest is
covering all the vessels of the sanctuary, lest they die.

 I RM   they shall [not] go in]   the Levites shall [not] go in

 I LM   [the High Priest] is covering...they die.]   the priests
         are covering the vessels of the sanctuary, lest they die.

II RM   when/is covering...the sanctuary]   when the priests
         are covering the vessels of the sanctuary

Nu. 10:29

    And Moses said to Hobab, son of Reuel the Midianite, Moses'
father-in-law: We are moving to the place of which the Lord
said: I will give it to you. Come with us, and we will do
well by you (lit., do you good); for the Lord has said by his
Word that he would bring good and consolation upon Israel.
  I RM the Lord/ it...upon Israel.]   the Word of the Lord
         [said]: I will give it to you.   Come with us, and we
         will do well by you, for the Word of the Lord has spo-
         ken (decreed) good for Israel.
 II LM the Lord (2)/ by his Word...Israel.]   it has been spo-
         ken from before the Lord from the days of the world
         (from eternity) to bring good upon Israel.

Nu. 12:12

    I pray, do not let Miriam be defiled in the tent like one
dead; for she would now be like the child that passed nine
months in its mother's womb, in water and in heat, and was not
injured; but, when the time arrived for (its) coming forth into
the world, its flesh was half-consumed. Even so, when we were
enslaved in Egypt and wandering and tossed about in the desert,
our sister witnessed our servitude; and--when the time has
arrived to take possession of the land--why should she be
parted from us? Pray for this dead flesh that it may live.
Why should her merit pass (from us)?
 II RM I pray...parted]   I pray, do not let Miriam our sister
         be like the pregnant woman who was struck with leprosy
         during her pregnancy and, when the time arrived to give
         birth, the child was dead in her womb.   Has not Miriam
         our sister suffered with us?   And now when the time has
         arrived to see the consolation, let her not, I pray, be
         separated (from us).
  I LM defiled...womb]   a leper in the tent like one dead,
         for she would be like a child who was in the womb
  I LM into the world...consumed]   from the womb of its mother
         [its flesh was half] consumed
  I RM Even so, when we were...and when]   Thus Miriam our
         sister was tossed about with us in the desert and was
         with us in our trouble, but when
  I RM the time...why]   the time [has arrived] to enter the
         land of Israel, why
  I RM Pray]   + now
  I RM this [dead body] that it may live...her merit   [pass

Nu. 12:12 (cont.)

(from us?)]]   this [dead body]   that it may live, that
we may not lose her merit.

Nu. 12:16

Although Miriam the prophetess had become liable to be
stricken with leprosy, there is nevertheless great (reward) for
the sages and for those who keep the Law. For the little good
that a man has done he receives for it a great reward.   Thus,
because Miriam stationed herself on the river bank to know
what would become of Moses, Israel -- they were sixty myriads,
which are equivalent to eighty legions -- and the cloud of
glory and the well did not move nor go forward from their places until the time that Miriam the prophetess was healed of
her leprosy.   The people went forward from Hatseroth and en-
camped in the wilderness of Paran.

I LM   Although]   morphological change
II LM Although...their places, or, from her leprosy.]   And
       because Miriam waited for Moses by the river for one
       hour, the Shekinah of the Lord of the world and the
       tabernacle and all Israel waited for her seven days
I LM   he receives]   pronoun omitted
I LM   which are]   morphological change
I RM   nor go forward]   grammatical change
I LM   of her leprosy/went forward]   of her leprosy.   And
       after the prophetess was healed of her leprosy, after
       this [the people] went forward

Nu. 16:1

And Korah, the son of Izhar, son of Kohath, son of Levi,
and Dathan and Abiram, sons of Eliab, and On, the son of Peleth,
sons of Reuben, made a division.

I LM   And/made a division.]   And [names] took counsel and
       made a division.
II RM And Korah/made a division.]   And [names] took evil
       counsel and quarreled.
  LM   sons of (2)]   from the tribe of the sons of

Nu. 16:30

But if the Lord creates a new thing and the earth opens
its mouth and swallows them and all that belongs to them, and
they go down alive to Sheol, then you will know that these
men blasphemed before the Lord.

II RM But if...opens]   If death in the world has been cre-
       ated from the days of the world (from eternity) for
       this world, behold, it is good; if not, let it be

Nu. 16:30 (cont.)
>   created now and let [the earth] open
>   I LM   the Lord/opens]   the Word of the Lord [creates a new
>   thing and the earth] opens
>   I LM   swallows]   orthographic change
>   I RM   alive to Sheol]   grammatical and orthographic changes

Nu. 20:17
>   Let us, we pray, pass through your land. We will not
>   pass through fields or vineyards, and we will not drink the
>   water of the wells.   We will walk the King's Highway; we
>   will not turn either to the right or to the left until the
>   time that we shall have passed through your territory.
>   I RM   We will [not] pass through fields...we will not turn]
>   We will [not] commit violence, and we will not seduce
>   virgins, and we will not seek men's wives. We will
>   travel on the King's Road; we will not turn
>   II RM   We will [not] pass through fields...We will walk]
>   We will [not] seduce virgins and we will not violate
>   men's wives; in the way of the King of the world we
>   will travel;
>   I RM   either to the right or to the left]   either (not) to
>   the right or (and not) to the left   (continues I RM)

Nu. 33:9
>   They went out from Moriah and came to Elim.   In Elim
>   were twelve springs of water corresponding to the twelve
>   tribes of Israel and seventy date-palm trees corresponding to
>   the seventy elders of the children of Israel; and they en-
>   camped there.
>   I RM   to Elim]   grammatical change
>   I LM   twelve...corresponding to (1)]   morphological and
>   grammatical changes
>   I RM   twelve (2)]   morphological change
>   II RM   twelve...tribes]   morphological and vocabulary changes
>   I LM   elders of the children of]   synonym for "elders"
>   II RM   there]   + by the sea

Deut. 7:7
>   Not because of your being more in number than all (other)
>   nations did the Lord choose you, for you are a people fewest
>   in number of all peoples.
>   LM   your/number]   your numerousness (possibly a correction
>   to the text)
>   II LM   [because of]/number...fewest]   because of your

Deut. 7:7 (cont.)

       pre-eminence did the Word of the Lord care for you and
       choose you, but because you are humble

 I RM the Lord]   the Word of the Lord

   RM fewest]   least

Deut. 8:9

     A land in which you will eat bread without poverty. You
will not want for anything in it. A land the stones of which
are hard and polished like iron and from whose hills you may
dig copper.

   RM poverty] want

   LM bread] + and food

 I RM You will [not] want...copper.] You will not want for
       anything in it. A land the stones of which are pol-
       ished like iron and the mountains bright like copper.

II LM the stones of which...copper.] whose wise men are
       strong like iron and the teachers tenacious like copper.

Deut. 10:20

     From before the Lord your God you shall fear, and before
him you shall pray, and you shall be well versed in the teach-
ing of the Law, and by his name, the Holy One, you shall swear
and live.

II RM From before...and live.] Before God, your God, you
       shall pray; and you shall serve him with sacrifice; and
       in his name you shall speak truthfully.

 I LM you shall fear...the Holy One] you shall fear, and
       you shall serve him, and in the name of the Word

Deut. 12:9

     Because you have not yet come to the rest and the inheri-
tance which the Lord your God gives you.

 I LM you have/come] synonym

II RM to the rest and the inheritance] to the sanctuary
       which is called 'house of rest' and to the land of
       Israel which is called 'the inheritance'

 I LM to the rest and the inheritance] to the sanctuary and
       to the inheritance

Deut. 14:1

     Beloved are you before the Lord your God. You shall not
make wounds, wounds of the kind required in idolatry, and you

Deut. 14:1 (cont.)

shall not put a mark upon your forehead on behalf of the souls
of the dead.

II LM   you shall [not] make...in idolatry]   you shall [not]
        have anything to do with wounds, wounds for doing evil
 I RM   in idolatry]   grammatical change
 I LM   a mark upon]   baldness above
 I RM   on behalf of]   to defile

Deut. 17:8

        If a matter for judgment should be unclear to you be-
tween the blood of virginity and the blood of homicide, between
the laws of property and the laws of life, between the affliction of leprosy and the affliction of scall, (any) quarrels in
your cities, you shall arise and go up to the place where the
Lord, your God, chooses.

 I RM   for judgment...affliction]   for distinction in judgment
        between the blood of homicide, the blood of virginity,
        the affliction
II LM   blood (1)...in your cities]   pure blood and defiled
        blood, between laws of life and laws of property, be-
        tween the actual affliction of leprosy and the supposed
        affliction of leprosy, dissension in your schoolhouses
 I RM   quarrels]   wrangling

Deut. 20:6

        And who is the man who has planted a vineyard and has not
gathered in its fruit?   Let him go and return to his house
lest he die in battle and another man pick it.

    LM   is]   is this [man]
 I LM   gathered in...and return]   picked it?   Let him go and
        return
II LM   gathered in its fruit?]   redeemed it from the priest?
 I RM   pick]   grammatical change
II RM   pick it]   redeem it

Deut. 22:3

        And thus shall you do to his ass and thus shall you do to
his garment and thus shall you do to every lost article which
he loses (lit., which is lost from him) and you find.   It is
not permissible for you to keep the article (lit., to cover
your eye from it.)

 I LM   And thus (1)]   Thus (synonym)

Deut. 22:3 (cont.)

I RM And thus (2)]   synonym

I RM to his garment]   to his festive suit

II RM lost article]   lost article of your brother

I RM which is lost]   orthographic and morphological changes

II LM lost from him]   orthographic and grammatical changes

I RM it]   orthographic change

I RM permissible for you to keep the article]   permissible
       for you to hide it

Deut. 22:12

   You shall make fringes for yourselves on the four corners
of your cloaks with which you cover yourselves.

I RM You shall make fringes]   You shall make borders of
       fringes (zizith)

II RM fringes...you cover yourselves.]   You shall make bor-
       ders of fringes for yourself (upon) the four corners of
       the shawl (tallith) with which you cover yourself.

I LM corners of your cloaks]   borders of [your] cloaks

I LM you cover yourselves]   you make a cover

Deut. 23:2(1)

   He who is cut or castrated shall not enter into the as-
sembly of the Lord.

II RM [He who is cut] or castrated]   [He] whose testicles
       [are cut] or whose male member is damaged

I LM He who is cut or castrated]   Any one who is cut or
       anyone who is castrated

Deut. 24:6

   My people, children of Israel, you shall not bind bride-
grooms and brides by charms, and you shall not take a millstone
as a pledge, because every one who does so takes lives in
pledge.

I LM My people...takes/ [in pledge.]]   You shall not take
       the upper or lower millstone in pledge because the
       pledge is a necessity of life, and you shall not bind
       bridegrooms and brides because any one who does this
       wipes out the life of the world to come.

II LM you shall not...takes/[in pledge.]]   you are not permit-
       ted to take as a pledge the upper and lower millstone.   For

Deut. 24:6 (cont.)

       that reason you are not permitted to join bridegrooms
and brides who are related because he (who does so) is
reckoned as a shedder of innocent blood and his life
is required in pledge.

Deut. 24:14

  You shall not oppress the hired servant who is poor and
needy, whether he is one of your brothers or one of your so-
journers who is in your land in your cities.
II RM You shall [not] oppress]   synonym
 I RM You shall [not] oppress]   grammatical change
 I RM who (2)]   grammatical change

Deut. 25:2

  And it shall be, if the guilty man is condemned to be
flogged as punishment, then the judge shall have him lie down
and shall have him flogged in his presence: in number: according to his guilt.
II RM if...[the judge] shall have him lie down]   if the
         wicked man [is condemned] by the judge to be flogged,
         then let him put him in stocks as punishment
 I RM the guilty man...lie down]   the guilty must be
         flogged, then [the judge] shall have him lie down

Deut. 29:14(15)

  Because all the generations who have arisen before us
from of old up to now are standing with us here this day before the Lord our God, and all the generations who are destined to arise after us are standing with us here this day.
 I RM who have arisen...old]   who arose from the days of
         the world (from the beginning)
II LM who have arisen...this day.]   who are standing here
         with us, standing this day before the Lord our God,
         and all the generations which are from the days of
         the world (from the beginning) and those who are not
         yet created, all of them, are standing with us this
         day.
 I RM after us]   morphological change
 I LM are standing (2)] is standing

2. <u>Two</u> <u>Sets</u> <u>of</u> <u>Variants</u>: <u>Similar</u>

Gen. 29:22

Laban gathered together all the people of the place and
prepared a meal. Laban answered and said to them: Seven
years now this pious man has dwelt among us. Our wells have
not diminished; our troughs have increased. And now, what advice do you give that we may make him dwell among us here sev-
en years more? They gave him deceptive advice: to marry him
to Leah instead of Rachel.

I RM Seven years . . . They gave] This man has dwelt among
     us seven years of days. Our springs have been blessed
     and our flocks of sheep have increased. But now give
     me advice. What should we do with him so that he will
     dwell among us another seven years? And the people of
     the land arose and gave

  LM what [advice] do you give...here [seven years] more?]
     Give advice that will make him dwell here among us yet
     [seven years].

I RM deceptive/ to marry him] deceptive [advice]: that
     they would have him marry

Gen. 35:9

O God of eternity -- may his name be blessed for ever and
forever -- your patience, your fairness, your righteousness,
your might, and your glory will never pass away. You taught
us to bless the bridegroom and the bride from Adam and his wife;
and, again, you taught us to visit the sick from our father
Abraham, the righteous, when you were revealed to him in the
Valley of the Vision while he was still suffering from circum-
cision. And, again, you taught us to comfort those who mourn
from our father Jacob, the righteous -- the way of the world
befell Deborah, the foster-mother of Rebekah, his mother; and
Rachel died beside him on his journey. And he sat down crying
aloud; and he wept and lamented and was desolate. But you, by
your good mercies, were revealed to him and you blessed him.
(With) the blessings of those who mourn you blessed him, and
you comforted him; for so the Scripture explains and says: And
the Lord was revealed to Jacob a second time when he came from
Paddan-aram; and he blessed him.

  LM O God] O God, etc.

I LM your patience...to bless] you taught us fitting com-
     mandments and beautiful statutes. You taught us to

Gen. 35:9 (cont.)

        bless, etc.

I LM   and, again, you taught (1)]   for so the Scripture ex-
        plains: the Word of the Lord blessed them and the
        Word of the Lord said to them: Be strong and multiply
        and fill the earth and subdue it.   And, again, you
        taught

I LM   while he was still...for so the Scripture explains and
        says]   and you had commanded him to circumcise his
        foreskin.   And he sat down by the door of his tent in
        the heat of the day; for so the Scripture explains and
        says: And the Word of the Lord was revealed to him in
        the Valley of the Vision.   And, again, you taught us
        to bless those who mourn from our father Jacob, the
        righteous, when the ways of the world were revealed to
        him on his return from Paddan-aram when it (death) be-
        fell Deborah, the foster-mother of Rebekah, his mother,
        and Rachel died beside him on the journey.   And our
        father Jacob sat down, crying aloud and lamenting and
        mourning and weeping.   And you, Lord of all the world,
        the Lord, according to the measure of your good mercies
        you were revealed to him; and you comforted him and
        (with) the blessings of those who mourn you blessed him
        on account of his mother.   That is why the Scripture
        explains and says:

  RM   (With) the blessings/you blessed him...and says/was re-
        vealed]   And (with) the blessing of the one who mourns
        you blessed him and comforted him; for so the Scripture
        explains and says: Because [the Lord] was revealed

  RM   a second time...and blessed him; or, add to verse]
        And, again, you taught us to bury the dead from our
        master, Moses, whom the Lord of the ages, the Lord, may
        his name be blessed forever, buried.

 I BM   the Lord...when he came]   the Word of the Lord [was
        revealed] a second time to Jacob when he came

Gen. 49:22

        My son who has grown: Joseph, my son, who has grown and
become strong.   And it is your destiny to become stronger. I
compare you, Joseph my son, to a vineyard planted by springs
of water that sends its roots into the earth and breaks through
the hardness of all the rocks and sends its branches high above

Gen. 49:22 (cont.)

and overshadows all the trees.   So you have overshadowed by
your wisdom, Joseph, my son, all the magicians of the Egyptians
and all their wise men.   When they mounted you on the second
chariot of Pharaoh and proclaimed before you: Long live the
father of the king, who is great in wisdom and young in years;
then the daughters of the kings and governors would gaze upon
you from the windows and listen to you from the lattices.
They would throw before you chains, rings, necklaces, brooches,
and every article of gold, hoping that you would raise your
eyes and look at one of them.   Far (be it) from you Joseph,
my son.   You did not raise your eyes and look at one of them.
The daughters of kings and governors would say to one another
that this is Joseph, the pious man, who has not gone after the
visions of his eyes or after the imaginations of his heart.
They cause man (lit., son of man) to perish from the world.
Therefore, there will arise from you two tribes, Manasseh and
Ephraim.   They will receive a portion and an inheritance with
their brothers in the division of the land.

    LM   And it is...to become stronger.]   And also, it is your
        destiny to become strong.

    LM   of water]   morphological change

    LM   and breaks]   and breaks ::

I LM   and breaks the hardness of all]   and splits the hard-
        ness of all

    RM   you have overshadowed]   you have taught

    LM   and all their wise men]   and all their magicians

I LM   of Pharaoh]   which is Pharaoh's

    LM   and young]   synonym

    LM   and/from the lattices...at one of them.]   from the
        lattices, and they would watch you from the beginning
        and would cast upon you chains, necklaces and brooches
        to see if you would raise your face and look at one of
        them.

    RM   You did [not] raise your eyes and look]   You did [not]
        raise your face and you did not look

    LM   of them.   The daughters of/would [say]]   of them in or-
        der not to be in her company in Gehenna in the world to
        come.   And the daughters of [kings and governors] would
        [say]

I RM   who has not]   morphological change

    RM   They cause/to perish...Therefore]   since they expel man
        from this world.   Therefore

I LM   They cause [man] to perish from the world.]   They cause
        man (lit., the son of man) to perish from the midst of
        the world.

Gen. 50:16

    And the tribes commanded Bilhah, the foster-mother of
Joseph, to say to him: Your father commanded before he died,
saying:

I RM   the foster-mother...Your father]   the handmaid of Ra-
       chel, to say to Joseph: Your father

    LM   Bilhah...Your father]   Bilhah to say to Joseph: Your
       father
I LM   he died]   he was gathered

Ex. 2:12

    And he looked here and there and saw that no one was
there, and he killed the Egyptian and hid him in the sand.

    RM   here and there...in the sand.]   in the spirit of proph-
       ecy in this world and in the world to come, and he saw,
       and behold, there was no innocent man to go forth from
       him. And he smote the Egyptian and buried him in the
       sand.

I LM   [looked] here and there...in the sand.] Moses in the
       holy spirit (lit., spirit of holiness) [looked into]
       both worlds and he saw, and behold, there was no pros-
       elyte destined to arise from that Egyptian. And he
       smote the Egyptian and buried him in the sand.

Ex. 12:30

    And Pharaoh arose in the night, he and all his rulers and
all the Egyptians; and there was a great cry in Egypt because
there was not a house there where there were no dead.

    RM   his rulers]   his servants
    LM   Egyptians]   orthographic change
    LM   a house...dead.]   a house of Egypt in which there was
       not a dead (one) of Egypt.
    RM   a house...dead.]   a house in which there was not dead
       one of the Egyptians.

Ex. 13:17

    And it came to pass when Pharaoh let the people go that
the Lord did not lead them (by) the way of the land of the
Philistines although that was near because, the Lord said:
Lest the heart of the people break when they see battle-array;
and they return to Egypt.

    LM   when/ let/ go]   at the time that [Pharaoh] let [the
       people] go

Ex. 13:17 (cont.)

   RM the Lord/the way of]   the Word of the Lord [did not
          lead them (by)] the road of
   RM it was]   grammatical change
   RM the Lord]   the Word of the Lord
   LM the Lord [said:] Lest]   the Word of the Lord in
          thought [said:] Lest

Ex. 15:7

   And in the greatness of your exaltation you destroy the
enemies of your people. You send on them the might of your
anger; you devour them just as fire burns in straw.

   RM And in the greatness...enemies] And in the greatness
          of your might you break the walls of the enemies
   LM you destroy the enemies] you break the walls of the
          enemies
   LM you devour them] and you do violence to them

Ex. 31:2

   See, Moses, that I have appointed and called by the good
name of Rabban, Bezalel, son of Uri, son of Hur, of the tribe
of the sons of Judah.

 I LM that I have appointed and called] behold, I have
          anointed (honored?) and called
   LM that I have appointed....of Rabban] that I have hon-
          nored (made great) and called by a good name from the
          days of the world (from eternity)

Lev. 17:10

   And any man of the house of Israel or of the strangers
that sojourn among them who eats any blood, I will set my
strong anger against the soul that eats the blood, and I will
destroy him from the midst of his people.

   RM of the house] of the children
   LM among them] among you
   RM eats any blood...the blood] eats any blood, I will
          set my angry face against the soul that eats the blood
   LM any blood...my [strong] anger] any blood, I will set
          my angry face

Nu. 11:7

   And the manna was like the seed of coriander, and its
appearance like the mirror of (identical to) bdellium.

Nu. 11:7 (cont.)

    LM was/ coriander]   was white [like the seed of] coriander
    LM like the seed of coriander]   white like the capsule of
        the coriander seed
    RM and its appearance like the mirror of bdellium]   and
        its appearance like the appearance of bdellium

Nu. 21:15

    When Israel was crossing through the valley of the Arnon,
the Amorites hid themselves within the caves of the valley of
the Arnon, saying: When the children of Israel are crossing,
we will go out against them and kill them.   But the Lord of
all the worlds signalled -- the Lord, who knows what is in the
hearts (minds) and before him is revealed what is in the kid-
neys (emotions) -- he signalled to the mountains, and their
heads (summits) were joined one to the other, and the heads of
their mighty men were crushed; and the valleys overflowed with
their blood.   But they (Israel) did not know the sign and
mighty act that the Lord had done for them in the valley.   And
afterward they (the mountains) were separated and went to their
places.   And Lechaiath, the city that was not among their op-
pressors, was spared, and behold, it is close to the borders of
the Moabites.

    RM the Amorites hid themselves...Israel]   the Amorites hid
        themselves in the caves, saying to one another: When
        Israel
    RM against them...their heads]   against them
        and destroy them and kill kings together with rulers.
        At that time the Lord signalled to the mountains and
        their heads
    LM and/ overflowed...Lechaiath, the city]   and the valleys
        flowed with their blood.   And Lechaiath, the city
  I LM with their blood...the sign]   with the blood of their
        slain.   But Israel walked above on the tops of the
        mountains and did not know the sign
  I LM in the valley...the city]   in the valley of Arnon.
        And Lechaiath, the city
  I LM of the Moabites.]   orthographic change.

Deut. 18:14

    Because these peoples whom you are destroying are obedient
to those who deceive eyes (magicians) and to those who practise

Deut. 18:14 (cont.)

divinations; but you, my people, children of Israel, the Lord
your God has decreed for you not (to be) like them.

    RM are destroying] synonym

I LM eyes]   the eyes

I RM are [obedient]/ divinations] [obey]/ the divinations

    RM but you/ not (to be) like them.] but you [the Lord
your God has decreed] not (to be) like them.

    LM my people...your God [has decreed for you not (to be)
like them.]]   not thus has the Lord your God decreed
as your share.

Deut. 20:8

    And the officers will continue to speak with the people
and they will say: What man is there who fears because of his
guilt, and his heart is broken on account of his deeds? Let
him go and return to his house lest it (his heart) melt, and
he break the heart of his brothers like his (own) heart.

    LM with]   to

    LM What...like his heart.] Who is the man who is afraid,
and his heart is broken from the guilt which is in his
hands? Let him go and return to his house lest he will
cause the heart of his brothers to break like his heart.

    RM it melt]   grammatical change

    RM like his heart]   morphological change

Deut. 24:15

    On his day you shall give (him) his wage and the sun shall
not go down upon it, because he is poor and for the wage for
(lit., of) his labor he places his life before you (in your
hands). Beware lest he complain against you before the Lord,
lest there may be sin with you.

I RM On his day...upon it] You shall give him his wage each
day (lit., on the day); you shall not let [the sun] go
down upon it

    LM [the sun shall not] go down...before the Lord] Let
[not] the sun go down, because he may bring charges
against you before the Lord

I RM and for the wage...sin [with you.]] and because he is
a hired servant. He has entrusted to you his life.
Let him not cry out against you before the Lord. Take
care lest there may be sin against you.

3. <u>Two</u> <u>Sets</u> <u>of</u> <u>Variants</u>: <u>Unclassified</u>

Gen. 9:21

And he drank of the wine and he became drunk and exposed himself in his tent.

   LM   wine]   synonym

   LM   became drunk]   synonym

   RM   and exposed himself]   and weakened himself

   LM   and exposed himself in his tent.]   Jerush/   and
       stretched himself out in the midst of the tents of the
       Syrians and was despised in the midst of (their?) tents.

Gen. 21:6

And Sarah said: A great joy has been made for me by [lit., from before] the Lord. All who hear will rejoice with me.

   RM A great joy...the Lord.]   My [lit., to me] great joy,
      the Lord has made for me.

   LM A great joy...will rejoice with me.]   The Word of the
      Lord has made for me a great joy.   Everyone who hears
      my voice rejoices for me and will rejoice with me.

Gen. 25:1

And Abraham again took a wife and her name (was) Keturah.

   RM Keturah.]   + She was Hagar who had been bound to him
      from the beginning.

   LM Keturah.]   + She was Hagar who had been tied to him
      from the first.

Gen. 27:8

And now, my son, obey me and go where I command you.

   RM and now]   morphological change

   LM and go where I]   in what I

   RM [where] I]   morphological change

Gen. 32:25 (24)

And Jacob was left alone. And the angel Sariel in the likeness of a man wrestled (with him) and he struggled with (lit., embraced) him until the time that the column of dawn arose.

   RM And/ was left...And/ wrestled; or, And wrestled] And
      [the angel Sariel in the likeness of a man] struggled

   LM And [the angel Sariel in the likeness of a man] wrestled...
      until the time]   And an angel in the likeness of a

Gen. 32:25(24) (cont.)

    man struggled with him until

  RM until the time...dawn [arose.]]   until daybreak.
    (Probably continues preceding M.)

Ex. 8:17(21)

    If (twice) you do not let my people go, behold I will un-
leash against you and against your rulers and against your
people and against the men of your house a swarm (of gnats);
and the houses of the Egyptians will be filled with the swarm
(of gnats), and the land in which they dwell.

  LM if you do not]   you do not
  LM will unleash]   will send
  RM and against your rulers]   against your servants
  RM a swarm (of gnats)]   a swarm (of gnats) and also
  LM [in] which they dwell]   morphological change
  RM in which they dwell]   on which they reside

Ex. 9:30

    And you and your rulers -- I know that you do not yet
fear from before the Lord our God.

  LM And you...[I] know]   And you, Pharaoh, and your ser-
      vants [I] know
  RM that...before]   that until the plagues came upon you
      you did not humble yourselves before
  RM that...fear]   that still [you] did not fear
  LM the Lord]   the Word of the Lord

Ex. 16:17

    And the children of Israel did so; and they gathered,
some more and some less.

  RM some more and some less.]   one tribe more; one tribe
      less.
  LM some more and some less.]   this one and that one,
      this one more and that one less.

Ex. 32:22

    And Aaron said to Moses: Let not the anger of my master
be enkindled; you know the people, that they are evil.

  LM that they [are evil.]]   that the evil inclination has
      power over them (singular in Aramaic) and it has led
      them (singular in Aramaic) to do [evil].
  RM evil.]   contrary.

Ex. 33:8

And whenever Moses went out to the tent all the people got up and stood, each man at the door of his tent, and watched after Moses until he entered his tent.

    RM And whenever...stood]   And when Moses would go out to the tent all the people would arise and stand

    LM went out]   would go out

    RM and watched]   and would watch

    RM until he had entered his tent]   until his entry into his tent

Lev. 11:10

And anything that does not have fins and scales in the seas and in the rivers, of every swarming creature of the waters and of every living thing that is in the waters, they are an abomination to you.

    LM scales]   orthographic change

    RM living [thing]...to you.]   [thing] which is living that is in the waters, they are an abomination to you.

    RM and of...abomination]   and of every living thing that is in the waters [they are] an abomination

Lev. 20:6

And the person that goes astray by inquiring of a necromancer and (by) bringing up apparitions [to stray][1] after them, I will set my strong anger against that person and I will destroy him from among his people.

    RM And the person...from among his people.]   And the man (lit., son of man) who takes into account conjurers and the bone of a yiddoa' [to stray][1] after them, I will bring my anger against that man (lit., son of man) [and I will destroy][1] him from the life of the world to come, and there will be no portion for him among his people.

    LM apparitions...after them]   apparitions to whore after [them]

    LM my strong anger]   my angry face

[1]Ms erased.

Nu. 11:22

If flocks and herds were slaughtered for them, would it suffice them?   If all the fish of the sea were gathered for them, would it suffice them?

Nu. 11:22 (cont.)
>   RM If flocks...suffice them? (2)]   If flock(s) and herds
>   ...of the great sea were gathered for them, would it
>   fully suffice them?[1]
>   RM If/were gathered(2)...for them(4)]   If [all the fish
>   of the] great [sea] were gathered for them, would it
>   fully suffice them?

[1]M is a continuous reading.

Nu. 17:3(16:38)

[For] the censers of these guilty ones who have sinned at
(the cost of) their lives [are holy].[1]   And they shall make
them (into) hammered plates as covering for the altar; because
they offered them before the Lord, they have been made holy.
And they will be a sign for the children of Israel.
>   RM censers]   orthographic change
>   LM [of] these [guilty ones]...at (the cost of) their lives]
>   [of] the [guilty ones] at (the cost of) their lives[2]
>   LM who have sinned at (the cost of) their lives]   a
>   blaze of fire at (the cost of) their lives
>   LM And they shall make...covering]   And they shall make
>   them (into) hammered plates as covering (change of
>   construction and vocabulary)
>   LM And they will be]   morphological change

[1]Verse is continued from preceding one. Bracketed words belong to preceding verse.
[2]So M.   Possibly one should supply "who have sinned" after
"the guilty ones."

Nu. 21:28

For a nation of warriors, burning like fire, went out
from Heshbon; wagers of war, like flames, went out from the
city of Sihon.   They destroyed the fortress of the Moabites
(censored) that were sacrificing before the high places of
the Arnon.
>   LM a nation of warriors...the fortress of the Moabites]
>   a king, strong as fire, went out from Heshbon; and le-
>   gions of wagers of war, like the flames of Gehenna,
>   went out from the city of Sihon, the fortress of the
>   Moabites
>   RM like fire]   synonym for "like"
>   LM like flames]   orthographic change
>   LM the fortress of the Moabites] morphological change
>   LM the high places]   the idols

Deut. 3:16

    To the tribe of the sons of the Reubenites and of the sons
of the Gadites I have given from Gilead to the River Arnon
(with) the middle of the valley as the boundary, to the River
Jubeka, the boundary of the sons of the Ammonites.

    RM to the tribe...of the Gadites]   to the Reubenites and
        to the Gadites
    LM the middle of the valley]   synonym for "middle"
    LM (with) the middle... as the boundary]   (with) the city
        which is built in the middle of the valley as the bound-
        ary
    RM Jubeka]   orthographic change
    RM Ammonites]   orthographic change

Deut. 15:14

    You shall surely outfit him from your flocks, from your
threshing floor, and from your winepress, from whatever the
Lord your God has blessed you with you shall give to him.

    LM You shall surely outfit him]   You shall surely be zeal-
        ous for him
    RM You shall/outfit]   from s. to pl.
    LM you (2)...him.]   from s. to pl.

Deut. 23:6(5)

    But the Lord your God would not hearken to the cursing of
Balaam, and for your sake the Lord your God turned the curse to
blessing; because the Lord your God loves you.

    RM hearken...of Balaam]   hearken to Balaam
    LM the curse to blessing]   the curses to blessings
    RM the curse]   the curse (Hebrew)
    RM loves you]   grammatical change

Deut. 25:9

    And his sister-in-law will approach him in the presence of
the elders, and she will take off the sandal from upon his foot
and spit before him.   And she will answer and say: In this
manner let it be done to the man who does not desire to build
the house of his brother.

    LM And / will approach...and she will take off]
        And his sister-in-law will approach him before the el-
        ders and she will take off
    RM and she will take off the sandal] and she will take off his

Deut. 25:9 (cont.)

      sandal

  RM his foot]   his right foot

  LM In this [manner]...of his brother.] So shall it be done
to the man who will not build the house of his brother.
(M in Hebrew)

  RM to the man]   to a man

    4. <u>Variants Marked</u>, ס"א

Gen. 12:3

    And I will bless the one who blesses you and the one who
curses you shall be cursed; and by your merit all the families
of the earth shall be blessed.

  LM the one who...shall be cursed]   another source: who
blesses you like Aaron the priest, and who curses you I
will curse like Balaam the wicked one

  RM the families of]   orthographic and grammatical changes

Gen. 15:12

    And the sun was about to set and a pleasant sleep fell
upon Abram; and, behold, Abram saw four kingdoms rising against
him: Dread: This is Babylon; Darkness: This is Media; Great:
This is Greece; Fell upon him: This is (censored).

  RM And the sun was...to end of verse]   another source: And
the sun was going down (Hebrew): And the sun was near
to setting when (lit., and) the deep sleep was cast upon
Abram; and, behold, (he saw) four kingdoms rising to enslave his sons: Dread: This is Babylon; Darkness: This
is Media; Great: This is Greece; Fell upon him: This is
(censored). And after this the rulership will return
to the people, the house of Israel.

I LM about to set]   going down to set

I LM [pleasant] sleep]   deep [pleasant] sleep

I LM kingdoms rising...Darkness]   the [four] kingdoms which
were destined to arise and enslave his sons: Dread,
Darkness

Gen. 15:17

    And the sun had now set, and there was darkness; and Abram
looked (lit., saw) as seats were being arranged and thrones
erected. And (he saw) Gehenna, which was like a furnace, like
an oven surrounded (by) sparks of fire, (by) flames of
fire, into the midst of which the wicked fell, because the
wicked had rebelled against the Law in their lives in this

Gen. 15:17 (cont.)
world.   But the righteous, because they had kept it, were being delivered from the affliction.   All this was shown to
Abram when he was passing between these pieces.

    LM And the sun...these pieces.]   And the sun was on the
        point of disappearing (lit., was going down to set), and
        there was darkness.   And Abram looked (lit., saw) as
        seats were being placed and thrones erected.   And (he
        saw) Gehenna, which was like a furnace which is prepared
        for the wicked in the world to come because they did
        not occupy themselves with the instruction of the Law in
        this world and did not keep the commandments.   All
        this Abram saw when Abram was passing between these
        pieces.

    RM of fire, into the midst...against the Law]   of fire,
        and in its midst wicked ones [fell] who renounced the
        Law

    RM But the righteous, because they had kept...All this]
        But righteous ones who fulfilled the Law were being de-
        livered from the affliction.   All this

    BM And the sun...these pieces.]   another source: And the
        sun set (Hebrew): And the sun had set and there was
        darkness: Abram looked (lit., saw) and (he saw) Gehenna,
        which was burning like a furnace with sparks of fire
        and glowing coals of fire (and) with smoke rising.   And
        (he saw) the wicked being thrown into it because they
        had rebelled during their lives in this world against
        the teaching of the Law and had not fulfilled the com-
        mandments.   But the righteous were being delivered from
        the judgment, because during their lives in this world
        they had served and had fulfilled the commandments.
        And for their merits the flame of fire is destined to be
        let loose at the end of days from the throne of glory.
        Every kingdom will be burned and dissolved.   Abram saw
        these great visions at the time when he passed between
        these pieces.

Gen. 18:2
    And he raised his eyes and saw that three angels in the
likeness of men were standing beside him.   And he looked
(lit., saw) and ran from the door of the tent to meet them.
And he greeted them according to the custom of the land.

    RM standing beside him.]   another source: standing before

Gen. 18:2 (cont.)
    him.   One of them was going to tell Sarah that she
    would bear a male child (lit., son); and one of them
    was going to destroy Sodom; and one of them was going
    to rescue Lot from the midst of the destruction.

LM standing...and he ran]   taking places beside him.   And
    he saw them and he ran

Gen. 27:41
    And Esau hated Jacob on account of the blessing (with)
which his father blessed him (Jacob).   And Esau said in (his)
heart: I am not going to do as Cain did who killed Abel during
the lifetime of his father and (his father) turned his face and
begat Seth and called his name by (according to) his (own)
name.   I will wait until the time that the days of mourning of
my father approach; then I will kill Jacob my brother and I
will be called a murderer and an heir.

LM And [Esau] hated Jacob]   And Esau kept hatred toward
    Jacob
LM his father/ And Esau said]   Isaac his father [blessed
    him.]   Esau answered
RM in (his) heart: [I] am not]   [I] am not
LM as]   orthographic change
RM who killed...of his father]   to Abel his brother, whom
    he killed in the lifetime of his father
RM and turned]   synonym
LM I(2)...approach]   that is, the slain; but [I] will wait
    until the time of [the days of mourning of my father]
    approach
LM I(2)...and an heir.]   another source: that is, Abel,
    but I will wait until the time that the days of mourn-
    ing of the death of my father arrive, and then I will
    kill Jacob my brother, and I will be found a murderer
    and an heir.

Gen. 34:31
    The two sons of Jacob, Simeon and Levi, answered and said
to Jacob their father: It is not fitting that they should say,
in their congregations and in their schools [uncircumcised][1]
have defiled virgins and worshippers [of idols][1] the daughter
of Jacob.   But it is fitting that they should say in the congregations of Israel and in their school house: uncircumcised
were slain on account of a virgin, [worshippers of idols][1] because they defiled Dinah the daughter of Jacob; so that after

Gen. 34:31 (cont.)

all this, Shechem, the son of Hamor, may not be proud in his
soul or exalted in his heart and say: Like a woman who has
no man (lit., son of man) as an avenger of humiliation, so
was it done to Dinah, our sister, like (as though she were)
a lost woman, a prostitute.

```
II LM   that they should say]    to be said
 I LM   that they should say]    that it be said
 I RM   and in their schools]    and in their schoolhouses
   LM   virgins]   another source:  vocabulary change
II LM   the daughter of [Jacob.]]   have violated the daughter
        [of Jacob.]
II RM   But it is fitting that they should]   But it is fitting
        that they should (synonym for "But" and grammatical
        change)
 I LM   that they should say in the congregations of [Israel]]
        that it be said in [the] congregations [of Israel]
   RM   and in [their school] house]   and in [their school]
        houses
II LM   on account of a virgin]   because of the daughter
II RM   because they defiled...so that/may not]   because of
        the daughter of Jacob; and not only this but also lest
 I LM   so that after...Shechem]   and after this it is not
        fitting for Shechem
 I RM   proud...exalted]   exalted
II LM   in his soul...in his heart]   in his words
II RM   who has no...a prostitute.]   [like a] lost [woman], a
        prostitute, who does not have an avenger, was it done
        to Dinah our sister. Therefore we have done this thing.
 I LM   man (lit., son of man)...prostitute.]   avenger of
        blood nor avenger of humiliation.  This is the way
        (lit., so) it happened to Dinah, the daughter of Jacob.
        And they said:  Like a woman of fornication and a pros-
        titute is [our] sister.
```
[1]Censored.

Nu. 34:8

    From Taurus Manos you shall draw a line to the entrance
of Antioch, and the outer edges of the boundary shall extend
to (lit., be) Abelas of the Cilicians.

```
   LM   Taurus Manos]   another source:  the mountains of
        Isminos
 I RM   to the entrance of]   when you enter
 I RM   to the entrance of]   to the entrance
```

Nu. 34:8 (cont.)

I RM of the boundary...of the Cilicians.]   [shall be] at
       the boundary of Abelas of the Cilicians.

5. Three Sets of Variants: Unclassified

Gen. 15:11

And the bird came down upon the pieces, but the merit of
Abram drove them away.   When the bird of prey came down they
(sic) hovered over the pieces.   What is this bird of prey?
This is the unclean bird of prey.   What is this unclean bird?
They are the kingdoms of the earth when they are plotting evil
against the house of Israel.   Through the merits of Abram,
their father, salvation is theirs.

II RM And/ came down...salvation is theirs.]   And the nations
       which are likened to the unclean bird came down to plun-
       der the possessions of Israel but the merit of Abraham
       protected them.

   RM bird of prey (2)]   bird

   RM bird of prey (2) or (3)]   synonym

   LM What is this (2)]   morphological and grammatical changes

   LM What is this (2)...They are]   They are

   RM They are...salvation is theirs.]   They are the four king-
       doms which are destined to enslave the sons of Abram;
       but the merit of Abram, the righteous, will deliver them.

Gen. 44:18

And Judah approached him furious in (his) words and sub-
dued in his language (lit., in tongue).   He roared like a lion
and said: I beg you, my lord, let your servant now say something and, my lord, don't let your anger rise up against your
servant.   Did you not tell us the first time that we came to
you: I fear the Lord (lit., from before the Lord)?   But now
your judgments have changed so that they are like the judgments
of Pharaoh your master.   And he said: I pray, our lord, the
first time that we came you said to us: (I) fear from before the
Lord.   But now you say: I fear Pharaoh (lit., from Pharaoh).
Perhaps it has not been said to you, or perhaps it has not been
heard by you, what Simeon and Levi, my two brothers, did in the
fortress of Shechem -- that they went into it and slew every
male in it because they had defiled within it Dinah, our sister,
who is not numbered with the tribes and who does not have any

158

Gen. 44:18 (cont.)

share or inheritance in the division of the land. How much
more for the sake of Benjamin, our brother, who is numbered
with the tribes and who does have a share and inheritance in
the division of the land! As for me, my strength is stronger
than the strength of Simeon and Levi. I swear (that) if I
unsheath my sword from the scabbard I will not put it back in
it until I have slain all the Egyptians. With you I will
begin and with Pharaoh your master I will end, because I am as
honorable as you and my father as (honorable as) Pharaoh your
master. For,[1] because you swear what is sworn you swear by
him,[1] I swear to you by the life of the head of my father, just
as you swear by the life of the head of Pharaoh your master,
that, if I unsheath my sword from within the scabbard I will
not return it to the scabbard until the whole land of Egypt is
filled with (the) slain. I will not return it to the scabbard
until we have made the whole land of Egypt desolate of inhabit-
ants. With you I will begin and with Pharaoh your master, by
whom you swear, I will finish; even though in doing (this I)
act against the will of my father. Has it not been heard by
you, or has it not been told to you, what my two brothers,
Simeon and Levi, did in the fortress of Shechem which was at
peace when (lit., and) they went into it and slew every male
at the edge of the sword, because they defiled Dinah, our sister, who is not numbered with us among the tribes and does not
receive with us the inheritance? How much more for the sake
of our brother who is numbered with us among the tribes and
does receive a share and an inheritance with us in the division
of the land! And how much more because I am more unyielding
than they! And how much more because my strength is more bru-
tal than theirs because (lit., and) I became surety for the
child with my father and spoke to him, saying: If I do not
bring him to you and place him before you, let me be far from
my father's greeting ever more (lit., all the days). But perhaps it has not been heard by you or not told to you that kings
and princes like you are we in the land of Canaan. Just as
you and Pharaoh your master are princes in the land of Egypt,
so I and Jacob my father are princes in the land of Canaan.

RM furious...and said, I beg you] and said: I beg you
RM and said: I beg you...I will end] and said: I beg
you, our lord, the first time that we came you said to
us: I fear from before the Lord but now you have said:
I fear Pharaoh (lit., from before Pharaoh). Perhaps

Gen. 44:18 (cont.)

it has not been told to you, or perhaps it has not been
heard by you, what Simeon and Levi, my two brothers,
did in the fortress of Shechem when they went into it
and slew every male in it because they had defiled in
it Dinah, our sister, who is not numbered with the
tribes and who does not have a share or an inheritance
in the division of the land. How much more for the
sake of Benjamin, our brother, who is numbered with the
tribes and does have a share and an inheritance in the
division (of the land)! And my strength is stronger
than the strength of Simeon and Levi. I swear, if I
unsheath my sword from the scabbard I will not put it
back in it until I have slain all the Egyptians. With
you I will begin and with Pharaoh your master I will
end.

RM and, my lord, don't]   in the hearing of our lord, and
don't

RM so that they are]   orthographic change

LM [and he said: I pray]...because I am as honorable]   Because I am as honorable

LM [For, because you swear]...[I] swear (2); or, [I] swear
(2)]   I swear   (either omission of corrupt section
and orthographic change; or, orthographic change only)

LM Dinah (2)]   grammatical change

RM indecipherable (apparently one word or abbreviation)

RM because my strength]   because (lit., with) my strength

RM until I have slain all the Egyptians]   until we have
made the whole land of Egypt desolate

LM until I have slain all the Egyptians]   until the slain
fill the whole land of Egypt

LM [until] the whole land/ is filled]   [until] we have
filled the whole land [of Egypt]

LM and with Pharaoh your master I will end...Has it not
been heard]   and with Pharaoh your master I will end.
Has it not been heard

RM who is not numbered with us...How much more]   and she
is not numbered with us (and) does not receive with us
a share and inheritance in the division of the land?
How much more

RM greeting]   grammatical change

Gen. 44:18 (cont.)

LM   and princes]   + also
$^1 \dots ^1$Corrupt reading in Ms.   Cf., FT.

Gen. 47:21

As for the people who spoke slanderously (lit., slandering
with evil language), Joseph displaced them.   And he exiled
them and moved them about from city to city, from one end of
the borders of the Egyptians to the (other) end.   And the
people who were in the cities he made dwell in the country,
and the people who were in the country he made dwell in the
city -- from one end of the land of Egypt to its (other) end --
so that the Egyptians would not taunt the brothers of Joseph
and say to them: "Homeless foreigners."

   LM As for the people..."Homeless foreigners."]   As for
       the people, he displaced them from city to city in or-
       der that they would not call his brothers "wanderers"
       or "homeless like chaff;" for this reason he displaced
       them from (one) end of the territory of Egypt to its
       (other) end.

   LM As for the people..."Homeless foreigners."]   And the
       people who had dwelt in the country he moved into the
       cities, and the people who had dwelt in the cities he
       moved into the country; so that they would not taunt
       the sons of Jacob and say to them: "Foreigners,"
       "Exiles."

   RM end (1)..."Homeless foreigners."]   end of the territory
       of Egypt to the opposite boundary on account of the
       brothers of Joseph, that they not call them "Foreign-
       ers," "Exiles."

Gen. 48:22

I have given to you a portion more than (that of) your
brothers, the garment of the first man.   Abraham, the father
of my father, took it from the hands of the evil Nimrod and
gave it to Isaac, my father.   And Isaac, my father, gave it to
Esau, my (text, his) brother, and I took it from the hands of
Esau, my (text, his) brother, not by my sword and my bow, but
by my merits and my good works; because these are better for
me than my sword and my bow.   And again, I have given to you
a portion more than (that of) your brothers -- Shechem -- which

Gen. 48:22 (cont.)

I took by my merits and my good works from the hands of the
Amorites, which are better for me than my sword and my bow.

RM to you a portion (1)...to end of verse] to you (pl.)
a portion more than (that of) your brothers [-- Shechem --] which I took by my merits and (my) good works
from the hands of the Amorites, which are better for me
than my sword and my bow.

RM to you (1)...of the Amorites, which are better] to
you (s) [a portion more than (that of)] your brothers
[-- Shechem -- which I took] from the hands of the Amorites by my merits and (my) good works which are better

LM first...to Esau...than my sword and my bow(1)] [of
the] first [man] which Abraham took from the hands of
Nimrod. And he gave them to Isaac and Isaac gave them
to Esau, who walked according to the customs of the Amorites...by my might...many (?) deeds which are pure...
than (text, between) swords and (text, than) bow(s).[1]

[1]M is a continuous reading.

Gen. 50:1

And Joseph fell upon the face of his father and wept over
him and kissed him. And Joseph laid his father on a bed of
ivory overlaid with gold, set with fine pearls and fastened
with articles of linen and purple. There were poured out
there precious liquids and aromatic spices; there were burned
there precious ointments. Kingdoms stood there: rulers from
the sons of Ishmael stood there; rulers from the sons of Esau
stood there; rulers from the sons of Keturah stood there;
Judah, the lion, mightiest of his brothers, stood there. Judah
answered and said to his brothers: Come, let us plant to our
father a tall cedar, so that its top may reach up to the height
of heaven and its roots extend to the generations of the world;
because from him have come forth twelve tribes, that is, the
sons of Israel, because from him have come forth priests with
their trumpets and Levites with their harps. Then Joseph bent
down over the neck of his father, and Joseph wept over him and
kissed him.

LM of ivory]   morphological change

RM of ivory]   orthographic and/or morphological change

162

Gen. 50:1 (cont.)

LM [gold,] set...and purple.]   fine [gold[and set with
    precious stones and pearls and fastened with rings of
    linen and purple.

LM There were poured out there...the lion/ [stood there.]]
    Poured out there were precious liquids, aromatic spices.
    Warriors from the house of Esau stood there; rulers
    from the house of Jacob stood there; the lion [mightiest
    of his brothers] stood there.

LM There were poured out there...the lion/ [stood there.]]
    Poured out there were wines, aromatic spices; and heavy
    incense was burned there.   Some from the house of Esau
    stood there; warriors from the house of Jacob stood
    there;...from the house of Ishmael stood there.   The
    lion [mightiest of his brothers] stood there.[1]

RM from the sons of Keturah]   orthographic change

RM from the sons of Esau]   orthographic change

RM let us plant to our father]   and let us plant upon our
    father

RM let us plant to our father]   and build upon our father

RM and its roots]   but its roots

LM and its roots...bent down]   its branches spread over
    all the inhabitants of the earth and its roots reach to
    the lowest part of the deep.   From him arose twelve
    tribes in Israel.   From him (priests arose?) to offer
    offerings, and from him arose Levites with their divi-
    sions to sing.   Then he bent down

[1]M is a continuous reading.

Ex. 20:2

The first word(s) that went out from the mouth of the Holy
One, may his name be blessed, was like shooting stars and like
lightnings and like torches of fire, a torch of fire to the
right and a torch of fire to the left.   It flew and winged
swiftly through the air of heaven and returned; and all Israel
saw it and feared.   And when it returned, it became engraved on
the two tablets of the covenant and said: My people, children
of.   And it returned and hovered over the camps of Israel; and
it returned and became engraved on the tablets of the covenant;
and all Israel saw it.   Then it cried out and said: My people,
children of Israel, I am the Lord, your God, who redeemed (you)

Ex. 20:2 (cont.)
and brought you out redeemed from the land of Egypt, from the
house of slavery.

> LM and returned; and all Israel...children of Israel] and
>   all Israel saw it and feared.   And when it returned,
>   it became engraved on the two tablets of the covenant
>   and said: My people, children of Israel [I am the Lord
>   your God, etc.]

> RM Reads as follows: And this is what (lit., thus) it
>   cried out and said and all Israel saw it.   Then it
>   cried out and said: My people, children of Israel

> LM Reads as follows: And this is what (lit., thus) it
>   cried out and said and all Israel saw it.

Ex. 22:14(15)
   If its owner was with it, he shall not make restitution;
if it was hired, it is received for the hire.

> RM received for the hire.]   he receives the hire.

> RM received for the hire.]   he shall take (?) the entire
>   loss of its hire.

> LM received for the hire.]   its hire goes with the
>   losses.

NOTES TO CHAPTER I

[1] An excellent introduction to the targumic literature is, Roger LeDéaut, Introduction à la Littérature Targumique. Première partie. (Rome: Institut Biblique Pontifical, 1966).

[2] The name "Onkelos" is owing to a corruption in the Babylonian Talmud of the name of Aquila the Proselyte, to whom is ascribed the translation of the Torah in the Palestinian Talmud. See, Encyclopedia Judaica, 1971, s.v. "Onkelos and Aquila."

The editio princeps of O was printed in Bologna in 1482 and has been reprinted in the Polyglots and Rabbinic Bibles. The most recent edition is, A. Sperber, ed., The Bible in Aramaic, I: The Pentateuch according to Targum Onkelos (Leiden: Brill, 1959).

Other Pentateuchal Targums are the Peshitta, which is the Syriac (Eastern Aramaic) translation, and the Samaritan Targum.

[3] Martin McNamara, The New Testament and the Palestinian Targum to the Pentateuch, Analecta Biblica 27 (Rome: Pontifical Biblical Institute, 1966), pp. 57-58, nn. 48-52.

[4] Bleddyn J. Roberts, The Old Testament Text and Versions (Cardiff: University of Wales Press, 1951), p. 205.

[5] Gustaf Dalman, Grammatik des Jüdisch-Palästinischen Aramäisch, 2nd ed. (Darmstadt: Wissenschaftliche Buchgesellschaft, 1960; photographic reproduction; first published 1905).

[6] The author of this Targum has been identified with the author of Targum Jonathan to the Prophets, but the attribution is universally considered false because of a wide divergence of language and style. Hence the designation, "Pseudo-Jonathan." The mistaken identity probably arose from a misreading, or a misunderstanding, of an abbreviation for "Targum Jeruschalmi" as "Targum Jonathan."

The editio princeps of PJ, Asher Forins, ed., was published in Venice in 1590/91 from a Ms of the Foa family and has been reprinted in the Polyglots and Rabbinic Bibles. The most recent edition is, D. Rieder, ed., Pseudo-Jonathan: Targum Jonathan ben Uziel on the Pentateuch, copied from the London Ms. (British Museum Add. 27031), (Jerusalem: Salomon, 1974).

[7] See, Encyclopedia Judaica, 1971, s.v. "Bomberg, Daniel."

[8] For publication of the FT see n. 20. The most recent edition of the FT (V with critical apparatus) is included in, Malcolm C. Doubles, "The Fragment Targum: A Critical Reexamination of the Editio Princeps, Das Fragmententhargum by Moses Ginsburger, in the Light of Recent Discoveries" (Ph.D. thesis, University of St. Andrews, 1962).

[9] "Toward the Publication of the Extant Texts of the Palestinian Targum(s)," Vetus Testamentum 15 (1965), 16-26.

P is the only extensive witness of its type; although Stras-
bourg Ms n. 4017, E. N. Adler 656, and possibly Codex Paris
75 at Gen. 38:25,26 and 44:18 are members of a "P group," according to Geoffrey J. Cowling, "The Palestinian Targum: Textual and Linguistic Investigations in Codex Neofiti 1 and
Allied Manuscripts" (Ph.D. thesis, University of Aberdeen,
1968), pp. 52-53.

[10]Masoreten des Westens, II (Stuttgart: W. Kohlhammer Verlag,
1930). The publication includes a seventh Ms, Ms G, but this
is not a Palestinian Targum.

[11]While Kahle's dating may be subject to revision, there is
consensus that these CG fragments antedate by several centuries the texts extant in the FT group. See M. McNamara,
Targum and Testament (Grand Rapids: Eerdmans, 1972), p. 183,
n. 21, for bibliography on discussion.

[12]A complete listing is found on p. XII of Kahle, Masoreten.

[13]Two additional Mss in the V 440 group are the Ms Sassoon 264
of the Sassoon Library, Letchworth, England, and the Ms Or
10,794, folio 8, of the British Museum. According to Cowling,
"Thesis," p. 50, the former differs from B "in a few scribal
errors."

Additional CG fragments include the E. N. Adler Mss 2578 and
2755 published by A. Díez Macho, "Nuevos fragmentos del Targum palestinense," Sefarad 15 (1955), 1-39, as well as unpublished fragments of the E. N. Adler Collection of the Jewish
Theological Seminary of New York.

[14]For an account of the discovery of the Codex see Díez Macho,
"Una copia de todo el Targum jerosolimitano en la Vaticana,"
Estudios Bíblicos 16 (1956), 446-47; M. Black, "The Discovery of the Language of Jesus," New Testament Studies 3 (1957),
305. For the history of the Codex see LeDéaut, "Jalons pour
une histoire d'un manuscrit du Targum Palestinien (Neofiti 1),"
Biblica 48 (1967), 509-33. For the paleographical character
of the Codex see S. Lund, "An Argument for Further Study of the
Paleography of Codex Neofiti 1," Vetus Testamentum 20, No. 1
(1970), 56-64.

[15]The editio princeps is currently being published: A. Díez
Macho, ed., Neophyti 1, Targum Palestinense Ms de la Biblio-
teca Vaticana, 5 vols. (Madrid: Consejo Superior de Investi-
gaciones Científicas), 1: Genesis (1968), 2: Exodus (1970),
3: Leviticus (1971), 4: Numbers (1974).

The following verses are partially or wholly missing from the
text but supplied in the margin: Gen. 7:3, 29:5, 35:10,
47:11-12, 47:23; Ex. 32:31, 35:15-16, 36:16, 38:25-26, 40:12-
13; Lev. 17:10, 23:29; Nu. 15:38, 20:18, 21:8-9, 29:27, 30:9,
31:12, 31:37-38; Deut. 2:7, 8:3, 17:19, 22:25, 23:12, 27:24,
28:6, 28:22, 33:10-11. Missing in whole or in part, without
marginal correction, are Gen. 25:25-26, 31:26-27, 35:14,
35:25-26, 36:13-14, 36:21-31, 36:41, 39:13; Ex. 12:14, 12:26,
12:32, 19:23, 21:17, 28:20-21; Lev. 26:42-44; Nu. 32:11,
32:18; Deut. 14:10. Most of these are errors of homoiote-
leuton; at Gen. 36:21-31 a whole page must have been skipped.
Other smaller omissions in the text occur when the Hebrew
verse-openings duplicate a word of the translation and the

Aramaic opening words are not given.   Cf.: LeDéaut, La Nuit Pascale, Analecta Biblica 22 (Rome: Institut Biblique Pontifical, 1963), p. 38.

[16]"The Relationship between the Arûk and the Targum Neofiti 1," Leshonenu, 31 (1966s), 23-32, 189-98; 34, No. 3 (1969s), 172-79 (in Hebrew).

[17]"Thesis," p. 233.

[18]J. W. Etheridge, The Targums of Onkelos and Jonathan ben Uzziel on the Pentateuch with the Fragments of the Jerusalem Targum (New York: Ktav Publishing House, 1968; first published 1862).

[19]A. Berliner, ed., Targum Onkelos, 2 vols. (Berlin: Gorzelanczyk and Co., 1884).

[20]Moses Ginsburger, Das Fragmententhargum: Thargum jeruschalmi zum Pentateuch (Berlin: S. Calvary & Co., 1899).

[21]Moses Ginsburger, Pseudo-Jonathan: Thargum Jonathan ben Usiël zum Pentateuch (Berlin: S. Calvary & Co., 1903).

[22]Leopold Zunz, Die Gottesdienstlichen Vorträge der Juden, 1st ed. (Berlin: A. Asher, 1832).

[23]Z. Frankel, Vorstudien zur Septuaginta (Leipzig: Vogel, 1941); Abraham Geiger, Urschrift und Übersetzungen der Bibel in ihrer Abhängigkeit von den inneren Entwicklung des Judenthums (Breslau: Verlag von Julius Hainauer, 1857); Theodor Nöldeke, Die alttestamentliche Literatur in einer Reihe von Aufsatzen dargestellt von Theodor Nöldeke (Leipzig: Quandt & Händel, 1868).

[24]Hermann Seligsohn, De Duabus Hierosolymitanis Pentateuchi Paraphrasibus (Breslau: Typis Sulzback, 1858).

[25]W. Bacher, "Targum," Jewish Encyclopedia, 1906, 12, 57-63.

[26]S. D. Luzzatto, Elementi grammaticale del Caldeo Biblico e del Dialetto Talmudico Babilonese (Padua: A. Bianchi, 1865).

[27]Dalman, Grammatik.

[28]Jacob Bassfreund, Das Fragmenten-Targum zum Pentateuch (Breslau: S. Schottländer, 1896).

[29]Marcus Jastrow, ed., A Dictionary of the Targumim, the Talmud Babli and Yerushalmi, and the Midrashic Literature, 2 vols. (New York: Pardes Publishing House, Inc., 1950. First published 1903).

[30]Kahle, Masoreten.

[31]Ibid., pp. 1*-13*.

[32]The lectures were published as The Cairo Geniza (London: Oxford University Press, 1947).

[33]Kahle, The Cairo Geniza, 2nd ed. (Oxford: Basil Blackwell, 1959), pp. 200-208. Evidence from Pseudo-Jonathan is considered relevant, since it is regarded as preserving some traditions belonging to the ancient Palestinian Targum not encountered elsewhere. The Exodus passage is discussed in detail by Georg Schelbert, "Exodus xxii 4 im Palästinischen Targum," Vetus Testamentum, 8 (1958), 253-63.

[34]Kahle, Cairo Geniza, 2nd ed., p. 208.

[35]Kahle, Masoreten, p. 11*, n. 3.

[36]Kahle, Cairo Geniza, 2nd ed., p. 203.

[37]Díez Macho, Genesis, p. 32*.

[38]See Joseph A. Fitzmyer, The Genesis Apocryphon of Qumran Cave I: A Commentary, 2nd rev. ed., Biblica et Orientalia 18a (Rome: Pontifical Biblical Institute, 1971), p. 10 and n. 24. The Targum to Job is published in J. P. M. van der Ploeg, O.P., and A. S. van der Woude, Le Targum de Job de la Grotte XI de Qumrân (Leiden: Brill, 1971). For a comprehensive bibliography see Fitzmyer, Genesis Apocryphon, p. 20, n. 55, and p. 28, n. 67.

[39]Kahle, Cairo Geniza, 2nd ed., p. 193.

[40]E. Y. Kutscher, "The Language of the Genesis Apocryphon: A Preliminary Study," Scripta Hierosolymitana, 4 (1958), 22.

[41]Ibid., p. 10, n. 44.

[42]Ibid., p. 1.

[43]Fitzmyer, Genesis Apocryphon, p. 22.

[44]See n. 14.

[45]Kahle, "Das palästinische Pentateuchtargum und das zur Zeit Jesu gesprochene Aramäisch," Zeitschrift für Neutestamentliche Wissenschaft (1958), 111. In the article Kahle responded to views Kutscher had expressed in "The Language of the Genesis Apocryphon." The article appeared, almost unchanged, as Chapter III of Cairo Geniza, 2nd ed., pp. 191-208. One very noteworthy change was made, however. In the article Kahle described the Genesis Apocryphon as "zwar in aramäischer Sprache, in der dem Volke der Bibeltext verdolmetscht wurde" (p. 106). In Cairo Geniza he described it as a text "written in literary Aramaic" (p. 200). This latter judgment is the correct one in terms of Kahle's own view.

[46]E. Y. Kutscher, "Das zur Zeit Jesu gesprochene Aramäisch," Zeitschrift für Neutestamentliche Wissenschaft, 51 (1960), 46-54.

[47]Ibid., p. 48.

[48]Ibid., p. 54.

[49]Kahle, "Das zur Zeit Jesu gesprochene Aramäisch: Erwiderung," Zeitschrift für Neutestamentliche Wissenschaft, 51 (1960), 55.

[50]For example, LeDéaut, "The Current State of Targumic Studies," Biblical Theology Bulletin, 4 (1974), pp. 1-32; John Bowker, The Targums and Rabbinic Literature (London: Cambridge University Press, 1969); Gerard J. Kuiper, The Pseudo-Jonathan Targum and its Relationship to Targum Onkelos, Studia Ephemeridis "Augustinianum" 9 (Rome: Institutum Patristicum "Augustinianum", 1972); Bernard Grossfeld, A Bibliography of Targum Literature (New York: Ktav Publishing House and Cincinnati: Hebrew Union College Press, 1972).

[51]At first, because the notations had been produced by many hands and were often carelessly written, the impression received was that these notations represented a diverse collection of notes, appended at various times during the lifetime of the manuscript. Closer examination revealed, however, that the great majority of these were copied at the same time as the main text from an earlier annotated manuscript, and that the variations in scribal hand cannot be correlated with a change in text-type of the material copied. See Lund, "Paleography," pp. 61-64.

[52]Díez Macho, Genesis, p. 9*.

[53]See Ch. IV, pp. 72-80.

[54]See Ch. II, Appendices, pp. 20-59.

[55]See Ch. V, pp. 83-117.

NOTES TO CHAPTER II

[1] For example, P. Grelot, "Les targums du Pentateuque: Étude comparative d'après Genèse IV, 3-16," _Semitica_ 9 (1959), 85; Lund, "The Sources of the Variant Readings to Deuteronomy 1:1-29:17 of Codex Neofiti 1," _In Memoriam Paul Kahle_, eds., M. Black and Georg Fohrer (Berlin: Töpelmann, 1968), pp. 168-72; LeDéaut, "Lévitique XXII 26 - XXIII 44 dans le Targum Palestinien," _Vetus Testamentum_ 18 (1968), 470; Cowling, "Thesis," pp. 215-25; Julia A. Foster, "The Language and Text of Codex Neofiti 1 in the light of other Palestinian Aramaic Sources" (Ph.D. dissertation, Boston University, 1969), p. 10; Díez Macho, _Exodus_, p. 24*; McNamara, _Targum_, p. 188.

[2] Cowling, "Thesis," p. 218; McNamara, _Targum_, p. 102.

[3] The verses transcribed in Appendix I were chosen, rather than others, in order not only to provide opportunity for comparison of texts but also to use texts with vocabulary and morphology helpful in later discussion. The words to be discussed are underlined.

[4] This is not to say that we have transcribed all passages with Type II Mgg, for sometimes this version appears without Type I.

NOTES TO CHAPTER III

[1] We have used S. Mandelkern, ed., Veteris Testamenti Concordantiae: Hebraicae atque Chaldaicae, 7th ed. (Jerusalem: Schocken, 1967). We are not hereby expressing the opinion that TJ II texts are translations based on the MT.

[2] See Foster, "Thesis," Ch. 3, pp. 66-113. The thesis study focused on correlation of Targumic usages with those given by Dalman as evidence for "Targumic" versus "Galilean" Aramaic (Grammatik, pp. 44-51). This survey has subsequently been much extended along the same lines. Many of the contrasts cited by Dalman involved morphological elements (cf., discussion of language of Type II Mgg above, pp. 66-68), whereas the greater part of the variation between Ni 1 text and margin is in vocabulary.

[3] For discussion of verbs רחש/רמס, see pp. 74,75.

[4] Cowling, "Thesis," has emphasized the importance of these sets of "differential" translation equivalents and has included in his thesis an exhaustive study of five Hebrew words with differential translation, pp. 119-83.

[5] A distinct pattern is evident in the use of כען/כדון in the Targums:

		O	TJ II	TJ I
MT	עתה	כען	כדון	כדון
MT	נא	כען	כען	כדון

See Cowling, "Thesis," pp. 261-2.

It should be noted that all Targumic texts use בבעו also, and occasionally other words, to render נא.

[6] למה כען is the regular TJ II translation for MT למה. Of forty-three occurrences of למה in the MT of the Pentateuch the text of Ni 1 reads למה כען thirty-three times. In six of the remaining ten instances כען is supplied by a marginal or interlinear reading. In the ten instances in eight verses extant for this word from the CG (Gen. 4:6 (twice), 29:25, 31:27, 30, 43:6, 44:4; Ex. 5:22 (twice); Deut. 5:22(25 in MT and English translations), the reading every time is למה כען. In the three instances extant for the word in the FT (Gen. 25:22, 42:1; Nu. 32:27), למה/א כען appears every time except for one of the three witnesses for Nu. 32:27 (B against VN). TJ I has this reading only at Nu. 9:7.

The Type II variant for the verse cited (Gen. 25:22) is of further interest because it translates MT למה זה as למה דין, in agreement with TJ I for this verse. TJ I and O usually render למה זה as למה דנן, whereas the TJ II texts do not translate זה, but instead render this phrase exactly as למה alone, i.e., למה כען.

170

[1]Lund noted that "beyond [Deut.] 29:17 there is a change in
the text and Mgg which warrants a separate study," "Variant
Readings," In Memoriam, p. 167, n. 5. According to Cowling,
"Thesis," "We may...deduce from the consistency of the marginal variants throughout the Pentateuch, that a manuscript
similar to E was extant for all the books, and was used
throughout. A doubt remains for Deuteronomy 29:17 [18] to
the end, and for the first few chapters of Genesis," p.
218.

[2]ס"א ("another book"), נ"א ("another version"), and ל"א ("another language") are used to mark variant readings. ס"א appears later to mark several Mgg (see p. 82 and pp. 109-12).
ל"א appears in the margin at Gen. 8:13, 14, marking two readings which agree with TJ I.

[3]Díez Macho, Genesis, p. 43*.

[4]M at 1:10 is not a variant but a correction to the text.

[5]The Tetragrammaton is written in several different ways in
the texts. We are using יי/ for all forms except ה, which
we render by ה.

[6]So far as the text is concerned, it would be possible to con-
clude that Gen. 1:24 is not the beginning of a new recension
but an interpolation into the text. Against this conclusion,
however, are the sigla, נ"א, from 1:24-2:5a and the use of
ממריה (cf. 2:2) in the text.

[7]Interchanges of כ and ב are common in the TJ II texts.

[8]Mgg are rare in P. Three other variants marked with נ"א are
found in the Ms at Gen. 18:1, 24:10, and Nu. 21:34. The variant reading at Gen. 24:10 is actually not in the margin, as
stated by Ginsburger, Das Fragmententhargum, but in the middle
of a line.

[9]גבר (2:23, 24) translates Hebrew איש here and regularly elsewhere.

[10]Two omissions from the text supplied in the margins are not
included in the count.

[11]In the preceding section this situation is reversed:
מ[י]/ מרה דיי, twelve times, מימריה דיי/, once.

INDEX OF VERSES